Praise for *The New Health Insurance S*

"*The New Health Insurance Solution* is   help a reader get the best possible insu   with helpful information and advice, Pilzer sh   .id outs of how to find the right plan without fallin   ..r spending too much money and not getting enough cover.   *Houston Chronicle*

"The real question for those considering an HSA is: 'Do I want a high-deductible health insurance plan?' says Paul Zane Pilzer, co-founder of Extend Benefits, a health-care services provider in Salt Lake City."
The Wall St. Journal

"Well, ladies and gentlemen, the book is called *The New Health Insurance Solution,* Paul Zane Pilzer. It's widely quoted these days; *Forbes* was talking about it just the other day. And I think this is something that you need to get. It's a real service to the country. You ought to take advantage of it." CBN: *The 700 Club with Pat Robertson*

"Paul Zane Pilzer offers living proof that even economists can have trouble finding good health insurance. He's since authored the book. . . . And now, he's among those championing a Congressional bill, the Health Care Choice Act, which would allow individual health insurance to be sold across state lines." *New York Daily News*

"*The New Health Insurance Solution* is the definitive guide to the new ways every American can now get affordable health care—without an employer." *SeniorCitizens.com*

"Economist Paul Zane Pilzer, whose latest book, *The New Health Insurance Solution* (Wiley, 2005), is on health savings accounts, says shopping intelligently for prescription drugs involves more than comparing the costs and benefits of particular pills. Consumers must also step back and reflect on why they are taking a given drug and what nondrug alternatives might be available, he says." *HR Magazine*

"In his latest book, *The New Health Insurance Solution*, published in September by John Wiley & Sons, Pilzer argues (not surprisingly) that most Americans—at least those without pre-existing conditions—can save money by choosing individual policies over those offered by their employers." *Newsweek*

The New Health Insurance Solution

How to Get Cheaper, Better Coverage *Without* a Traditional Employer Plan

PAUL ZANE PILZER

John Wiley & Sons, Inc.

For general information on our other products and services or for technical
support, please contact our Customer Care Department within the United
States at (800) 762-2974, outside the United States at (317) 572-3993 or
fax (317) 572-4002.

Wiley also publishes its books in a variety of electronic formats. Some content that
appears in print may not be available in electronic books. For more information
about Wiley products, visit our web site at www.wiley.com.

ISBN-13: 978-0-470-04021-8 (paper)
ISBN-10: 0-470-04021-1 (paper)   365/9/54

ISBN-13: 978-0-471-74715-4 (cloth)   "/67
ISBN-10: 0-471-74715-7 (cloth)

Printed in the United States of America.

10 9 8 7 6 5 4 3 2 1

CONTENTS

PART I

How to Better Protect Your Family While Saving $5,000+ Each Year: Savvy and Affordable New Health Insurance Strategies

PART II

How Businesses Can Fix Their Health Insurance Nightmare and Still Hire Great Employees

Executive Summary: New Health Insurance Solutions for Individuals, Families, Self-Employed, and Businesses

Two basic solutions apply to most readers of this book.

New Solution #1

Individual/family health insurance policies (that you purchase yourself, just like auto insurance) are better for most people, especially if they are healthy and less than 60 years old. This is because they are:

> *Safer*—Individual/family health insurance isn't dependent on an employer, so you don't lose your health insurance if you lose your job. (Losing job-related health insurance is how up to 1 million Americans each year end up in medical bankruptcy.)

> *Less expensive*—The cost is about one-half (or less) the price of an employer-sponsored group plan for similar coverage (low deductible/ doctor co-pay). Many families will pay less for high-quality individual/ family health insurance than they are currently paying in monthly contributions to their employer plan.

New Solution #2

For most people who are healthy, high-deductible health insurance, which is required to open a Health Savings Account (HSA), is better than a low-deductible plan. (High-deductible, HSA-qualified health insurance is available from either an employer-sponsored group plan or as an individual/family policy.) It is better for most people because it:

Lets you save whatever you don't spend—Whatever you don't spend each year is saved and invested tax-free in your Health Savings Account for future medical expenses or retirement.

Is far less expensive—The average cost of high-deductible, HSA-qualified health insurance is only $92 per month for a single person, nation-wide—about half the price of similar low-deductible/co-pay plans. This mean millions of uninsured Americans can now afford health insurance. In addition, you get to make tax-deductible contributions to your Health Savings Account.

Following are summary solutions for many typical situations. Please refer to the appropriate chapter(s) for more complete information.

Summary Solutions for Individuals, Families, and Self-Employed

Problem: I work for a company that pays 100 percent for my health insurance but charges me $450 a month to include my spouse and children in the company plan.

Solution: You should get your spouse and children their own individual/family policy as described in Chapter 5—a policy for a female, age 35, with two children, costs about $264 per month in California, for example. You would save $2,232 per year, and your family members would not lose health insurance coverage should you lose your job. Nationally, employer-sponsored plans cost about twice the price of individual/family policies with similar low-deductible/doctor co-pay coverage.

Problem: I am self-employed and do not have health insurance.

Solution: You should get an HSA-qualified high deductible individual/family policy before you or a family member develops a health problem—no one should ever go without health insurance, especially since it has now become affordable for most working people. See Appendix A for examples of affordable policies and rates in your state, which nationally average $92 per month for a single person and $272 per month for a family. Health insurance premiums recently became tax deductible for self-employed people, so your after-tax cost will be even less. Also, you should open an HSA and make the maximum tax-deductible $5,450 (family) annual contribution (in 2006).

Problem: I just lost my job and lost my health insurance.

Solution: You should apply and get accepted for your own individual/family health insurance policy as soon as possible. If you already have a Health Savings Account, you are allowed to withdraw money tax-free from your HSA to pay health insurance premiums while receiving unemployment benefits. When you purchase your individual/family policy, if you are healthy you can get up to three and a half months of free coverage from your former employer, typically worth $1,400 or more, if you follow the "COBRA loophole" described in Chapter 3.

Problem: I cannot afford health insurance.

Solution: If your annual income is below the federal poverty line (FPL)—about $20,000 for a family and $10,000 for a single individual—you probably qualify for Medicaid. If your family income is above the FPL but below $48,000 a year and you live in certain states (e.g., California or New York), you may qualify for other income-based programs—see Chapter 8 for more on Medicaid and other ways to get health insurance if you cannot afford it. You should also check out the new high-deductible HSA-qualified plans, which cost less than $90 per month for a single individual in most states—see Appendix A for examples in your state and who to contact to get one.

Problem: What's the best way to shop for my own individual/family health insurance policy?

Solution: There are three basic methods to shop for a policy: (1) Call insurance companies yourself. (2) Find a local agent in your state. (3) Shop online. See Chapter 4 for specific instructions on each method, including recommended phone numbers and web sites. The cost is the same regardless of which method you choose, since all states prohibit carriers and agents from discounting the stated prices of their policies or rebating commissions to consumers. Most people prefer to shop online and then work with a licensed agent—Chapter 4 explains how to locate a qualified agent in your state.

Problem: My employer is offering a high-deductible health insurance option for the first time. Should I take it?

Solution: In general, if you are healthy, you should choose high-deductible health insurance. The amount you save is likely to be more than the total of your out-of-pocket medical expenses. See Chapter 5 for the best options to choose from your employer's health insurance plan, and see Chapters 9 and 10 for how to save money once you have high-deductible health insurance.

Problem: A member of my family has a preexisting condition that has prevented my family in the past from getting an individual/family health insurance policy.

Solution: First, you should get the healthy members of your family their own policy before one of them develops a preexisting condition. Then, for the member of your family with the preexisting condition, carefully read Chapter 4 on how to apply for affordable individual/family health insurance without getting rejected, how to get a free copy of your Medical Information Bureau (MIB) file, and how to locate an agent in your state who knows which carriers may accept the preexisting condition. Also, read Chapter 7, which discusses six options for your unhealthy family member, including how to get state-guaranteed coverage, which, for example, costs about $194 per month for an adult in Maryland (see Appendix A for the rates in your state). Although state-guaranteed coverage is about twice as expensive, you typically need it for only the one family member with a health issue, so the blended price is not that much more for your entire family.

Problem: I work for a company that supplies me with free health insurance, but I would like to quit before age 65—either to retire or to start my own business.

Solution: You should get yourself an individual/family policy as soon as possible because if you or a family member should develop a health problem, you may not be able to get one after age 55—see Chapter 4 for how to buy an individual/family policy and Chapter 8 for more solutions for early retirees. Because of your age, your employer will save a lot of money when you drop out of its group plan, so you should ask your employer to reimburse you tax-free for the premiums on your individual/family policy. Chapter 8 tells you how to do this.

Problem: If someone in my family has a significant monthly prescription drug expense, what are our options?

Solution: See Chapter 9 for how to save up to 75 percent on prescription drugs by using drug discount cards, choosing the right pharmacy coverage, shopping overseas pharmacies, substituting generics, and using different, less expensive prescriptions. Also see Chapter 10 for how to save

100 percent—by working with a doctor to stop taking prescriptions entirely. If you or your parents are seniors, make sure you know about the new Medicare Part D prescription drug program that began in 2006 and costs only about $37 per month. This is explained in Chapter 8, along with how to enroll immediately before you experience a permanent life-time price increase.

Problem: I am about to change jobs. How can I transfer my family's health insurance coverage between employers?

Solution: When you leave your current employer, you should get a "Certificate of Creditable Coverage," as described in Chapter 3. This will prevent your new employer from excluding from coverage any preexisting conditions you or a family member may have. Under HIPAA, employers cannot exclude from coverage conditions for which you have had "contin-uous coverage" for the previous 12 months. See Chapter 3 for more details and other advice on what to do when changing or losing your job. You should also consider getting your spouse and children their own cov-erage, as described in Chapter 5, so you don't have to worry the next time you change jobs.

Problem: My parents are getting older and needing more medical care. What is the best health insurance solution for seniors?

Solution: Medicare is almost always the best solution for Americans over age 65, since the government pays most of the cost. However, the average senior on Medicare still spends about $4,000 a year for out-of-pocket medical items and supplemental insurance that Medicare does not cover—which is why every senior should have a Health Savings Account. Chapter 8 explains the components of Medicare, how to choose the best options for your parents, supplemental "Medigap" insurance policies, and the new Medicare Part D prescription drug insurance that began in 2006.

Problem: My parents would like to leave money to their grandchildren but are concerned about home-care or nursing home expenses destroy-ing their nest egg as they age.

Solution: Your parents are right to be concerned. The average nursing home today costs $82,500 per year per person, and Medicaid has closed the loopholes for government assistance unless you and your family are very poor. As explained in Chapter 8, there are four basic ways to finance your long-term care and, since it is unknown how long anyone will live and how much care each person will need, the best financial choice is usually long-term-care insurance. Chapter 8 also explains how to choose a long-term-care policy and how to pay the premiums with tax-free dollars from your HSA.

Problem: My wife and I want to have a baby. What are our insurance options?

Solution: If you or your spouse work for a company with a good employer-sponsored health plan, you are in luck—under HIPAA, employers must cover maternity and offer coverage to newborns regardless of their health. If you don't work for a company with a good health plan, consider switching employers, even if you are pregnant—HIPAA also requires employers to immediately cover pregnancy and newborns, even in cases where an employee marries a pregnant woman (see Chapter 3). If you choose to buy or have an individual/family policy, most carriers offer either a $5,000 separate deductible for pregnancy or optional pregnancy coverage, but will not cover pregnancy until at least six months after you obtain the policy or elect maternity coverage.

Problem: I work for a company with a good company health plan, but I don't know which options (HSAs, high deductible, FSAs, etc.) I should choose.

Solution: If you have a spouse or family, you can probably buy them their own permanent individual/family policy for less than you currently pay your employer to cover them. If you choose a high-deductible plan, you should get $1,000 to $2,000 tax-free contributed by your employer to your HSA for future medical expenses or retirement. If you have any medical or child-care expenses not covered by your employer (and who doesn't!), you can gain 50 to 90 percent additional spending power by paying these expenses with pretax dollars through an FSA or Section 125 salary redirection plan. If your employer doesn't provide it, you can (and should) also purchase long-term-disability insurance funded with pretax salary contributions. See Chapter 5 for specific strategies to follow on these and other options offered by your employer group health plan.

Summary Solutions for Businesses

Problem: I own a small business and would like to see all my employees have health insurance, but we cannot afford a traditional group plan.

Solution: You should (1) create a Health Reimbursement Arrangement (HRA) that reimburses employees tax-free for at least the price of an individual/family health insurance policy for a typical employee—about $92 per month for a male, age 35, and (2) establish a Section 125 salary redirection plan that allows your employees to redirect some of their wages to tax-free contributions to their HSA—you save 7.65 percent on FICA on the amount they redirect, and employees save up to 50 percent in FICA plus state and federal income taxes. Chapters 11 to 13 explain in detail how to set up a simple HRA and Section 125 HSA plan and how to help your employees obtain the best individual/family policies.

Problem: I own a small business that has group health insurance, but we no longer can afford the rising annual premium on our group policy.

Solution: You should terminate your existing "defined benefit" group health insurance plan and set up a fixed-cost "defined contribution" health plan as follows: (1) Establish an HRA to reimburse employees, say $100 to $200 per month, for their own individual/family policies, which typically cost only 25 to 50 percent of the price of your group plan; and (2) contribute 100 percent of the savings to HRAs and/or HSAs that cover employee medical expenses and allow employees to save unspent funds for future medical expenses or retirement. This will lock in your health benefit expense at today's level, and your employees will have equal or better coverage than they have now. Chapters 11 and 12 explain how to do this and how to get your employees to enthusiastically embrace your new "defined contribution" health plan.

Problem: My organization has an expensive traditional group health insurance plan. What new solutions can save money without hurting benefits?

Solution: There are many new things you can do to save $2,000 to $6,000 each year per employee on your group health insurance without hurting benefits for existing employees. For example, instead of offering new employees coverage from day of hire, you should have a 180-day waiting period and offer employees an HRA for company-paid short-term health insurance during the waiting period. Short-term coverage typically costs about one-eighth the price of an employer group plan because it lasts only six months—but this time limit is acceptable since new employees automatically get group benefits at the end of their waiting period. Chapter 13 explains how you can save $1,950 per single or $6,528 per family for each new hire using waiting period coverage and offers other new ways to save thousands per employee on COBRA, older employees, dental, vision, and more, without decreasing benefits.

To Miriam, Maxwell, Michael, Mark, and especially Lisa

I n 1999, my wife and I were elated to learn that she was pregnant, but our joy turned to panic that same month when we lost our employer-sponsored health insurance. If our baby was born prematurely, it could cost up to $60,000 a day for four months. And this amount didn't include care that a preterm child might need afterward or any medical care for my wife.

Fortunately, our baby was born healthy, and I found a new way to buy affordable health insurance for my family. But in the process of researching our health insurance options, I discovered that I had been wasting thousands of dollars a year by getting health insurance from employers instead of purchasing health insurance myself.

Here are some of the problems I discovered with employer-sponsored health insurance:

■ Employer-sponsored health insurance has become so expensive that most employers are cutting benefits, raising employee contributions, or no longer offering health insurance at all.

■ Employees receiving "free" health insurance from their employers are often paying their employer twice what they should be paying for health insurance coverage on their spouse and children.

■ Many employees feel trapped in jobs they don't want only because they don't know how to get affordable health insurance without an employer.

■ Employees of large companies who often feel the safest are actually the most at risk for "medical bankruptcy" because they lose their company-sponsored health insurance if they become ill and can't work.

■ Many Americans are wasting thousands of dollars a year paying for health insurance benefits that they don't need—such as pregnancy coverage when they are single.

■ Most health benefit plans pay enormous sums when you become ill, but contribute nothing to help you prevent illness from developing in the first place.

How I Found Solutions to These Issues, Saved $4,000 a Year, and Became an Expert on Health Insurance

After earning an MBA from Wharton in 1976, I began my career with Citibank, where I received traditional company benefits. Like most people, I never thought too much about health insurance as a potential threat to my financial future. Later, I became an entrepreneur and experienced firsthand the enormous economic burden health insurance places on small businesses.

In 1979, I began teaching finance at New York University and studying the problems surrounding employer-provided health benefits. I wrote articles on the economics of healthcare, testified before Congress in the 1980s, and served as an appointed economic adviser for two White House administrations. I began writing popular books on economics, wealth, and personal finance—five of which became international best sellers. Although I wrote about health insurance in my books, I didn't realize how easy it is to lose your health insurance until I faced my own crisis in 1999.

I solved my crisis by buying "individual/family" coverage directly from the Blue Cross Blue Shield carrier in my state—after researching for months to understand health insurance and how self-employed individuals could get their own individual or family policy. Amazingly, the brand-new type of individual/family policy I bought cost my family $4,000 less per year than we had been paying for the employer-sponsored policy that was canceled. Furthermore, this policy could not be canceled, nor could the monthly premium be increased due to someone in our family becoming ill.

As an economist and businessman, I realized that millions of self-employed Americans faced the same problems but were completely unaware of these individual/family policies and the options available to them. In late 1999, I cofounded a company to help other self-employed

Americans get these new affordable health insurance policies. As the company grew, we hired some of the top health insurance executives in the nation, most of whom had spent their entire working lives in the field.

In the period from 2003 to 2005, the floodgates opened. The federal government passed revolutionary legislation that made Health Savings Accounts and other related health insurance products (originally designed for self-employed people) legally available to all Americans—independent of whether they worked for a company that provided health insurance. Unlike traditional employer-sponsored health benefits, this new kind of health insurance is affordable and stays with you when you leave your job.

As a result of these changes in the law and in the health insurance industry, America's entire $2 trillion healthcare industry is undergoing the biggest change since health insurance was created during the Great Depression: it is shifting from employer-based health insurance to consumer-directed plans that individuals buy themselves. These new individual/family plans reward you for staying healthy and are better, cheaper, and safer than traditional employer-sponsored health insurance.

Two Reasons Why the Individual/Family Policy I Purchased Cost $4,000 Less than I Was Paying for an Employer-Sponsored Group Policy

Most working Americans and their families receive health insurance through their employer's group policy. Among these working Americans, 80 percent are healthy and consume less than $1,000 a year for health care. In contrast, 20 percent have major health problems in their families and, on average, consume more than $25,000 a year for health care. If you are closer to the 80 percent healthy group, new legislation allows you to purchase an "individual or family" policy directly from a carrier that is priced extremely low based on the fact that your actual health costs are closer to $1,000 a year. These individual/family policies typically cost less than half of what you and your employer are paying for your current traditional group policy. Insurance carriers offer this enormous discount because they only accept the 80 percent of applicants who are healthy and will most likely stay that way.[1]

Don't despair if you are in the 20 percent group (typically because of the preexisting health problems of one member of your family). In this book I explain ways to get "state-guaranteed coverage" for individual family members who are unhealthy so that the rest of your family can still qualify to be in the 80 percent pool of healthy applicants.

Not only can you now purchase an individual/family policy for yourself and/or your spouse and children, in 2007 employers can reimburse employees tax-free for the cost of health insurance premiums on individual/family policies.

The second reason my policy cost $4,000 a year less was because it had a higher annual deductible than our canceled employer policy. Insurance carriers will typically lower your annual premium by $3,000 a year for a $2,000 increase in your annual deductible—putting a guaranteed $1,000 a year in your pocket! Insurance carriers offer this great deal because it saves them $1,000 in paperwork costs on the 20 or so transactions that typically make up your first $2,000 in annual medical expenses.

In addition to saving thousands on our annual premium, we also received a Health Savings Account (HSA) to pay medical expenses tax-free until we reached the annual deductible on our policy—the HSA also allowed us to keep anything we didn't spend, up to $4,500 each year, for future medical expenses or retirement. Until 2004, HSAs were called "Medical Savings Accounts" and were legal only for a limited number of self-employed people. New legislation has now made them universally available for all working Americans.

Higher deductible Health Savings Account (HSA) plans are now being offered by most major employers—HSAs allow you to choose any medical provider and accumulate hundreds of thousands of dollars tax-free for future medical expenses or retirement.

The Health Insurance Revolution Has Begun

In the past two years, new legislation and regulations have dramatically altered the landscape for health insurance. However, very few individuals, and even fewer employers, are aware of the revolution that is taking place and of the following potential solutions to their problems:

1. Most Americans can now buy their own health insurance that is better, cheaper, and safer than their employer's insurance. But even if you choose to get health insurance from your employer, you can still save thousands of dollars every year by paying for only the health insurance benefits you need (this book describes how).

2. Employees receiving "free" health insurance for themselves from employers can purchase their own private policies covering their spouse and children for half the price their employer may be charging for their dependents.

3. Employees no longer need to stay in jobs they don't really want, because today they can get affordable health insurance without their employer.

4. Employers finally have an option to end their health insurance nightmare—instead of offering a very expensive one-size-fits-all group policy, they can offer every employee their own permanent individual/family policy and reimburse each employee tax-free for the cost of their monthly premium.

5. Americans can choose health insurance plans that provide wellness and preventive care to keep them from becoming ill—ranging from weight loss to smoking cessation.

These and many other changes discussed in this book have permanently changed the landscape for health insurance in the United States.

The purpose of *The New Health Insurance Solution* is to show you how to take advantage of these changes. This book explains how to get better, cheaper, safer insurance than you are getting from your employer, save thousands of dollars each year, and protect you, your family, or your business from the greatest threat to your financial future—our nation's broken employer-based health insurance system.

Vive La Revolution!
Paul Zane Pilzer
Park City, Utah

For the latest health insurance information please visit the web site for this book: *www.TNHIS.com* (also *www.TheNewHealthInsuranceSolution.com*).

The first acknowledgment goes to my friend and business partner, Tony Meyer, who for 22 years has found ways to bring consumers the benefits of my research through our business adventures. In 1999, when my family lost our health insurance, then found our own health insurance solution, Tony helped turn what I learned into the company that is now Extend Benefits Group (EBG)—dedicated to bringing affordable health benefits to millions of American families.

Continuing in chronological order, my next acknowledgment goes to everyone at EBG and especially Brian Tenner (who helped edit every chapter) and to our new investors at Revolution Health Group. Thank you all for allowing me, as former Chairman and cofounder, to shine by your achievements.

Next is my new team at Zane Benefits LLC. There will be many more of you by the time this is published, but I'm not sure I'll ever have more fun than when we were all crammed into my home office, with my wife cooking us breakfast, lunch, and dinner. Thank you, Josh, Ben, David, and Tom, for believing in our mission and for the better health benefits we are about to bring to millions of American families.

Then there is my brilliant editor, Richard Narramore. Richard was the first to realize that what I had learned over six years at EBG could be turned into a book to help every American get affordable lifetime health insurance. Richard originated the concept for this book, moved into my home in Utah to help produce the outline, and kept me focused throughout the most intense writing process of my career.

The next team member is my lead researcher, Catherine Chou, a second-year law student at BYU, who painstakingly researched state-guaranteed coverage in all 51 jurisdictions. Catherine approached this daunting task as if she, personally, were the parent of an ill child requiring government assistance to stay alive. The United States is in good hands if Catherine is representative of our next generation of legal and business professionals.

More than a hundred other individuals helped me research and summarize the information in this book—including Michael Ashkin, Tod Cooperman, Mike Fillon, Richard Jaffe, Allison Garrett, Patrick Gentempo, Scott Lingle, Kimberly Lankford, Fabrizio Mancini, and Toby Rogers.

Like all my previous books, this book benefited enormously by the same key individuals in my professional life: my literary agent Jan Miller, my brother and copy editor Lee Pilzer, my manager Reed Bilbray, my savant John Hauge, and my sages Gerry and Charles Pilzer.

And finally, my highest level of gratitude is reserved for my wife, Lisa, and our four children, Miriam, Maxwell, Michael, and Mark, who make everything worthwhile.

PART ONE

How to Better Protect Your Family While Saving $5,000+ Each Year: Savvy and Affordable New Health Insurance Strategies

You Are One Serious Illness Away from Bankruptcy: The Huge Gaps in Your Employer's Health Insurance Plan

Forty-five million Americans lack any form of health insurance and live in fear of a major medical problem. Yet surprisingly, 80 percent of these people are employed and 16 million earn more than $40,000 per family ($20,000 per single).* The good news is millions of these uninsured working Americans can now afford to buy good Health Savings Account (HSA-qualified) health insurance for an average of $92 per month for an individual or $272 per month for a family.† If you or a loved one is in this category, you may want to skip ahead to Chapters 2 and 4 to learn how.

Most Americans get health insurance from their employers and never think too much about it until they or a family member develops a serious health problem. That's when they first learn the details of their health insurance benefits, which medical providers they can use, and what their out-of-pocket expenses will be. In an ideal world, this is how it should be. As a resident of the greatest nation on earth, you should not need a book on health insurance solutions any more than you need a book on life insurance, car insurance, or property insurance. Sadly, this is not the case.

---

*The poorest 38 million Americans (those who earn less than $20,000 a year) receive free health insurance through Medicaid. See Appendix B.
†Average price in all states for policies offering coverage for 2006. See Appendix A.

Healthcare costs now consume almost one-sixth of America's economy, and, during your lifetime, medical and health insurance costs are likely to be your largest or second largest expense after housing. That's if you're lucky enough to have health insurance. However, as this chapter explains, even if you have health insurance, your traditional employer-sponsored plan is arguably the number one threat to your financial future.

This book describes great new ways you can save thousands of dollars each year while getting better coverage than your employer offers.

The problems with our current health insurance system are deep:

- Up to 1 million mostly middle- and upper-middle-class families file bankruptcy each year due to medical bills they can't pay—yet amazingly, three-quarters of these families had health insurance when they first became ill. A family bankruptcy typically affects three individuals and lasts for seven years—meaning up to 21 million people, including children, are living in economic purgatory at any given time due to failed health insurance.[1]

- Tens of millions of Americans are modern-day slaves—unable to retire early, or working in jobs they don't really want, just for the health insurance they need to take care of themselves, a spouse, or a child with a "preexisting condition."

- Health insurance is a crisis for employers as well as individuals. As I write, GM is in serious trouble because health insurance adds $1,550 to the cost of every car it sells. The cost of health benefits now exceeds profits for most of the Fortune 500.

- Small businesses are the backbone of our economy, yet many of them fail because they cannot afford to pay the premiums for their group health insurance plan. Our current employer-based health insurance system is injuring American competitiveness in the world marketplace and costing jobs here at home.

- Millions of self-employed and independent contractors go without health insurance because they don't realize it has recently become affordable and tax deductible.

- American seniors who have fought wars and saved enough money to pay off their home mortgages now live with a new daily physical and economic threat—their monthly prescription drug bill. The largest monthly expense in most senior households is prescription drugs, and many seniors make the terrible choice between buying their food or their medicine—24 percent of the prescriptions written each year are not filled because of price.*

■ Many seniors who have saved up hundreds of thousands of dollars for retirement or for their grandchildren's education sadly live to see their assets completely wiped out by medical or nursing care expenses not covered by Medicare.

None of these situations should exist. Recent changes in law and new health insurance options have made it possible for most Americans to get high-quality, affordable health benefits for themselves, their families, or their employees. This book explains how.

This book also teaches you how to save $5,000 or more each year on your health benefits and create a Health Savings Account nest egg of $200,000 to $500,000 or more for your retirement or future medical expenses.

Let's get started.

What Would Happen If You Became Ill and Could Not Work?

Don't despair as you start to read this chapter about the problems with employer-sponsored health insurance. Beginning with Chapter 2, this book is mostly about solutions that you can take advantage of now.

Have you ever thought about what would happen if you became ill, lost your job and your health insurance, and couldn't get another job? Every year this happens to millions of Americans, with dire consequences, and it doesn't have to be a major heart attack or cancer to lead you to the poorhouse.

Few employers can afford to keep paying absent employees for more than a few weeks after those employees have used up their available sick time and vacation. Such employees are then let go, and their financial problems, which are the leading cause of bankruptcy in the United States, begin. Employees who lose their jobs can get government-mandated health insurance coverage through COBRA for up to 18 to 36 months, but many cannot afford the high cost of COBRA, or their COBRA coverage runs out while they are still sick.

What are the chances that something like this could happen to you? There are hundreds of circumstances in which you could exceed your

---

*This situation will improve for many seniors with Medicare prescription drug coverage, which began in 2006 (see Chapter 8).

allowable sick and vacation leave, and the chances of this happening at some point in your working life are greater than 50 percent.

Outdoor activities. Do you play sports, ski or snowboard, go boating, or ride bicycles? Any one of these outdoor activities could cause an injury that would prevent you from being able to work. Even without a specific injury, many active people will require some type of knee or leg surgery during their working lifetime.

Home accidents. Although most people feel safest at home, the home is actually the place where you are most likely to have an accident requiring medical treatment or one that could prevent you from being able to work. Common causes of home accidents include falls, choking, shootings, poisoning, and improper use of medications.

Commuting/driving. Do you commute to work? More than 3 million people are hurt each year in auto accidents, and common injuries include fractures, broken bones, and spinal damage resulting in short- and long-term disability.[2]

High blood pressure. About 65 million Americans over age 20 have high blood pressure, a chronic disease requiring medication and one that dramatically increases the chances of having heart disease during your working lifetime.[3]

The overweight/obese. Almost two-thirds of Americans are overweight or obese; primarily because of this, 18 million Americans have diabetes and another 41 million over age 40 have prediabetes. Most people with prediabetes develop type 2 diabetes in 10 years. Diabetes virtually guarantees that you will have health issues requiring time away from work at some point in your life, and 65 percent of people with diabetes die from heart disease or stroke.[4]

Cancer, heart attack, or stroke. One in four men and one in five women will develop one of these debilitating diseases before age 65.[5]

Most Americans will develop some type of major medical condition at least once over a 45-year working life—a condition that could likely lead to job termination and loss of their health benefits. Are you and your family prepared for this eventuality?

The Gaps in Your Coverage When You Lose Your Job or Change Jobs

Once you lose your job, you lose your employer-sponsored health insurance unless you elect to go on COBRA. As explained more thoroughly in

Chapter 3, COBRA is the acronym for the short-term extension of your employer health insurance. Basically, COBRA allows you to continue your employer-sponsored health insurance for 18 months as long as you pay 100 percent of the cost of your former employer's plan plus a 2 percent administration fee (102 percent total).

COBRA is unaffordable for most people.

Nationally, COBRA premiums average about $700 a month for an individual and about twice that, $1,400 a month, for a family. Since total unemployment benefits average about $1,000 a month, only one in five COBRA-eligible individuals elect to go on COBRA—few people can afford to spend 100 percent or more of their unemployment check on health insurance. Worst of all, after 18 months on COBRA you are out on your own without health insurance. Yet, despite the enormous cost and lack of security, about 5 million people at any given time are on COBRA—mostly because they don't know any better or believe that they will soon get another job with health benefits.

You can get the equivalent of free health insurance for 60 days, saving you $1,000 or more, if you know the "COBRA loophole." Employers are required to offer you COBRA within 14 days of termination, and to keep their COBRA offer open for 60 days. By delaying to choose COBRA until day 59, you can get a free 60-day health insurance option while you shop around for a new employer or new health insurance or both. If, on day 59, you do elect COBRA coverage because you have had a medical issue, you are required to pay for COBRA from day 1. But if you haven't had a medical issue, you just received the equivalent of free health insurance for 60 days. (See Chapter 3 for more details on this strategy, on getting an additional 45 days of free coverage when you change jobs, and on getting 30 days of free coverage when you come off COBRA.)

You should only go on COBRA as a last resort. It is expensive, temporary, and if you should develop a health condition while on COBRA, it could prevent you from getting permanent affordable health insurance. There are much better solutions, which are all explained in this book.

If you have recently lost your health insurance (perhaps because you are accepting a new job), or if you aren't eligible for COBRA, or if your COBRA benefits just expired, you need to pay particular attention to another five-letter acronym, HIPAA, which is explained in Chapters 3 and 7. Most employers today (1) have 30- to 360-day waiting periods before health benefits begin for new employees and (2) exclude covering employees and their dependents for health conditions that preexisted their date of employment. Yet, under federal HIPAA law, if your new employee benefits begin less than 63 days after your old benefits terminate, your new employer is not allowed to exclude you or your family's preexisting medical conditions from your new health insurance.

In many states, health insurance carriers offering individual/family policies are required to accept HIPAA-eligible applicants without any exclusions for preexisting medical conditions (although typically at a higher premium). However, if you become HIPAA-eligible you will have to act fast—your HIPAA eligibility is limited to just 63 days from the first day you lose your health insurance.

Do not depend on HIPAA eligibility alone if you are changing jobs and need insurance for a family member with a preexisting medical condition—the median length of time between jobs has increased from 56 days in 1996 when HIPAA became law to 70 days today.[6] Once you know you are changing jobs, you should apply for individual/family health insurance immediately. If you get a new job with health benefits quickly and no longer need the individual/family policy, you can cancel your policy without charge before it takes effect.

What Happens When You Lose Your Health Insurance

Once you lose your employer-sponsored health insurance, your nightmare has begun. Not only are you going to have to worry about how to pay for healthcare, you are also going to have to worry about how to get good healthcare. Many medical providers refuse to schedule an appointment for people without health insurance, and those who do agree to see you will typically charge from 150 to 500 percent of what they would have charged you or your insurance carrier had you had health insurance.

Since the 1980s, each year between 1 and 2 million American families file personal bankruptcy. Until recently, the causes of these bankruptcies were unknown, and most people assumed credit card spending, divorce, and loss of employment to be among the major reasons. In February 2005 Harvard University released the results of its study, "Illness and Injury as Contributors to Bankruptcy."[7]

The study interviewed 1,771 Americans in bankruptcy courts and determined that about half were "medically bankrupt"—driven to bankruptcy by medical bills not covered by health insurance. Equally surprising, the study concluded:

- Three-fourths of the medically bankrupt had health insurance at the beginning of their illness.
- The majority of the medically bankrupt owned their own homes and had attended college.
- Many people filing medical bankruptcy were middle-class workers with health insurance who were unable to pay their co-payments, deductibles, and exclusions in the employer-sponsored health insurance plan.

This book teaches you how to avoid the insurance gaps that drive millions of Americans into medical bankruptcy.

To protect yourself and your family, you will need to evaluate employer-sponsored health insurance and individual plans that you purchase yourself, paying particular attention to terms like *annual out-of-pocket maximum* (OOP max)—which means the maximum out-of-pocket expense you could incur in a given year from coinsurance, deductibles, and exclusions.

Many employer health insurance plans have annual OOP maximums of tens of thousands or more. You can start to see why 75 percent of medically bankrupt middle- and upper-middle-class Americans mistakenly think their health insurance will cover them.

Chapter 5 reveals how to make sure your employer plan does not have an OOP max that would send you to the poorhouse if you had to pay it and how to get disability insurance to pay your salary if you cannot return to work after an illness. Chapter 6 shows you how to build a Health Savings Account (HSA) nest egg to cover your OOP max plus pay your health insurance premiums tax-free during any period of unemployment or illness, and you learn insider HSA tricks that can add hundreds of thousands to your HSA nest egg.

How to Avoid Losing Your Health Insurance When You Lose Your Job

The best way to avoid losing your health insurance when you lose your job is to purchase your own affordable individual/family policy—just as you purchase your own auto insurance. Unlike traditional health insurance you get from an employer, loss of employment has no effect on an individual/family health insurance policy. Also, unlike most employer/group policies, premiums on most individual/family policies cannot be increased, nor can the policy be canceled, if you become ill.

As explained in Chapter 4, the best time to buy your own policy is while you are healthy and still have your employer-sponsored health insurance. If you have a good company plan and wish to keep it, Chapter 5 explains how to choose the best options from your employer-sponsored plan and how to transfer your spouse and children onto their own less-expensive individual/family policy.

No one reading this book should ever go without health insurance. Despite what you read in the newspapers, there are health insurance options available for every American, although it may take you some time, effort, and expense to get them. In most cases, because of recent changes in the insurance industry, you can get good health insurance for an individual or a family for $150 to $300 per month. See Chapter 2 and Appendix A for details.

The Other Huge Gaps in Your Employer's Health Insurance Plan

By now you understand that employer-sponsored health insurance has some serious shortcomings:

■ It offers no permanent protection when you lose your job.

■ It offers only limited protection when you change jobs.

■ It exposes you to serious financial risk even if you keep your job—due to low lifetime maximum benefits, not to mention hidden co-payments, deductibles, and exclusions that you learn about in Chapter 5. Moreover, as you learn in Chapter 3, if your company goes bankrupt or is taken over, federal law (ERISA) protects your pension but not your health insurance—employers may terminate company-provided healthcare at any time.

In addition, your employer-sponsored health insurance plan probably has the following disadvantages:

■ It does not provide dollars to spend today on preventive care that can save you thousands of dollars tomorrow.

- It does not provide retiree health benefits if you choose to retire before age 65, and even if it does (as you learn in Chapter 8), many employers today are considering using bankruptcy and reorganization to bail out of their retiree health benefits obligations.

- It does not provide long-term or home care options if you should desire to live out your golden years in your own home versus in a nursing facility.

- It may not provide Health Savings Accounts and other new options that allow you to choose your own medical providers, lower your prescription drug costs, and save what you don't spend on healthcare today for your future healthcare tomorrow.

This book shows you how to get affordable solutions to cover all of these gaps, or to avoid the gaps altogether by buying your own individual/family policy.

How Employer-Sponsored Health Insurance Works

The term *employer-sponsored health insurance* is misleading since, basically, the *insurance* terminates when you lose your job—often the time when you are most financially vulnerable.

Employer-sponsored health insurance is also misleading because *insurance* means spreading the risk among a large group of people or organizations so that no single entity bears the cost of a catastrophic illness. That's not how employer-sponsored health insurance works. Each time an insured employee in your organization runs up large medical bills, your organization pays these costs the following year with a directly proportional increase in its annual health insurance premium.[8] The "insurance" employers pay for is actually little more than a delayed bill-paying mechanism. Because most very large employers realize this, they are *self-insured,* which means they simply pay for employee medical expenses through a third-party administrator.

In 1985 I testified before the U.S. Congress as follows:

> Show me a person who owns their own 100-employee business, and I'll show you an employer who knows the first name of each child of an employee who has diabetes—even though they are not supposed to know. A small employer with a $35,000-a-year employee should not be burdened with the $75,000-a-year medical cost for a child of that employee who has diabetes—or have to face the terrible choice between staying in business versus taking care of the sick child of an employee.

Sadly, until recently Congress has done very little to address this national tragedy. Many employers wish all they had to worry about was paying $75,000 a year for the medical costs of a diabetic child. Some medical situations today, from preterm births to kidney dialysis, can literally cost hundreds of thousands or millions of dollars—making the entire employee health plan unaffordable, or potentially even driving the employer out of business.

Suppose you work for a 51-person company where one participant develops a health condition costing $500,000 a year or more. Next year, the health insurance premium paid by your company will go up by $500,000. The cost of your employer-sponsored medical plan would increase more than $900 a month per participant, forcing your employer to cut benefits or possibly terminate the plan. What would happen if two people developed such a condition? Employer-sponsored group health insurance plans are ticking time bombs as their workforce ages.

Company health insurance worked well 45 years ago when most Americans worked for very large companies and for the same employer all of their life. It no longer works for employers or for employees for these reasons:

- Most employee groups today are too small to absorb the risk of a few catastrophic illnesses.

- Most people today change jobs every 1 to 4 years versus every 25 years, and they are often out of work (and thus without health insurance) for months between positions.

- Some employees pick their next job based on near-term medical requirements like pending knee surgery or heart operations. Employers providing good health benefits are under siege from desperate people who have no other place to turn for life-saving treatments.

- U.S. annual healthcare costs have skyrocketed from $27 billion, 5 percent of our economy in 1960, to almost $2,000 billion, 17 percent of our economy today.[9] In 1960 there were no heart transplants, kidney dialyses, and many other treatments that today cost many times the annual salary of an employee.

- For reasons primarily related to employers footing most of the bills, U.S. healthcare costs are rising at 15 percent per annum, almost four

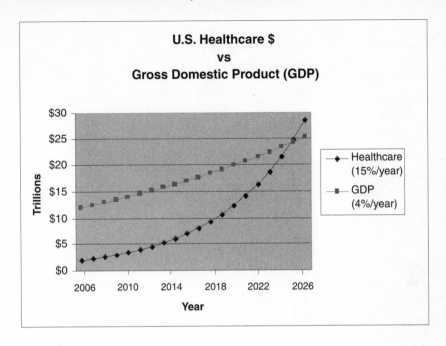

times the 4 percent projected growth rate for the U.S. gross domestic product (GDP). If this trend continues unchecked, U.S. healthcare costs will exceed GDP in 18 years and will cause the collapse of the U.S. economy long before then.

How We Got into This Mess

During the Great Depression, more people began using hospitals and less of them were able to pay. In response, hospitals created Blue Cross non-profit health insurance entities, which provided guaranteed service in return for a fixed fee—originally paid by either individuals themselves or their employers.

During World War II workers demanded wage increases that were pro-hibited by wartime wage and price controls. To grant a concession to labor without violating wage and price controls, Congress exempted employer-sponsored health insurance from wage controls and income taxation—in effect allowing off-the-books raises for employees in the form of nontaxable health benefits. This created an enormous tax advan-tage for employer-sponsored health benefits over health insurance pur-chased by employees with after-tax dollars (e.g., auto insurance). By the mid-1960s employer-sponsored health benefits were almost universal.

This huge government subsidy, which still exists today, results in the following:

■ It allows employers to deduct from their taxable income 100 percent of the cost of employer-sponsored health benefits.

■ It allows employees to receive unlimited employer-sponsored health benefits without having to pay wage or income taxes on these benefits.

Originally, employers thought providing health insurance was a great way to compensate employees, with federal and state governments paying about half the bill through a hidden tax subsidy.

With third-party employers and government footing the consumer's medical bill, the medical industry was given free rein to develop thousands of new treatments. Some of these were powerful, but others were not economical or merely preyed upon the hopes of desperately ill people and their families. Another problem that drove up costs was that the pharmaceutical industry began inventing solutions to problems that weren't previously defined as medical issues: prescription drugs to allow people to eat bad foods, Viagra to treat impotence caused by old age, and so forth. By classifying these solutions as "prescription drugs" rather than over-the-counter medicines, the pharmaceutical industry was able to sell them to consumers with a 50 percent tax subsidy through their employer-sponsored health insurance plans. The American taxpayer was thus forced to provide billions of dollars in unintended tax subsidies to the pharmaceutical industry to develop these lifestyle drugs, driving up costs for everyone.

As a result of this and other problems, U.S. healthcare costs, funded mostly through tax-free employer-sponsored health benefits, rose from $27 billion in 1960 to about $2,000 billion today. Today the cost of employer-sponsored health benefits exceeds profits for most large companies and threatens the viability of many of our best employers. In 2004–2005, despite a rising Dow over the same time period, GM's value dropped 50 percent after the company announced a $60 billion healthcare obligation.

Looking back, by making employer-sponsored health benefits tax deductible, Congress created more problems than just escalating medical costs:

■ The U.S. healthcare marketplace has been discouraged from developing innovative healthcare solutions for consumers at affordable prices because it has focused only on solutions that could be "sold" to employer health benefits and insurance company executives. This is in contrast to the dramatic innovation in every other part of the U.S. economy such as automobiles, restaurants, personal computers, telecommunications, and so forth, which are focused on solutions sold directly to consumers.

- The U.S. insurance industry has been preempted from developing affordable health insurance policies that could be sold direct to all consumers—just as it did with automobile insurance, homeowner's insurance, and life insurance.

- Employers and insurance companies have become the nation's healthcare gatekeepers, deciding, in advance, what type of medical care employees should receive—which by definition often means yesterday's treatments versus today's treatments. This also prevents entrepreneurial medical providers and alternative medical providers from developing better treatments, since they cannot get paid for them.

- As the average length of employment fell from 25 years to only 1 to 4 years, employers and their insurance carriers shifted to paying for short-term fixes versus long-term cures—treating the symptoms of disease instead of curing disease. Most of the major illnesses on which you can spend $1 today to save $100 in the future (e.g., heart disease from obesity or cancer from poor nutrition) will not show up until an employee is long gone or retired, at which time the $100 cost is picked up by another employer or by taxpayers through Medicare.

As you will see throughout this book, all of this has recently changed thanks to new federal legislation and regulations that have leveled the playing field between employer-sponsored health insurance and individual/family health insurance policies that you purchase yourself.

The New Health Insurance Solution: How We Are Getting Out of This Mess

Millions of working Americans believe that the only way they can get health insurance is from their employer. Until recently, their belief was accurate. But in the past few years, a quiet revolution has changed the health insurance options available to employees, self-employeds, and small businesses:

- *Individual/family health insurance has become cheaper and safer than traditional employer health insurance.* When my employer-sponsored policy (described in the preface) was canceled, I purchased an individual/family health insurance policy directly from the Blue Cross Blue Shield carrier in my state. This policy saved my family more than $4,000 each year in annual premiums and was much safer than my previous employer policy. Other than normal cost-of-living increases, our premium could not be raised, nor could our policy be canceled, because of job loss or a catastrophic illness.

■ *Health Savings Accounts are now available.* The individual/family policy I bought qualified me to contribute up to $4,500 a year tax-free to a Health Savings Account (HSA) for preventive care and for future medical expenses. However, at that time very few people qualified for Health Savings Accounts (at that time they were called "Medical Savings Accounts").

In 2004, Congress made Health Savings Accounts (HSAs) available to all Americans with high-deductible employer-sponsored health insurance or their own high-deductible individual/family policy.[10] Despite the higher deductible, HSAs save most consumers thousands of dollars each year. They also provide funds for preventive medicine, and allow you to save tax-free for your future medical expenses or even retirement. Individual/family policies that qualify for an HSA are now offered in almost every state, and 70 percent of the largest U.S. employers have announced plans to offer them to their employees.

■ *Premiums for self-employeds are now tax deductible.* In 1999, when I purchased my individual/family policy, the annual premium was not fully tax deductible even though I was self-employed. It seemed terribly unfair that health insurance premiums were 100 percent tax deductible for businesses offering group health insurance, but not for self-employed individuals. But, beginning 2003, Congress authorized a 100 percent income tax deduction for health insurance premiums for self-employed people.

■ *New Health Reimbursement Arrangements (HRAs) are now available for individual/family health insurance.* Prior to 2005, government and insurance regulations prohibited employers from reimbursing employees for individual/family premiums. But the IRS now allows Health Reimbursement Arrangements (HRAs) whereby employers can reimburse their employees tax-free for amounts spent on individual or family health insurance premiums.[11] As you will learn in Part II, these types of changes mean that businesses can now get out of their health insurance nightmare while still enabling their employees to obtain high-quality health benefits.

Three Trends behind the Changes

These and other changes are part of three major trends that are reforming U.S. health insurance. These trends are not dependent on Congress passing any new legislation or public policy—the legislation and regulations for them are already in place. The three trends are:

1. *Consumer-directed healthcare is making increasing inroads.* Health Savings Accounts are part of a much larger movement called *consumer-directed healthcare* (CDH), whereby individual patients choose their medical provider or service, and patients get to keep what they don't spend, tax-free, for future medical or retirement expenses. CDH also means that employers are shifting a larger percent of the healthcare burden to employees, especially employees with an unhealthy family member. CDH products and services are already incorporated into most employer-sponsored healthcare plans and individual and family policies. All types of health insurance will have CDH features within five years except for some existing union-type plans that have fixed contractual obligations.

2. *Individual/family insurance is replacing employer-sponsored health insurance.* Employer-sponsored group health insurance will decline over the next 10 years and be mostly eliminated within 20 years. Instead, employees will be given tax-free money to purchase their own individual or family health insurance policies. Government programs to protect the unhealthy and the indigent, and to provide limited coverage for the uninsured, will be expanded as health insurance responsibility is shifted from employers to individuals and government.

3. *Defined contribution plans are replacing defined benefit plans.* To accelerate the first two trends and to keep from going bankrupt, employers are shifting from paying the direct cost of employee health insurance (*defined benefit plans*) to giving each employee a fixed annual healthcare allowance (*defined contribution plans*)— and requiring that every employee obtain private or government-sponsored health insurance in order to receive this tax-free benefit.

The objective of this book is to teach you how best to take advantage of these trends to enable you to better protect your family and save money.

Why Buying Your Own Health Insurance Is Better, Cheaper, and Safer Than Your Company Plan

Nationwide, the average individual/family policy sold in 2004[1] cost less than half of what an employer-sponsored plan cost in 2004.[2]

Annual Health Insurance Premium Cost (2004)

	Single	Family
Individual/family policy	$1,800	$3,684
Employer-sponsored plan	$3,695	$9,950

Annual premiums in 2006 for employer-sponsored group plans cost approximately $4,500 per single and $14,000 per family. Comparable individual/family "traditional co-pay policies" for 2006 cost less than half this amount. Even better, the newest individual/family insurance plans that qualify for a Health Savings Account (HSA) cost 50 percent less than these individual/family "traditional co-pay" plans (see Appendix A).

Annual Health Insurance Premium Cost (2006)

	Single	Family
Individual/family traditional co-pay policy	$2,076	$ 6,492
Individual/family Health Savings Account policy	$1,104	$ 3,264
Employer-sponsored (2006)	$4,500	$14,000

See Appendix A for the cost of both "traditional co-pay" policies and Health Saving Account (HSA) individual/family policies in your state in 2005–2006.

If you are like most Americans, there are probably things you do not like about your employer-sponsored health insurance plan. Or you may not have insurance at all because you don't work for a company with a health benefits plan. Until recently, there was very little you could do about your situation. Thanks to new legislation and developments in the health insurance industry, you now have a good alternative to traditional employer health insurance— it's called an *individual policy* or an *individual/family policy.*

If you are relatively healthy and don't have free employer-sponsored health insurance, you will probably be able to save thousands of dollars by purchasing your own individual/family health insurance policy without your employer—just as you buy your own auto insurance. You may even get your employer to reimburse you tax-free for the monthly premium (see Chapter 11).

If you receive free health insurance from your employer, an individual policy may be safer (since you will not lose coverage if you lose your job) but it will not save money right now. However, if you pay extra to your employer to cover your spouse and children on your company plan, you may be able to save thousands of dollars now by taking them off your company plan and buying them an individual/family policy—and they will be safer because their health insurance will not be at risk if you lose your job. (See Chapter 5 for details.)

In 2004, 13 million Americans, about 4 percent of the U.S. population, were covered by an individual/family policy, and 157 million Americans were covered by an employer-sponsored plan. (See Appendix B.) These figures are about the same today. Because individual/family policies used to be unaffordable and difficult to obtain, few people are familiar with them and how they differ from the traditional employer-sponsored health insurance plans that most Americans have now. In this chapter we address the following questions:

What is individual or family health insurance?

How do I obtain individual or family health insurance?

How much does individual or family health insurance cost?

Why haven't I ever heard about individual or family health insurance?

What Is Individual/Family Health Insurance?

An individual or family health insurance policy is a policy purchased from an insurance company or government entity covering a single individual or selected family members.

The terms *individual policy, family policy, individual and family policy, individual/family policy,* and *individual or family policy* all mean the same thing—a policy purchased by a consumer directly from an insurance carrier (similarly to auto insurance) covering an individual or a family. (The terms *policy, plan, company,* and *carrier* are also used interchangeably and mean the same thing.)

There are two main differences between employer-sponsored "group policies" and individual or family policies:

1. **Employers and their group-policy insurance carriers are legally required to accept all applicants regardless of their health. In contrast, insurance carriers offering individual policies can reject applicants with preexisting medical problems, and therefore can typically offer far lower rates to healthy applicants (except in five states).**
2. **The premium paid by employers for their group policies is typically increased every year based on the previous year's healthcare costs of the employee group. In contrast, the premium you pay for an individual or a family policy cannot be raised each year, nor can the policy be canceled based on your health or your prior year healthcare costs.**

When you purchase an individual health insurance policy, you become a member of an insurance "group." But it's not the relatively small group limited to the employees of one company—it's the large group of people in your state who purchased a similar policy from the carrier in a given time frame. Monthly premiums paid for individual policies typically increase annually with the level of inflation or overall medical costs. The insurance carrier is allowed to ask the state insurance regulator for a rate increase based on the actual prior year's health costs for everyone in your group.

However, unlike with employer group policies, these groups of individuals are so large that even the catastrophic illness of hundreds of members would not result in a significant increase in your monthly premium. In contrast, in a small company, if one of the employees gets an extremely expensive illness like diabetes or cancer, the following year the carrier could double the cost that employer is paying for health insurance. Many companies are forced to pass increased costs on to employees or drop health insurance coverage because of catastrophic employee illnesses. Huge, sudden increases in health insurance costs can't happen with individual/family health insurance because your "group" is so much larger.

Moreover, competitive market forces limit potential increases in premiums for individual policies. Unlike with life insurance, the premium for individual and family health insurance is paid monthly, with no penalty for cancellation. When a carrier increases the premium, healthy policyholders start looking around to see whether they can obtain less expensive health insurance from another carrier. As explained in Chapter 4, even if your premium is not increased each year, you should always get new health insurance quotes annually to ensure you are getting the best deal.

State regulations also protect you from significant increases in your monthly premium. Insurance carriers are generally prohibited from raising premiums on existing group members above the levels paid by new people choosing to join the group—which protects you if you become unhealthy and are not able to shop around for a better rate from a different carrier.

Most states also have laws or regulations requiring individual health insurance policies to be renewable—meaning you can't be dropped by your carrier for any reason except nonpayment of your premium. If you live in a state that doesn't require individual policies to be guaranteed renewable, you are still protected as long as you choose a major carrier—policies from major carriers, such as Golden Rule or the Blue Cross Blue Shield plans, typically have a "guaranteed renewable" clause in their policy documents.

Unlike employer-sponsored health insurance, individual and family health insurance is real "insurance" because it "guarantees protection or safety." As long as you pay the premium, your policy cannot be canceled nor the premiums increased just because you lose your job, change jobs, or have a catastrophic illness in your family.

As with employer-sponsored health insurance, individual or family health insurance also includes access to a network of medical providers who charge 15 to 90 percent less to those in the network than to those outside the network, or to those who have no health insurance.

However, you get to choose which network of doctors and medical providers you wish to use for your family instead of having this choice made for you by your employer. As you will learn in Chapters 4 and 6, the ability to choose your own medical providers and type of network discounts is one of the best features of individual health insurance. Even if you have a high-deductible individual policy where you pay your own medical expenses, you pay each medical provider only the discounted price it would otherwise have received from an insurance carrier or large employer.

Individual/Family Insurance versus Employer-Sponsored Insurance

Feature	Employer-Sponsored	Individual/Family
Protection when job lost	Limited	Yes
Protection when changing jobs	Limited	Yes
Choice of medical providers	Limited	Yes
Protection from co-payments, deductibles, and exclusions	None	Available
Preventive and wellness care	Limited	Available
Retiree health benefits[a]	Limited	Yes
Long-term-care options	None	Available
Long-term disability	Limited	Available
Healthy financial incentives (e.g., HSAs)	Limited	Yes
Lifetime maximums for coverage[b]	Limited	Yes

[a]Employers are terminating retiree health benefits (see Chapter 8), while individual/family policies are guaranteed renewable until age 65.
[b]State law requires minimum lifetime maximums of from $1 to $6 million—employers are exempt from this requirement under ERISA (see Chapter 3).

Obtaining Individual/Family Health Insurance

Individual and family policies may be purchased directly from an insurance carrier such as a Blue Cross Blue Shield company, or through an insurance agent licensed to do business in your state and appointed by insurance companies to represent them. A good place to start is an online search engine like www.ehealthinsurance.com or www.zaneben.com, which provide quotes for thousands of policies from many different carriers.[3]

TIP: Be careful when you shop online for health insurance, and watch the fine print. Most web sites offering "online quotes" request personal contact information and then don't deliver any online quotes—they sell your information to third parties along with your express permission to phone you. A good online insurance web site will not ask for your name or contact information until you have seen quotes and are ready to choose a policy.

Insurance companies are legally required to charge the same premium whether you purchase your policy directly from the carrier or through a licensed health insurance agent. You should always get quotes from several carriers before choosing a policy, and choose an agent appointed by several of the major carriers in your state, particularly if a member of your family has a health issue.

See Chapter 4 for step-by-step instructions on how to buy your own low-cost, high-quality individual/family policy.

As I mentioned earlier, employers offering employee health benefits and their insurance companies must blindly accept every applicant regardless of their health—which is why employer-sponsored group policies are so expensive. In contrast, in almost all states, individual/family insurance carriers may choose the individuals whom they accept after analyzing the health risks of each family member applying for coverage. This process is called *underwriting*. The underwriter for an insurance company examines the healthcare experience, age, current health, family history, and lifestyle for each member of your family. The underwriter then makes three decisions regarding your application:

1. *Acceptance.* The underwriter may accept your entire family, or accept only certain members of your family, based on their assessment of the health risk of each individual.

2. *Uprating.* If the underwriter decides that a member of your family poses a moderate health risk, the underwriter may accept your application with a typical 15 to 200 percent rate increase over the normal monthly premium for a healthy individual in your age group.

3. *Exclusions.* The underwriter may accept your application with exclusions for "preexisting conditions" for one or more family members. For example, if you have a child with moderate diabetes, certain carriers will accept your child excluding all claims related to, or resulting from, diabetes. Such preexisting conditions may be excluded for a certain period of time or for as long as you keep renewing the policy.

Generally, about 80 percent of the applicants for individual/family insurance are accepted without being uprated or having exclusions.

In five states, state law requires carriers to accept 100 percent of all applicants "without upratings or exclusions." Because they are required to charge drug addicts, smokers, or clinically obese people the same rates as healthy people, few carriers offer policies in these states, and those that do typically charge everyone premiums 300 to 400 percent higher than in other states—effectively uprating all individual and family policies 300 to 400 percent. (See Chapter 7 on community rating and guaranteed issue policies if you live in New York, New Jersey, Massachusetts, Maine, or Vermont.)

There is no standard underwriting process, and insurance carriers vary widely in their assessment of the same health risk. Chapters 4 and 7 explain how to use this to your advantage if a member of your family has a preexisting condition. For example, you should get quotes from several carriers and consider applying to two or more carriers simultaneously. You can also get separate coverage for an unhealthy member of your family from your state (called "state-guaranteed" coverage) or a different carrier, while insuring the healthy members of your family under a policy that will likely cost thousands of dollars less.

If possible, try to avoid applying for individual health insurance if you have a preexisting medical condition or think you may be rejected for any reason. If you ever get rejected, you will have to state the reason for rejection on every subsequent application, and your premium could be higher.

A good agent knows which carriers will accept and reject applicants with preexisting conditions, and can advise you before you submit an application. Sometimes, agents who have a close relationship with a carrier can get a verbal preapproval before they even submit an application. You should also never blindly accept an insurance company's decision to exclude you or "uprate" your policy—since your initial premium will form the basis for all future increases. If you need health insurance right away, you may choose to accept an offer for insurance with an uprating or exclusion, and then appeal the decision of the underwriter.

For example, in December 2004, I applied to Blue Cross Blue Shield (Utah) to change the deductible on my family policy. The underwriter accepted my application with an uprating of 30 percent because it claimed I had once had a minor back problem. This uprating would have raised our monthly premium from roughly $400 (for a family of six) to $520, except that I counteroffered and we settled at an uprating charge of 15 percent, or $60 per month ($460 total premium). Then, after accepting the individual underwriter's 15 percent uprating offer, I filed an appeal with the carrier, which I won in 2005—resulting in a retroactive premium reduction of $60 a month. Assuming I renew this policy until my children are adults, this $60 a month reduction in premium saves my family $31,242 over the life of the policy.[4]

Employer-Sponsored Health Insurance Is Double or Triple the Price of Individual/Family Insurance

Employer-sponsored health insurance premiums cost about twice as much as individual or family health insurance premiums *for similar coverage.* As I mentioned earlier, the reason is that insurance companies have to accept every employee in your organization's group plan, no matter what their health risk may be. As explained in the preface, 80 percent of Americans consume less than $1,000 a year in medical care, while 20 percent consume, on average, more than $25,000 a year in medical care. With individual/family policies, insurance companies accept mostly healthy people in the 80 percent group and can charge much lower prices as a result.

Actually, the cost employers pay, per employee, is closer to three times as much as the actual cost for individual/family policies. This is because people who spend their own money to buy an individual/family policy do not choose policies *that are the same as those offered by employers*—they choose only those features and options they really want. (For example, employer-sponsored policies cover maternity, which is optional on individual policies.)

A leading U.S. health insurance agent for individual and family policies, eHealthInsurance, published the results for 82,000 individual and family policies purchased by its clients over a six-month period in 2004. Nationwide, the average family policy sold cost $307 per month, and the average single policy sold cost $150 per month ($3,684 and $1,800 per year, respectively). In contrast, a comparable Kaiser Foundation survey showed the average pro rata cost of employer-sponsored health insurance in 2004 to be $829 per month per family and $308 per month per single ($9,950 and $3,695 per year, respectively).[5]

Annual Health Insurance Premium Cost (2004)

	Single	Family
Individual or family	$1,800	$3,684
Employer-sponsored	$3,695	$9,950

Industry experts consider this enormous cost discrepancy between individual/family and employer-sponsored policies to be even larger today. The national average for employer-sponsored coverage is estimated to have been $14,000 per family ($4,500 per single) per annum in 2006.

This does not mean that average American workers are themselves paying too much for their own health insurance by having employer-sponsored coverage—most Americans receive free or heavily subsidized health insurance from their employers.

However, most Americans also typically pay their employer 50 to 100 percent of the prorated group health insurance premium for their spouse and children. If you are in this category, as explained in Chapters 4 and 5, you could save thousands of dollars a year by switching your spouse and children to a safer, better, and cheaper individual policy—and save even more if you carefully choose only the features you need to best protect your family.

Employees don't care how much their employer-sponsored health insurance costs because they typically don't pay for it—except for the $100 to $600 per month they typically pay to cover family members under the same plan.

Personally, I am currently paying $466 a month (in 2006) for a superdeluxe family policy covering me, my wife, and our four children ages 4, 3, 2, and 1—our only out-of-pocket costs are $20 for doctor visits and $5 for most prescriptions. An employer buying this same policy would pay more than twice as much.

The largest factor determining the cost of an individual/family policy is the age of the oldest adult member of the family. For example, even though I am healthy, because I am older (age 52) my share of our family's health insurance bill is as much as that of my wife and all four children combined. This is because on average, for example, a male's healthcare spending doubles from age bracket 35–44 to age bracket 45–54, and then rises another 50 percent in age bracket 54–65.[6]

Annual Cost of Healthcare by Age

Age Group	35–44	45–54	54–65
Healthy male	$ 500	$ 1,000	$ 1,500
Unhealthy male	$10,000	$20,000	$30,000

In Appendix A, for an HSA-qualified high-deductible policy from Blue Shield of California, the premium is $97 per month for a 35-year-old healthy male. This premium drops to $65 per month for a 25-year-old male, but rises to $149 per month for a 45-year-old and to $250 per month for a 55-year-old.[7]

TIP: Once you understand that health insurance costs on individual/family policies rise significantly as you age, you can use this principle to save thousands of dollars a year (see Chapters 4 and 5). If one family member is much older, you

> can remove that person from your family policy to lower your
> premium by 50 percent and get separate coverage from an
> employer, a different carrier, or a government entity.

On a national level, the largest determinant of your monthly premium for individual health insurance is not your age, but the state in which you live. Incredibly, the average cost of an individual policy for a single person in 2004 was $138 per month ($1,656 per year) in Pennsylvania, and the same coverage rose to $340 per month ($4,080 per year) by just walking across the Delaware River into New Jersey.[8] (See chart that follows.)

This is because a handful of states (New Jersey, New York, Massachusetts, Maine, and Vermont) have made it illegal for insurance carriers to offer lower premiums to healthy families and have mandated that every ill person, even chain smokers or drug addicts, be automatically accepted and pay the same premium as a healthy individual. As a result, of course, few carriers operate in these states and prices are high. A smart strategy for healthy individuals in these states may be to wait until they have a medical problem before buying health insurance. (New York recently closed this loophole by requiring a 12-month waiting period for coverage of pre-existing conditions.)

Fortunately, at the time of this writing, proposals are circulating in Congress to allow insurance carriers offering any policy in a single state to freely sell such policies in all other states—just as they do with life insurance, credit cards, and other financial products (see epilogue).

For now, when it comes to individual/family health insurance, you are stuck purchasing a policy only from a carrier willing to meet the laws and regulations of the state in which you live.

Following is the average cost of an individual policy for a single person sold in 2004 by eHealthInsurance in the 10 largest states representing 55 percent of the U.S. population.

Average Cost of Individual Policy per Single Person in 2004

10 states (55% of U.S. population)	Monthly Premium	Annual Premium
California	$140	$1,680
Texas	$133	$1,596
New York	$295	$3,540
Florida	$148	$1,776
Illinois	$140	$1,680
Pennsylvania	$138	$1,656
Ohio	$132	$1,584
Michigan	$112	$1,344
New Jersey	$340	$4,080
Georgia	$159	$1,908

Appendix A, "State-by-State Guide to Health Insurance," contains representative single and family health insurance costs for 2005 to 2006 in every state and the District of Columbia, as well as the cost of the average policy actually sold in 2004.

Why Haven't I Heard of Individual/Family Health Insurance?

In 1976 I joined the workforce in New York City, and for the next 23 years I received health insurance from my employer or from one of my companies. When my employer-sponsored policy was canceled in 1999, I was surprised to discover that I could simply pick up the telephone and purchase an individual or family health insurance policy directly from the Blue Cross Blue Shield carrier in my new state of residence (Utah). I discovered that in almost all states there were multiple carriers offering affordable individual and family policies. However, most of my friends in these states also didn't know that such affordable policies were available.

There are many reasons that most people haven't heard of individual/family health insurance policies:

Simple inertia precludes action. The majority of people living in the United States today have always received free or low-cost employer-sponsored group health insurance as a job benefit. Most people are unaware that better options exist because they have never had to go looking for them.

Families used to be covered by employers. Until recently, most employers providing employee health insurance included free or heavily subsidized coverage for the employee's spouse and children. Today most private employers charge employees 50 to 100 percent of the cost for insuring their spouse and children. Many employees aren't aware they are paying from half to all of the cost and not just a co-payment.

Employers won't tell you. If you are currently paying your employer for the cost of insuring your healthy spouse or children, your employer doesn't want you to know about much less expensive individual or family health insurance. The $4,000 or more you pay in annual premiums for your family goes to support other, less healthy group members. Your employer's group health insurance premium would increase dramatically if healthy people were to leave the group.

People think individual or family policies cost more. The average cost of an individual/family health insurance policy used to be higher than the cost of an employer-sponsored policy, but today it is less than half the pro rata cost of a group policy in most states.

U.S. income tax laws did not encourage it. Until recently, people wanting to purchase their own individual or family health insurance had to earn almost $2 of pretax income to have $1 left over to pay their health insurance premium. As explained in Chapters 11 and 13, this is no longer the case now that employers are allowed to reimburse employees tax-free for health insurance premiums on individual and family policies. In addition, health insurance premiums only recently became 100 percent tax-deductible for self-employed people.

Insurance carriers don't advertise. Advertising the availability of individual policies attracts mostly applications from unhealthy and/or unemployed people who typically do not qualify for, or cannot afford, individual health insurance. These applications are expensive to process and can cause regulatory problems for the carriers when most of them are rejected. Instead, carriers rely on a select group of agents who are trained to send in applications only from healthy applicants who can afford the premium.

Individual/Family Health Insurance Policies in 2006

Appendix A, "State-by-State Guide to Individual/Family Health Insurance Costs," contains representative prices and details for individual/family health insurance policies available in every state for coverage in 2005–2006. Policies shown are from the top-rated insurance carriers in each state, mostly Blue Cross Blue Shield plans.

The average monthly premium for an employer-sponsored policy in 2006 is $1,166 per month per family and $375 per month per single individual—more than twice the average price of the roughly comparable traditional individual/family policy that is available now for 2006.

Moreover, when spending their own money, many people purchasing their own individual/family policies will choose an even less expensive, higher-deductible Health Savings Account (HSA) policy—so the thousands they save in premiums each year can go into a tax-free savings account for their retirement and future medical expenses (see Chapter 5).

Average Monthly Premium for Individual/Family Health Insurance Policies (2005–2006)

	Traditional Policy (Low Deductible with Co-Pays for Doctor Visits)	Health Savings Account Policy (Higher Deductible of $2,500–$7,500)
Single	$173	$ 92
Family	$541	$266

Individual/family health insurance policies are not only much cheaper, but also offer better benefits and are much safer—particularly when you lose your job or change jobs, as you will see in the next chapter.

Your Legal Rights to Health Insurance When You Lose Your Job or Change Jobs: ERISA, COBRA, and HIPAA

"Dad, what's the difference between a recession and a depression?"
"That's easy," my father replied, citing a common adage. "In a recession,
your neighbor loses his job. In a depression, you lose your job."

If you have just lost your job or are thinking about changing jobs or retiring, keep reading—you need to know your legal rights under COBRA and HIPAA—the two most important federal laws that protect your rights to health insurance coverage. (If you think you know them, think again, the rules changed in 2005.)

If you have a stable job and need help choosing options from your employer-sponsored plan, or want to purchase your own individual policy, you may wish to jump ahead to Chapter 5 or Chapter 4 and refer back as necessary.

If you own your own business you'll want to carefully read everything in this chapter, since hidden in the rules of COBRA and HIPAA are the ways to secure affordable permanent health insurance for your chronically ill employees.

ERISA, COBRA, HIPAA, and the IRS Code effectively dictate the healthcare benefits you receive—from the medicines your doctor can prescribe to how long your employer must provide coverage if you've lost your job. COBRA and HIPAA laws are particularly important if you need health insurance for a family member with a preexisting medical condition, or if a family member should develop a preexisting condition in the future. These laws apply whether you obtain health benefits from your employer or through your own individual/family policy, and they are particularly important if you are transferring between employers and/or individual healthcare plans.

ERISA—Protects Your Pension but Not Your Health Benefits

Between 1913 and 1974 there were thousands of scandals involving employer abuses of retirement health benefits; numerous overlapping and often conflicting laws and regulations were passed to stop them. Finally, Congress consolidated the regulation of retirement and health benefits into a massive piece of legislation called the Employee Retirement Income Security Act of 1974 (ERISA).

When it comes to retirement benefits, ERISA law contains elaborate provisions to protect workers should their company try to reduce their pension obligations or should the company go bankrupt.[1] In 1974, when ERISA was passed, it was accepted that companies would always provide their workers and retirees with health benefits—thus ERISA has no requirements for employers to continue their health benefits plans and is virtually silent on what happens to employee health benefits when an employer goes out of business.

If you are retired or planning to retire from a large corporation and take advantage of your company's retiree health insurance benefits, be aware that these benefits could be reduced, the premiums raised dramatically, or the policies canceled altogether. See Chapter 8 for details.

Moreover, if your employer is self-insured—as are most U.S. employers with more than a few thousand employees—your employer is exempt under ERISA from complying with state and local insurance regulations.[2]

This means, for example, that your state may require all health insurance plans to have at least a $2 million per person lifetime maximum, but under ERISA, your employer-sponsored plan may have only a $500,000 lifetime maximum. Your state may limit annual premium increases to 15 percent a year, but under ERISA, your employer-sponsored plan may increase your premium contribution 100 percent or more.

If you receive your health benefits from a self-insured employer, no matter which state you live in, assume nothing—read carefully the complete Summary of Plan Document (SPD), a description of your health benefits, that your employer must provide to every employee.

When you read your SPD, you will not be able to miss the following paragraph, which is contained in virtually every employer-sponsored health benefits document:

> Employer has the right to change or terminate a plan at any time and for any reason. A change also may be made to premiums and future eligibility for coverage, and may apply to those who retired in the past, as well as those who retire in the future.[3]

Nothing in ERISA law prohibits employers from unilaterally terminating their health benefits plans or increasing the premiums they charge employees.

As explained in Chapter 2, individual/family insurance polices sold by private insurance carriers are required to be "guaranteed renewable," even if you have a catastrophic expensive illness. Insurance carriers are also required to limit increases in their premiums. In contrast, self-insured employers offering employer-sponsored health insurance have no such requirements and, under ERISA, are generally exempt from any state insurance regulations to the contrary.

In the 1980s and 1990s corporate raiders such as Boone Pickens and Carl Icahn made hostile tender offers for companies whose stock was selling below the price that the companies' assets would fetch at a liquidation sale. As explained in Chapter 8, new corporate raiders may soon be purchasing companies whose stock prices have fallen because they are spending billions providing health benefits to current and past employees—most of whom are no longer contributing to the earnings of those companies. These new corporate raiders will simply terminate the companies' retiree health benefits plan and in some cases reduce or terminate current employee health benefits.

Those Americans who feel the safest—individuals receiving health insurance through their employers—are actually the most at risk. It is only a question of time before they find themselves out of work and without health insurance—or their employer may be forced to terminate its health insurance plan.

Most employees today don't even know what ERISA is, but they do know about ERISA's most common amendments, COBRA and HIPAA, which set legal guidelines for cases in which a company remains in business and decides to keep its employer-sponsored health benefits plan.

COBRA—A Temporary "Last Resort" if You Lose Your Employer-Sponsored Health Insurance

The first major amendment to ERISA, which has become almost a household word for people who have changed jobs, is the Consolidated Omnibus Budget Reconciliation Act of 1985 (COBRA). If you lose your job, COBRA allows you and/or your family to continue to participate in your employer's group health benefits plan, at your own expense, for 18 to 36 months.

You should choose COBRA only as a very last resort. It is expensive (typically $1,200 per month or more for a family, $400 per month for an individual), temporary, and if you should develop a health condition while on COBRA, could prevent you from getting permanent affordable health insurance. Most people are much better off buying an individual/family policy. However, COBRA can be enormously beneficial to employees and their families in times of a health crisis. You might have a child who needs a $200,000 operation or takes $3,000 worth of medications a month—either of which would prevent you from qualifying for affordable individual/family health insurance.

> COBRA should almost always be your last choice because it is both expensive and temporary; however, for people with expensive preexisting medical conditions that prevent them from qualifying for an affordable individual/family policy, it is a critically important backstop. You should always be familiar with your COBRA rights and obligations.

In some states, if you have a family member with a serious preexisting condition, you can save tens or hundreds of thousands of dollars by becoming HIPAA-eligible, but to do this, you may have to accept and exhaust your COBRA benefits (as explained in Chapter 7). Some states require you to be HIPAA-eligible to qualify for "state-guaranteed" permanent coverage (discussed later in the chapter).

Many people are under the misconception that COBRA is "ordinarily less expensive than individual health coverage."[4] This is false in almost all cases. COBRA typically costs individuals 102 percent of the full pro rata cost of an employer-sponsored group plan—which, as discussed here and in Chapter 2, is two to three times the average premium paid for an individual or family policy.

Summary of COBRA Rules and Eligibility

Employers. COBRA applies only to individuals eligible to be covered by group health plans maintained by employers with 20 or more employees in the prior year (on more than 50 percent of business days). Part-time employees count as a fraction of an employee based on hours worked. COBRA does not apply to plans sponsored by the federal government and certain church-sponsored organizations.

Beneficiaries. A qualified beneficiary is a covered employee, his or her spouse, or a dependent child who was eligible to be covered by the employer's group plan the day before the qualifying event.

Qualifying event that makes the covered employee eligible for COBRA

1. Voluntary or involuntary termination of employment for reasons other than "gross misconduct"
2. Reduction in the number of hours of employment

Qualifying event that makes a spouse and/or dependent eligible for COBRA

1. Voluntary or involuntary termination of employment by covered employee for reasons other than "gross misconduct"
2. Reduction in the number of hours of employment by covered employee
3. Covered employee eligible for Medicare
4. Divorce or legal separation from the covered employee
5. Death of covered employee
6. Loss of "dependent child" status

Cost of COBRA health insurance coverage. Beneficiaries are allowed to be charged 100 percent of the pro rata cost of the employer's group plan (plus a 2 percent administration fee) of similarly situated individuals who have not had a qualifying event—including both the portion paid by employees and the portion paid by employers. (An example follows.)

Period of coverage

■ Covered employee may have up to 18 months following a qualifying event.

- Spouse or dependents may have up to 36 months following a quali-fying event.

- Disabled persons may be allowed an additional 11 months at 150 percent of premium (versus 102 percent).

The High Cost of COBRA

For example, you might work for a typical company that has a generous health benefits package for existing employees but makes no payments toward COBRA coverage for ex-employees. Your existing health benefits plan probably costs $1,400 per month per family. (Contact your health benefits administrator to get the actual numbers for your company.) Your employer pays 100 percent of the cost for your individual health benefits ($400 per month) and 60 percent ($600 per month) of the cost ($1,000 per month) for your spouse and dependents (you pay the remaining 40 per-cent). Your family's COBRA coverage in this case, with you paying 100 percent of the costs, would be $1,428 a month, or $17,136 a year ($1,400 per month, or $16,800 per year, plus 2 percent administration fee).

A few employers do voluntarily pay part of the cost of COBRA during the first few months of unemployment, so check carefully with your plan administrator before rejecting COBRA entirely because of cost.

Employer-Sponsored Group Policy Cost
(Prorated for an Employee and Dependents)

	Total Premium	Employee Contribution	Employer Contribution
Employee cost per month	$ 400	$ 0	$ 400
Family cost per month	$ 1,000	$ 400	$ 600
Total cost per month	$ 1,400	$ 400	$ 1,000
Total cost per year	$16,800	$4,800	$12,000

Note: Typical cost for family coverage through COBRA is $1,428 per month, or $17,137 per year. Typical cost for yourself or one family member on COBRA is $408 per month, or $4,896 per year. (These figures include the 2 percent administration fee.)

COBRA Timeline—How to Get COBRA Coverage if You Need It

If you need COBRA because you or a family member has an expensive med-ical problem and can't get an affordable individual/family policy, you must carefully follow COBRA's qualifying rules. Neither your employer, your spouse's employer, nor your ex-spouse's employer is likely to make any exception for you if you fail to follow the exact COBRA timeline required. The reason is that employers typically dislike COBRA coverage and provide it only because it is legally required. This dislike is compounded by the fact that some people who accept COBRA consume many times their COBRA premium in healthcare costs—which raises the cost of the employer's group health benefits plan for the employer and for participating employees. There have been hundreds of legal cases in which ex-employers claimed people who got cancer or had a heart attack were not covered under COBRA because they had either missed the last date to accept COBRA or had sent in their COBRA premium too late.

To prevent these misunderstandings, the Department of Labor has issued new, very explicit rules for COBRA acceptance and premium payments for plans beginning in 2005 or later.[5] The new rules follow.

After a qualifying event, employers must send a "COBRA Qualifying Event Letter" to employees and/or their covered dependents. Most employers send this letter immediately. The letter must state the date your coverage ended and whether you are eligible for COBRA. If you are eligible, the letter must state the cost of each benefit option and the time frame within which you must elect coverage—which is the longer of 60 days from the date your coverage ended (*qualifying event*) or the date the letter was posted. You may opt for separate COBRA benefits coverage for each family member—spouse or dependent children.

This means that if you must choose COBRA, you should choose COBRA for only those family members with a preexisting condition that would prevent the rest of your family from getting a normal affordable individual/family health insurance policy.

From the day you elect COBRA coverage during this 60-day period, you then have 45 days to submit your first premium payment, which must cover the period back to the date of your qualifying event. The postmarked date of your acceptance and payment, not the date it is received, is considered the applicable date.

Once you have accepted COBRA within 60 days of your qualifying event and paid your first premium within another 45 days, you then must continue to pay your premium every month. You have a 30-day grace period for each successive payment. If your payment is received late, your plan administrator may immediately terminate your benefits, but must retroactively reinstate them if your payment is then received within the 30-day grace period. If your payment is short by the lower of 10 percent or $50, your plan administrator must temporarily accept this minor deficiency as payment in full, notify you, and allow you 30 days to make up the difference.

Most important, after sending you the initial "COBRA Qualifying Event Letter," your plan administrator has no obligation to send you monthly statements or confirmation of payments received (except for an initial minor shortfall of $50 or 10 percent). If you accept COBRA coverage, it is solely your obligation to maintain records that your acceptance has been sent to your employer on time and that all of your premium payments are up-to-date. The only obligation of your employer or the plan administrator is to send you an Early Termination Notice after you have lost your coverage.

Employers can permanently terminate your COBRA coverage, without prior notice, if you fail to make the monthly premium payment before the end of each 30-day grace period.

The COBRA Loophole—How to Get Three Months of Free Health Insurance Protection from Your Employer, Saving You $1,400 When You Change Jobs

If you've been following this closely, which you should be if you or your spouse just became unemployed, you may already see the "COBRA loophole." This loophole can save you the cost of 105 days (three and one-half months) of health insurance coverage if you are healthy, worth roughly $1,400, which you can put toward the purchase of your own individual or family health insurance policy at $400 a month.

You could also use this COBRA loophole if you are planning to take another job that includes health insurance but for which there is a 30- to 180-day waiting period before new employees are eligible to join the group plan.

The COBRA Loophole When You First Leave Your Job

Day 1	You officially leave your job and your employer sends you the "COBRA Qualifying Event Letter"—you now have until day 60 to accept COBRA coverage.
Days 1–105	You purchase your own family insurance policy for $400 a month, or you start a new job with health benefits, but you request that your new coverage begin on day 105.[a]
Day 60	You send in your COBRA acceptance notice retroactive to day 1[a]—you now have 45 days, until day 105, to send in your first COBRA premium payment of, for example, $4,998 for 105 days (prorated at $1,428 per month).
Day 105	If your family has had no major medical problems during this time, then don't send in your $4,998 COBRA premium payment; your COBRA coverage will automatically terminate retroactive to day 1. According to COBRA law, the only result of your nonpayment is that your COBRA coverage is terminated effective day 1, and you owe nothing to your ex-employer.
Day 105	Your new family coverage begins, costing $400 a month, and, assuming you did not have any major medical claims during the previous 105 days, you just received the equivalent of 105 days (three and one-half months) of health insurance protection worth $1,400.

[a]You should send all notices via certified mail and make sure your new family coverage is in place before day 105.

Of course, this COBRA loophole works only if you are healthy during this 105-day period. If you have a medical expense, you will have to decide whether to pay it yourself or actually send in all or part of the COBRA premium so you can get coverage from your former employer. Similarly, if you know you are going to need medical coverage from an earlier date, say day 60, you should request that your new insurance coverage begin on day 60—saving you $800, or about two months of your $400 per month new health insurance premium.

If you are healthy and already on COBRA, here's a second COBRA loophole that can save you the cost of 30 days of coverage, worth about $400.

The Second COBRA Loophole—If You Are Already on COBRA

Day 1	While on **COBRA**, you purchase your own family insurance policy for $400 a month, or you accept a new job with health benefits but request that your new coverage begin on day 30.[a]
Day 1	If you and your family stay healthy, hold off sending your ex-employer your monthly **COBRA** premium payment of $1,428 per month.
Day 30	Assuming you haven't had a major health claim since day 1, don't send in your **COBRA** premium payment. According to **COBRA** law, your **COBRA** coverage automatically terminates retroactive to day 1—you owe your ex-employer nothing since your **COBRA** coverage was terminated effective day 1.
Day 30	Your new health insurance coverage begins, costing $400 a month; assuming you did not have any major medical claims during the previous 30 days, you just received the equivalent of 30 days (one month) of health insurance protection worth about $400.

[a]You should make sure your new family coverage is in place before day 30, when you fail to send in your **COBRA** premium payment.

This second COBRA loophole also works only if you are healthy during this 30-day period. If you have a major medical expense, you will have to send in the COBRA premium to secure coverage from your former employer.

HIPAA—Your Legal Protection When You Change Jobs or Get a New Job

The second major amendment to ERISA law, which is extremely important to employees who have a family member with a preexisting condition, is the Health Insurance Portability and Accountability Act of 1996 (HIPAA).

HIPAA generally does the following:
1. Guarantees continuous health insurance coverage for a preexisting condition when you change employers if your previous employer covered it
2. Limits to 12 months the time period a new employer can exclude a preexisting condition from coverage if your previous employer did not cover it

3. **Requires each state to offer some type of coverage with no exclusions for preexisting conditions to individuals who have accepted and exhausted COBRA**
4. **Sets privacy standards for medical providers and insurers**
5. **Prohibits discrimination against employees on the basis of their health**

If you have a family member with a serious health condition and are on COBRA, HIPAA can save you tens or hundreds of thousands on medical bills if you qualify to become "HIPAA-eligible." However, to become HIPAA-eligible, you must closely follow HIPAA regulations (see following), especially toward the end of your 18 to 36 months of COBRA coverage. You must also make sure you maintain "creditable continuous coverage" when changing employers.

This section summarizes the key provisions of HIPAA and how they affect you when you change jobs or have expiring COBRA coverage. See Chapter 7 for specific strategies should you or a family member have a major health problem.

Summary of HIPAA Law and How It Affects You

Applicability. HIPAA's rules and provisions apply to:

■ Group employer-sponsored health benefits plans with two or more participants

■ Individual and family insurance policies including "state-guaranteed" plans or their equivalents

Offers protections when you take a new job with health insurance benefits. HIPAA limits to 12 months (18 months in certain cases) the time period in which your employer can apply preexisting-condition exclusions to your personal coverage. HIPAA also prohibits your employer from charging you more or less than other employees for your health benefits and from discriminating among employees in any way based on their health history or lifestyle. HIPAA specifies midyear enrollment procedures that apply when an eligible participant loses other coverage or acquires a new dependent.

Guarantees "continuous coverage" when you change jobs. Continuous coverage is based on the concept that a person should be given credit for previous health coverage when moving between healthcare plans. HIPAA law prohibits new employers and insurance carriers from excluding from coverage any preexisting conditions you may have— provided you have had "continuous creditable coverage" for at least 12 months without a "significant gap" (defined as 63 days) in health insurance coverage. If you had creditable coverage for less than 12 months, the 12- to 18-month period in which your employer can exclude a preexisting condition from coverage is reduced by the number of months you had creditable coverage from prior employers or health insurance carriers. Chapter 7 explains how to maintain continuous coverage between jobs should you or a family member have a major health issue.

Provides for certificate of creditable coverage. Basically, all issuers of health insurance are required to automatically give you a Certificate of Creditable Coverage when your coverage is terminated, on request during coverage, and for up to 24 months following coverage termination. You should always request such a certificate when terminating any health insurance plan. You will need to show this to your next employer or health insurer to prevent that entity from excluding from coverage any possible preexisting conditions you or a family member may have.

Defines a "preexisting condition." HIPAA defines a preexisting condition as a condition for which medical advice, diagnosis, care, or treatment was recommended or received during the six-month period prior to an individual's enrollment date in the health insurance plan.

Prohibits exclusions for some preexisting conditions. Certain medical conditions, like pregnancy, genetically inherited diseases, and medical problems of a newborn or adopted child, can never be excluded from coverage in an employer-sponsored group plan. This means that all employer-sponsored group plans must cover pregnancy and newborns, even in cases where you marry a pregnant woman.

Guarantees renewability. HIPAA requires health insurance companies to give employers the option of renewing their group health plan. (However, since there are no limitations on the price insurers can charge, this provision is, in effect, meaningless to employers.) Employers are specifically under no obligation to continue their group health policies and may cancel them at any time. In contrast, individual policies are "guaranteed renewable," and premiums cannot be raised because of a catastrophic medical problem. The only way you can lose your individual/family coverage is if your health insurance company goes bankrupt or if you default on a payment, commit fraud, move outside the service area (in a network plan), or move outside the state (if you have "state-guaranteed" coverage).

Ensures privacy. HIPAA establishes privacy standards for individual medical records and sets criminal and civil penalties for medical providers, employers, and health plan providers who fail to maintain these standards. Your HIPAA privacy rights are particularly important if someone contacts your doctor, current or past employer, or health insurer for a reference.

Provides for HIPAA-eligible classification. Certain people, called "HIPAA-eligibles," are guaranteed by HIPAA the extremely valuable right to purchase individual health insurance coverage with no exclusions for preexisting conditions. See following for how to become HIPAA-eligible and Chapter 7 for more information on your rights as a HIPAA-eligible individual.

Your Rights as a HIPAA-Eligible Individual

For people who have no choice but to accept COBRA and who have exhausted their COBRA coverage after 18 to 36 months, HIPAA creates a new class of health insurance applicant called *HIPAA-eligible*.

Basically, HIPAA-eligible individuals are those with an expensive preexisting condition who have exhausted their COBRA coverage (if they were eligible for COBRA).

All states are required under HIPAA to guarantee individual/family health insurance to HIPAA-eligible individuals without exclusions for preexisting conditions. See Chapter 7 and Appendix A for summary information regarding your state.

Should you or a family member have an expensive preexisting health condition, becoming HIPAA-eligible could save you from bankruptcy.

A HIPAA-eligible applicant might be consuming $75,000 or more in annual medical care and must be accepted by insurance carriers by paying $2,500 to $6,000 in annual premium.

In California, a HIPAA-eligible individual may apply to any insurance carrier offering individual insurance policies and must be offered at least two choices for health insurance: a deluxe and a standard policy with no exclusions for preexisting conditions. California limits the cost of this policy for HIPAA-eligible applicants to 200 percent of a regular policy. As shown in Chapter 7, a typical policy in California for a HIPAA-eligible individual costs $356 per month.

In Texas, a HIPAA-eligible individual is guaranteed acceptance into the Texas Health Insurance Risk Pool with no exclusions for preexisting conditions. Texas limits the premium charged for this state-guaranteed coverage to twice the premium charged by major Texas health insurers for individual health coverage. As shown in Chapter 7, a typical state-guaranteed policy in Texas for a HIPAA-eligible individual costs $364 per month.

If you are HIPAA-eligible and live in Florida, after you have exhausted your COBRA coverage the state requires the same group insurance carrier that provided your COBRA to offer you an individual policy called a *conversion policy,* with no exclusions for preexisting conditions. The premium cannot exceed 200 percent of the typical rate for an individual policy. You must be offered two conversion policy options that meet minimum state requirements, and if your group plan covered maternity, dental, and other benefits, these must also be included in your conversion policy. No preexisting conditions can be excluded. If you are HIPAA-eligible but do not qualify for a conversion policy, you are guaranteed the right to buy an individual insurance policy from any insurance company that sells individual policies in the state of Florida on terms similar to those in other states that offer this option to HIPAA-eligibles.

If only one member of your family has a preexisting condition, you need to pay these higher premiums only for that single individual. As illustrated in Chapter 7, the correct strategy is almost always to get separate coverage for the family member with a preexisting condition—thus making the remaining family members eligible for a traditional healthy family policy at normal rates.

However, it is not easy or inexpensive for you or a family member to become a HIPAA-eligible individual—unless you are lucky enough to have the HIPAA-eligible loophole apply to you as explained next.

How to Become HIPAA-Eligible

To become a HIPAA-eligible individual you must meet *all* of the following six conditions:

1. You must have at least 18 months of continuous "creditable coverage" without a break in coverage of more than 63 days.

2. Your most recent coverage must have been through a group plan (either employer-sponsored or through an association).

3. You must not be eligible for any other group plan, Medicare, or Medicaid.

4. You must not have other health insurance.

5. You must not have lost your insurance for premium nonpayment or fraud.

6. You must have accepted and used up your COBRA continuation coverage (or similar state coverage) if it was offered to you.

To become HIPAA-eligible, you must typically first work for a company with an employer-sponsored group plan, then quit or be fired and become eligible for COBRA benefits, and finally accept and exhaust your COBRA benefits. This can be very expensive and time-consuming.

Normal 18- to 36-Month Timeline for HIPAA Eligibility

		Cost/Single
Month 1	You quit or lose your job and accept COBRA.	$400/month
Months 1–18	You exhaust your COBRA benefits if you are a covered employee.	$400/month × 18 months = $7,200
Months 1–36	You exhaust your COBRA benefits if you are a dependent.	$400/month × 36 months = $14,400
Month 18 (or 36) + 63 days	You are HIPAA-eligible and must be accepted for an individual policy without exclusions for preexisting conditions.	Depends on state (typically $300/month)
After 20–38 months	You have a permanent individual health insurance policy.	$300/month (typical single policy)

The HIPAA-Eligible Loophole

Review the six-condition list for HIPAA eligibility. Conditions 1 and 6 appear to be redundant, since you automatically have 18 months of creditable coverage once you have exhausted your COBRA coverage for the required 18 to 36 months. Actually, they are not redundant.

Condition 6 requires that you accept and exhaust your COBRA coverage if it is offered to you. If COBRA is not offered to you, you are HIPAA-eligible from the day you lose your employer-sponsored health benefits. Here are three legal reasons you might not be offered COBRA if you work for an employer with a group benefits plan.

1. You lose your job and the employer has 19 or fewer employees.

2. Your employer's health insurance company went out of business.

3. Your employer voluntarily terminated its entire employer-sponsored group health benefits plan.

We examine the rules and ramifications of item 3 more in Part II, which is devoted to small businesses.

If you are a business owner, you may wish to jump ahead to Part II and learn how you can:

Terminate your expensive group health benefits plan

Give your employees tax-free money to buy their own individual/family health insurance

Simultaneously make your employees instantly HIPAA-eligible, which guarantees them immediate coverage without exclusions for preexisting conditions

---

If you have an employee with a preexisting condition that costs your employer-sponsored health insurance plan $25,000 to $75,000 each year, HIPAA-eligible individual premiums of $3,000 to $4,800 a year ($250 to $400 per month) look like the deal of a lifetime for your business. But the real person getting the best deal could be your employee with a preexisting condition—since now that individual could get permanent health insurance, guaranteed renewable until age 65, independent of any employer.

CHAPTER 4

How to Buy Your Own Low-Cost, High-Quality Health Insurance Policy

To open a Health Savings Account (HSA), as explained in Chapter 6, you first need to have either group (employer-sponsored) HSA-qualified health insurance or your own HSA-qualified high-deductible health insurance policy. This chapter will show you how to obtain such a policy. As illustrated in Appendix A, HSA-qualified high-deductible policies in most states cost about half the price of traditional lower-deductible policies.

If you have a family member with a preexisting health condition that makes it difficult to medically qualify for the affordable insurance described in this chapter, see Chapter 7.

There are three ways to shop for and buy an individual/family health insurance policy:

1. Call insurance companies directly to ask for a quote—your state insurance department has a list of all carriers licensed to offer policies in your state (see Appendix A for phone numbers and web sites).

2. Find a local licensed health insurance agent to help you choose and apply for a policy—see following for how to find and choose an agent.

3. Use an online insurance web site like ehealthinsurance.com or zaneben.com to get quotes, and then either apply online or proceed to option 1 or 2 above.

Most of the 13 million Americans who have individual/family policies chose option 2 or 3 and had a licensed health insurance agent submit their application. There is no cost difference between using an agent or applying directly to a carrier yourself.

The Two Major Components of Health Insurance

Health insurance is different from all other types of insurance. When you buy life insurance, automobile insurance, or homeowner's property and casualty insurance, you do not expect to have a claim in the near future. You purchase these types of insurance for financial protection against the occurrence of an unlikely event that you wish to avoid—like a death, an auto theft, or a fire. If such an event occurs, you generally receive money that you are free to spend any way you wish.

In contrast, with health insurance, you expect to have claims in the near future and you almost never receive money when you have one. Instead, your insurance carrier directly pays the medical providers that have taken care of you—typically paying them either a flat monthly fee or a small fraction of what they would charge you directly if you didn't have health insurance.

This is because what we call "health insurance" in the United States consists of two separate but related components:

1. Access to a network of physicians, hospitals, and other medical providers who provide services at greatly discounted rates

2. Financial protection against the medical expenses of an accident or illness

Here's the first question you need to ask when choosing a health insurance policy: "How good is the network of doctors included in the plan?" Your policy won't do you much good if you don't like the physicians it covers, or if it works only at a hospital many miles from where you live.

Once you have located a few policies that offer access to the medical providers you desire, as explained in this chapter, you need to analyze the financial protection offered by each policy—the monthly premium and how much you will pay out of pocket under different potential scenarios, from a routine physical exam to a catastrophic illness.

How Medical Provider Networks Work—HMOs and PPOs

Health insurance began in the United States during the Great Depression, when local hospitals began adopting the Blue Cross plans—providing groups of individuals with hospital care in return for a fixed monthly fee. Around the same time, employers began contracting with individual doctors to provide care to their workers for a fixed monthly fee—these were called Blue Shield plans. Over the subsequent decades, thousands of these plans were merged and consolidated into the 70 independent Blue Cross Blue Shield health insurance companies that exist today. These companies, collectively known as "the Blues," maintain their own networks of independent doctors and hospitals to provide benefits at discounted prices to their policyholders.

Hundreds of other health insurance companies and independent noninsurance companies also developed their own networks—contracting with medical providers in their local areas to provide service to their policyholders or members for either a flat monthly fee or a discounted rate.

As new medical providers entered the marketplace, from ordinary physicians to specialized blood testing laboratories, the only way for them to get patients was to offer great discounts to the largest purchasers of healthcare—the medical provider networks. As medical providers lowered their prices to these large purchasing networks, the same medical providers raised their prices to patients *outside* the network—sometimes just to show the networks that they were giving them increasing discounts off the prices they charged others.

Today, most medical providers, from local pediatricians to big-city hospitals, charge patients who don't belong to their health insurance network far higher prices (sometimes 10 times higher) than they charge to those in their network for the exact same service.

Here is a personal example of how a medical provider network (and a high-deductible individual/family health insurance policy) can get you a 90 percent or greater discount on healthcare.

In 2003 and 2004 my family had a low-premium, high-deductible, individual/family health insurance policy that required us to pay the first $5,150 (the *deductible*) of our annual medical expenses—so we were very motivated to make sure we weren't paying too much for our healthcare. During this time period my children saw our pediatrician for wellness exams and my wife saw her ob-gyn for pregnancy exams—on eight of these visits the medical providers drew seven blood samples and one urine sample, which were sent to Laboratory Corporation of America (LabCorp) for analysis.

Each time our medical provider sent one of these samples to LabCorp, we received a bill marked "insurance pending" from LabCorp for the amount shown under LabCorp Charge. Then, a few weeks later, we received an "Explanation of Benefits" (EOB) notice from our insurance provider (Blue Cross Blue Shield of Utah) stating the claim had been reviewed and that we should pay the bill, minus the PPO discount amount, which we received because we were using an in-network medical provider. We had to pay the discounted bill ourselves because we had not yet met the annual deductible on our policy. If we had met our annual deductible, our insurance company would have paid this same amount directly to LabCorp. For example, we paid $8.86 to LabCorp for the lab test done on July 18, 2003, versus the $94.00 we would have had to pay without our PPO in-network discount.

Note the incredible discrepancy—if we did not have health insurance granting us access to our health insurance carrier's medical provider network we would have paid more than 10 times the price for the exact same service!

LabCorp Bills to Pilzer Family 2003–2004

Date of Test	LabCorp Charge	PPO Discount	Price We Paid	% Paid if No PPO
2/13/2003	$ 286.00	$ 241.36	$ 44.64	641%
3/11/2003	$ 388.00	$ 334.76	$ 53.24	729%
6/9/2003	$ 102.00	$ 93.81	$ 8.19	1245%
7/18/2003	$ 94.00	$ 85.14	$ 8.86	1061%
8/12/2003	$ 83.00	$ 63.22	$ 19.78	420%
3/19/2004	$ 498.00	$ 439.78	$ 58.22	855%
5/24/2004	$ 410.00	$ 165.19	$244.81	167%
10/19/2004	$ 84.00	$ 64.94	$ 19.06	441%
Total	$1,945.00	$1,488.20	$456.80	426%

The marginal cost to LabCorp for performing these routine analyses is just a few dollars—the blood is dropped into a machine and the computer prints out the results. Our health insurance carrier knows this. That's why it was able to negotiate the price charged by LabCorp to a small fraction of the going rate paid by people outside of a medical provider network. As a high-deductible policyholder, I was given the same discounted price our insurance carrier would receive if paying LabCorp directly.[1]

Here's another example of the importance of belonging to a good medical provider network. The daughter of my partner Brian Tenner was hospitalized for a viral infection at the famous Cleveland Clinic in Ohio. If his family had not had health insurance or if the hospital had not been in their health insurance carrier's network, the hospital would have charged the Tenners $14,366.63. Instead, the hospital charged their insurance company just $3,009.73. The hospital was charging five times as much to out-of-network patients as to in-network patients.

Hospitalization Charges for Viral Infection (April 2002)

Medical Service	Cleveland Clinic Charge	PPO Discount	Price Paid	% Paid if No PPO
One week hospitalization	$10,614.72	$ 8,776.02	$1,838.70	577%
Medicines	$ 2,355.36	$ 1,660.25	$ 695.11	339%
Tonsillectomy	$ 723.00	$ 436.13	$ 286.87	252%
Lab and pharmacy	$ 263.80	$ 248.14	$ 15.66	1685%
Lab and pharmacy	$ 409.65	$ 236.26	$ 173.39	236%
Total 2002	$14,366.53	$11,356.80	$3,009.73	477%

The epilogue examines the problems caused by different patients paying widely varying prices for the same product or service. However, I want to point out here that the majority of patients who are overpaying LabCorp, Cleveland Clinic, and other medical providers are the working poor, the uninsured, disadvantaged minorities, and/or recent immigrants who do not belong to a medical provider network. The typical pediatrician or ob-gyn who orders a routine blood test is simply unaware of how much the less affluent patients are gouged.

Health Maintenance Organizations (HMOs)— More Restrictions, Lower Cost

A health maintenance organization (HMO) is a group of medical providers who are often permanent full-time employees of the HMO. They collectively provide service to HMO members for a flat monthly fee or salary. HMOs often own their own hospitals. HMOs can be independent entities, like Kaiser Permanente in California, or virtual HMOs run by insurance companies that contract with independent medical providers to provide unlimited service for a flat monthly fee.

Most HMOs are fairly restrictive—you typically can see only those medical providers who are members of the HMO, and you must see your assigned or chosen HMO primary care doctor first to get a referral to a specialist. Some HMOs give their doctors daily patient quotas—limiting the time they can spend with each patient.

In return, the premium for an HMO health insurance policy is sometimes less than for a PPO, and the out-of-pocket expenses like co-pays and prescription costs are far less—many HMOs even have their own pharmacy on the premises. In addition, HMO members rarely have to fill out claim forms.

Preferred Provider Organizations (PPOs)—
Fewer Restrictions, Higher Cost

When I obtained our family health insurance policy, I selected a type of medical provider network called a preferred provider organization (PPO). A PPO is a network of private, independent medical providers that have contracted with the PPO to supply services at either a fixed or discounted rate for each specific service—with the same medical providers also providing services to non-PPO members or other networks at different prices.

PPO health insurance plans typically charge higher monthly premiums than HMOs but offer you a larger choice of physicians and medical providers. PPO policyholders pay a discounted or flat co-pay fee for seeing a provider in the network, and they typically pay just the $20 to $30 co-pay (or perhaps nothing) after they have met their annual deductible.

PPO policyholders may also typically choose any out-of-network medical provider they wish by paying a greater percentage of the charges.

Indemnity Plans, EPOs, and POS Plans

Indemnity plans look more like other types of insurance—you can choose any medical provider you wish at any time, pay the provider yourself, and submit the receipt to your insurance carrier for reimbursement. However, your insurance carrier will typically reimburse you or pay your claims only at a percentage of the "usual, customary, and reasonable" rate for the service you received. Moreover, indemnity plans often have very high deductibles and are very expensive, so few people choose them over an HMO or a PPO.

TIP: If you use primarily alternative medicine providers or if you live in an area where the doctors you prefer are not in a network accessible to you, you might be better off with an indemnity plan. The only way to know is to phone your medical providers and ask whether they are covered by the network. You should also find out how much an indemnity plan would cover for each service.

Exclusive provider organizations (EPOs) are similar to PPOs except that no coverage is offered to policyholders for out-of-network medical providers. EPOs are not popular because few people want to bet that every doctor they ever need to see will be a member of their network or will have time available to see them when they have a medical crisis. You should choose an EPO only if you are confident you will not want to see a specialist out of the network.

Point of services (POS) plans are like PPOs, with some of the cost-saving features of HMOs (e.g., you must see your assigned or chosen primary care doctor first to get a referral to a specialist). They are a good choice for healthy people who want to save money on a PPO but don't mind having to go through a gatekeeper physician to see a specialist.

Choosing between a PPO or HMO

HMOs cost less, and PPOs offer more medical provider options, but there is no general way to compare the differences between an HMO and a PPO health insurance policy. As explained next, you can analyze all the financial components regardless of whether the provider is a PPO or an HMO. But trying to compare them side by side would be like trying to compare a Lincoln to a Cadillac—it is a matter of personal preference.

Moreover, each HMO and PPO is very different, so the best way to choose is to locate members of a specific HMO and/or PPO in your area and ask how satisfied they are with their health insurance. *Consumer Reports* recently surveyed 42,000 readers about their experiences with HMOs and PPOs and found that there was no difference between HMOs and PPOs in levels of satisfaction among people with chronic conditions; however, billing and customer service problems are more common to PPOs.[2]

How to Choose a Medical Provider Network When Buying Health Insurance

You should pay more attention to choosing the right network than to whether it is an HMO or a PPO. Here are some suggestions for how to choose the right network.

Make a list of all the good physicians you know of in your area. Then, when you first select a specific health insurance policy and network to analyze, check to see if these physicians are in that network. You can do this online or by phoning the physician or the insurance carrier. Be sure to also ask how much you will be paying per doctor visit, because different networks have very different pricing discounts.

Should you or a family member have a specific condition, like diabetes, you might ask around for names of good endocrinologists and pick your network based on them.

TIP: If you are new to the area or don't have time to prepare a list of doctors, just look to see which major hospitals are in a specific network. The best doctors are usually in the network with the best hospitals.

TIP: Most doctors today practice with other professionals in their own specialty, like a group pediatric practice. Although only one doctor in the group technically joins a network, all doctors in the group can provide network service. Never assume that a doctor is not in the network just because he or she is not listed—call and ask.

Once you have selected a few health insurance carriers, networks, and policies, you are ready to analyze the financial protection they offer.

Beware—Many Health Benefits Products Are Not "Health Insurance"

As you locate specific insurance carriers and policies, you should be aware that many products in the market are disguised to look like health insurance but do not qualify as such. Real health insurance is both (1) access to a network of medical providers at discounted rates and (2) real financial protection from medical bills.

Medical Discount Cards with No Insurance

Many products that look like health coverage policies are actually nothing more than poor network discount cards. Their marketing materials make them sound like "guaranteed-issue, no-questions-asked" health insurance, but they pay nothing for medical expenses.

The easiest way to spot these fake insurance policies is to ask for the state insurance license number of the person trying to sell them to you—these products are not "insurance" and are rarely sold by legitimate, state-licensed insurance agents.

Another easy way to spot these fake policies is to look carefully for the word *insurance* in their written sales materials—they rarely use this term because they wish to evade the scrutiny of your state insurance regulators.

When it comes to network access, the companies behind medical discount cards sometimes contract with legitimate medical provider networks, but at much lower discounts than those received by major insurance companies like the Blues. For example, a network discount card might offer you discounts of 15 to 20 percent off the price of retail medical expenses, like the bills from our LabCorp example, which would have you overpaying by "only" 800 to 850 percent instead of 1,000 percent.

TIP: If a salesperson or web site for one of these discount cards tells you to see whether your doctor is listed, check it out. Then call the doctor's office manager and ask how much of a discount you would actually be receiving with this plan versus with the local Blue Cross Blue Shield plan.

Medical discount cards should be considered only after you have exhausted all possibilities to get health insurance. See Chapter 7 for more information.

Association Plans with Limited Financial Protection

Another common scheme is to sell health insurance with a very low life-time maximum—typically offered by impressive-sounding associations like the "National Association of Contract Workers" (not a real name). These types of policies often promise low cost and easy underwriting or "no one can be turned down." If the deal looks too good to be true, it probably is.

These policies are often actual insurance polices sold by a licensed agent who sells policies for only one association. Often, an insurance company behind the policy forms the association specifically to evade the minimum insurance requirements required in your state for legitimate health insurance. For example, most states require individual/family health insurance policies to have a minimum lifetime maximum of $1 to $5 million. Some of these fake health insurance policies use legitimate medical provider networks—but they are easy to spot because they typically have lifetime maximums of $50,000 or less. If you develop a chronic condition, or get into an accident, you could run through the $50,000 lifetime limit in a week.

The saddest thing about medical discount cards and some association plans is that many of the people who buy them think they have real health insurance—until they have an accident or illness.

Financial Protection—What to Look for in a Health Insurance Policy

Once you have selected some policies to analyze, look at these seven major financial items in each policy:

1. Doctor visit co-pay or discount

2. Prescription co-pay or discount

3. Annual deductible

4. OOP max (co-insurance + deductible)

5. Lifetime maximum coverage

6. Premium

7. HSA-qualified

Doctor Visit Co-pay or Discount

The doctor visit co-pay is the amount that you pay each time you visit the doctor. In a traditional low-deductible plan, this ranges from $10 to $30 per visit per patient. Most higher-deductible plans do not offer any doctor co-pay, but do offer substantial network discounts off the $100 or more standard doctor visit fee. When considering a plan without a doctor visit co-pay, you should phone your physician first to ask how much you will pay per doctor visit (typically 30 to 50 percent off a typical $100 fee per doctor visit).

Prescription Co-pay or Discount

This is the amount you will pay per prescription filled. Most healthcare plans offering pharmacy coverage break their coverage into three tiers: *generic, formulary brand*, and *nonformulary*. A typical plan for a 30-day prescription might charge a $10 co-pay for a generic drug, a $20 co-pay for a formulary-brand drug that is on a list (the "formulary") maintained by the carrier, and a discount from full retail for a drug that is neither generic or on the formulary list. There is no standard pharmacy coverage, so the only way to know what you will pay is to ask your carrier or look up your prescription on its web site.

TIP: If you are having doubts about whether to get pharmacy coverage, get it; then analyze your situation next year to see whether you want to keep it. If you don't accept it initially, then want to add it later, once you start using prescriptions, you won't be able to—or your insurance carrier will use your request as an excuse to try to uprate your policy (see my personal experience, which follows shortly).

TIP: If you decline pharmacy coverage, most policies from major health insurance carriers still include free drug discount cards that offer you up to 15 percent off brand-name prescriptions and 50 percent off generic ones—see Chapter 9 for more on drug discount cards.

Annual Deductible

This is the annual amount of your medical expenses that you must pay before your health insurance company begins paying providers or reimbursing you for claims. Traditional healthcare plans have deductibles of up to $1,500 as well as co-pays for doctor visits and prescriptions. High-deductible plans have deductibles from $1,000 to $10,000—but much lower premiums.

TIP: Pay attention when calculating your medical payments to reach the deductible—doctor visit co-pays and prescription co-pays are excluded. Also, the lower in-network price is used rather than the medical provider's full price.

Out-of-Pocket Annual Maximum (OOP Max = Coinsurance + Deductible)

Coinsurance is the amount, typically about 20 to 30 percent, that most insurance carriers expect you to pay on your annual medical expenses after you have met your deductible. Fortunately, most coinsurance clauses have an upper limit of about $10,000. Your maximum coinsurance obligation, plus your annual deductible is called your OOP max—referring to the maximum out-of-pocket annual expense you could incur under the policy. Some newer high-deductible plans, including many HSA plans, do not charge you coinsurance; they pay 100 percent of your medical expenses once you have met the deductible (see Chapter 6).

TIP: The industry term "OOP max" is confusing because it does not include doctor visit co-pays or prescription co-pays, nor does it often include payments to out-of-network medical providers.

Lifetime Maximum Coverage

This is the maximum amount of benefits that could be paid out over the life of the policy. Some states require individual/family policies to have a certain lifetime maximum—California requires all individual/family policies to have a lifetime maximum coverage of at least $5 million per person. You may not think today there is a big difference between a $1 million and a $5 million lifetime maximum, but you might think differently if you needed an organ transplant, which typically requires decades of expensive follow-up treatment.

TIP: Pay careful attention to the lifetime maximum. Should you or a family member develop an illness, you may not be able to switch carriers and could have the same policy for the rest of your life. For example, if you need $35,000 worth of care per year, this could add up to more than $1 million dollars over a working lifetime.

TIP: If you need a higher lifetime maximum, it may be advantageous to insure your family members under different carriers. Check to see whether the lifetime maximum is per person or per family and whether there is a maximum annual benefits level. If you need maternity coverage, you might want to choose a $5 million lifetime max policy for yourself but choose a less expensive policy for the rest of your family (e.g., one with a lifetime max of only $1 million). One or more preterm births can use up a $1 million lifetime max fairly quickly.

Premium

This is the monthly amount you will pay for the policy and the options you have chosen. It is often paid quarterly, in advance, or monthly, with required automatic drafts from your checking account.

TIP: If there is any doubt about different policy options, you should initially choose the higher-priced option and cancel it later to lower your premium if you find you don't use it. Carriers freely allow you to reduce benefits, but typically will re-underwrite your policy (i.e., review your health risks and possibly raise your premium as a result) if you want to increase a benefit. This makes sense, since many people wanting to increase their medical benefits probably have a good reason (e.g., illness) for doing so.

HSA-Qualified

This is the newest feature to look for in a policy. To open a Health Savings Account, which allows you to save up to $5,450 tax-free for future medical expenses or retirement, you have to first have high-deductible health insurance that meets the federal qualifications—which in general means that the deductible must be above $2,100 per family or $1,050 per single (in 2006) and your OOP max must be less than $10,500 per family or $5,250 per single. These qualifications are discussed in detail in Chapter 6. High-deductible insurance policies that meet these qualifications are clearly marked "HSA-qualified."

Other Considerations

Do you travel often? If so, you should probably consider a policy from a Blue Cross Blue Shield carrier, because the 70 Blues typically offer out-of-area coverage to other Blues members throughout the United States. Most other national health insurance carriers, like Golden Rule, Humana, and Fortis, offer similar out-of-area coverage.

If you are often in the United States but are not an American citizen or resident, there are affordable international plans. These typically offer you excellent health insurance while you are not in your country of residence, at premiums that are even lower than those paid by U.S. residents for the same coverage. This coverage is also available for U.S. residents and citizens working abroad.

Comparing Different Health Insurance Policies

The most useful comparisons entail first estimating your future healthcare needs and then reviewing the major features of each policy item by item.

Estimating Your Future Healthcare Spending

To compare different health insurance policies, you have to first make assumptions about your future healthcare needs. If you haven't had a major illness recently, the best way to do this is to look at what you spent on medical care last year. After you have prepared this list, think carefully about the health of each family member and estimate what you might spend next year.

You should be able to come up with your exact out-of-pocket expenses for healthcare last year (including your health insurance premium) and an estimate of next year's spending (assuming you keep your current health insurance).

Current and Future Healthcare Estimate Worksheet

	Last Year	Next Year
Pharmacy	How many prescriptions filled? Total dollars spent?	What will be different versus last year?
Doctor visits	How many visits? Total dollars spent?	What will be different versus last year?
Therapists	Physical and/or emotional therapy: How many visits and how much was spent?	What will be different versus last year?
Hospitalization	What were the causes, and how much was spent?	Are there any major items pending?
Other items	Special items (crutches, etc.)	Are there any major items pending?
Health	Premium paid last year	Are there any major insurance items pending?
Total	$	$

Comparing Policy Features

Once you have estimated what you may spend next year, you need to collect the following basic information for each policy you are considering. All of this information should be readily available in any brochure or web site describing an individual/family policy. Once you have the information, make up your own worksheet similar to the one shown here.

Insurance Policy Analysis Worksheet

Name of Policy	Monthly Premium[a]	Annual Deductible	Annual OOP Max	Doctor Co-pay	Drug Visit Co-pay	Lifetime Maximum
Policy #1	$243	$2,000	$5,000	No doctor visits covered	No coverage	$1 million
Policy #2	$364	$1,500	$7,000	$30/visit for two visits, then 20–40%	$20 with $1,000 deduct.	$5 million
Policy #3	$402	$1,000	$6,000	$10/visit	$10 with $100 deduct.	$2 million

[a]Numbers have been chosen for illustrative purposes only.

Using the two worksheets, figure out what your total healthcare costs will be next year under each different policy you are considering.

TIP: There are virtually unlimited ways to analyze this data, and no single correct way to do so. A good health insurance agent can help you by asking the right questions, but ultimately you will have to make the final decision on which policy feels right for you.

TIP: There is no way to financially compute the lifetime max amount you will need, since very few people ever come close to using this much money in healthcare. Ultimately, buying insurance (protection) is more about purchasing peace of mind than about securing a financial return; only you can value the peace of mind you get from having a given lifetime max on your health insurance. In general, if you don't expect to keep the policy for a long time because you are over age 60 and approaching Medicare eligibility, a lifetime max of at least $1 million should be sufficient.

Submitting Your Application—
Be Careful!

Once you've chosen the policy that best meets your requirements and budget, you are ready to submit your application along with a check or bank debit authorization for the first month's premium. This is the "art" versus the "science" part of getting good health insurance, so read carefully.

What Health Insurance Companies Look For in Your Application

Health insurance companies make their money over the long run by rejecting applicants who are likely to have large medical expenses that will cost more than those people will ever pay in premiums. Conversely, insurance companies want to accept applications from people whose medical expenses are likely to be average or below average. Think about health insurance from the perspective of a carrier—unlike your employer, a health insurance carrier is a privately owned company with whom you have no relationship. When you apply for an individual/family policy you are asking a third party to take an amazing risk on your continued good health.

If a carrier accepts you for, say, a policy costing $300 a month, it will probably receive about $9,000 in premiums from you over the 30-month average life of an individual/family policy—and pay out about $2,500 in claims for a healthy family during this same 30-month period ($1,000 a year). The carrier will also have to pay a commission of typically 6 to 20 percent on the first-year premium if you were represented by a health insurance agent. The gross profit per policy in this case is about $6,100 ($9,000 premium − $2,500 claims − $400 commission = $6,100).

If you or a member of your family develops a problem with your health, you are probably going to keep your policy for a lot longer than 30 months—since you won't be able to get a job while you are ill or get cheaper health insurance anywhere else while you have a preexisting condition. Your treatment might cost $10,000, $50,000 or even $100,000 for each year you keep the policy until you hit the lifetime maximum of $1 to $5 million. Insurance companies will go bankrupt if they accept too many people with preexisting conditions who are likely to cost the company far more than they pay in premiums.

This is why about 20 percent of the millions of applications submitted every year for individual/family health insurance are formally rejected. Applying and being rejected is very bad because it will be recorded on your permanent health insurance record (your "MIB" report is discussed later in the chapter). This could make it more difficult to get insurance or could permanently raise your premium.

If you think your application may be rejected because of a preexisting condition or any other reason, *do not apply!* Instead, call a health insurance agent. The good ones can help you determine before applying if you will be accepted or can help you withdraw your application once submitted if it looks like you are going to be rejected.

It is also very important that your application be complete and accurate before it goes to the underwriter for review. In this example, the carrier makes a gross profit of $6,100 if your family stays healthy; conversely, it potentially loses from $1 million to $5 million when it insures someone whose health deteriorates or who has an accident. The carrier has to sell 820 policies to healthy families to cover the cost of one family who hits a lifetime max of $5 million (820 × $6,100 = $5 million). The general rule of thumb when it comes to underwriting health insurance applications is "when in doubt throw it out"—meaning the underwriter will not consider an application with incomplete or confusing information.

When you fill out your application for health insurance, be clear and concise and do not leave anything out. If you do not understand a question, call and ask—do not leave it blank. As explained next, if possible, you never want to get turned down for health insurance.

Missing or Inaccurate Information on Your Application Could Cause Your Policy to Be Canceled When You Need It Most

There are two types of mistakes that you could make on your health insurance application—an honest mistake, when you forget or don't know something, and a dishonest mistake, when you deliberately omit something. Here's what happens with each type of mistake.

A typical health insurance application has about 100 specific questions about prior diseases, illnesses, birth defects, and so forth, followed by a dozen or so questions to catch something that the exhaustive list might have missed, such as:

Do you or does any listed family member have any serious medical problems not asked here?

Have you or any listed family member *ever* experienced any condition for which future consultation, treatment, or surgery is contemplated or advised?

You might have forgotten about a potential medical issue from 30 years ago that turned out to be benign, or your spouse might have had an issue before you met him or her that you didn't know about. Or you might have just seen a doctor on your vacation who suspected you have cancer, which is why you are now applying for an individual/family policy before you go to see your local physician.

Most insurance policies and state insurance laws have a two-year period of contestability for an honest mistake. If you make such a mistake, and the insurance carrier does not contest your mistake within two years, the carrier is stuck with your policy as if the mistake had never been made.

However, insurance policies and state laws have no statute of limitations for fraud. If you lie about or omit a major item, such as cancer or major surgery in the past few years that you couldn't possibly have forgotten about, your carrier may retroactively rescind the policy at any time—canceling your future benefits, returning your premiums, and holding you personally liable for all benefits you may have received under the policy.

Many insurance carriers don't spend a lot of time or money checking the accuracy of your statements when you initially apply. However, once you have a major claim, they are likely to investigate and retroactively cancel your policy if you committed fraud when you submitted your original application.

How Underwriters Verify the Information on Your Application

Underwriters have several tools at their disposal to confirm information provided by prospective applicants.

The Medical Information Bureau

Insurance underwriters often check the information you put on your application against your Medical Information Bureau (MIB) report.* Your MIB report is to your medical history what your credit report is to your financial history or what a Dun & Bradstreet rating is to the creditworthiness of your business. MIB, a central database on the health history of tens of millions of Americans, is shared by approximately 600 life and health insurance companies. When you apply for individually underwritten life or health insurance, or when you participate in a group insurance plan in which an insurance carrier underwrites the health of your group, you typically give the underwriter permission to send your health information to the MIB. MIB keeps information on file for seven years.

MIB is not subject to HIPAA privacy regulations, but MIB is a consumer reporting agency subject to the Fair Credit Reporting Act. As with a credit report, if you are denied insurance based on an MIB report, you are entitled to a free report and the opportunity to have any erroneous information corrected.

TIP: You should always obtain a copy of your MIB every year—even if you are not applying for health or life insurance. MIB recently began providing the following information, free once a year, to consumers who request it by contacting MIB at 866-692-6901:

- The nature and substance of your MIB
- The names of MIB member companies that have reported information on you

---

*MIB Group, Inc., home page, 2005, MIB Group, Inc., 6 May 2005, www.mib.com. Contact P.O. Box 105, Essex Station, Boston, MA 02112; phone 866-692-6901; infoline@mib.com.

■ The names of MIB member companies that have received a copy of your MIB during the preceding 12 months

Telephone Verification Calls

Most carriers do telephone verifications of the information on your application. After you apply, you should expect to receive a telephone call from the insurance company to verify at least a few questions on your application. A verification call is always recorded and is typically with a junior-level employee rather than with a senior underwriter with whom you can discuss your health issues.

> **TIP:** When answering a telephone verification call, listen to each question carefully, pause, think about the question, and then answer only and exactly what has been asked. A simple yes or no without comment is often your best reply. Don't start a conversation. Don't elaborate on your answers. The person at the other end of the telephone is not your friend, and any extra information you provide can only be used against you—and may end up in your MIB.

Requests for More Information

If you have checked yes to any of the hundred or so checklist questions on specific diseases or treatments, the underwriter may request a specific medical report from one or more of your medical providers. This is usually done without your knowledge since your signature on the application gives the underwriter permission to obtain this information and gives the medical provider permission to share it. It also typically gives the underwriter permission to share such information with the MIB.

About 5 percent of the time, the underwriter is not comfortable with the paper trail of your medical history or wants a professional to examine you for a specific issue and requests an Attending Physicians Statement (APS). In such a case, you are directed to see a local physician for a medical exam, or a doctor who has seen you recently is requested to send his or her medical notes to the carrier.

> **TIP:** Physicians' offices do not often respond to APS requests from carriers in a timely manner. You can speed up this process by calling your doctor and picking up your own APS, and then mailing or faxing it directly to the carrier.

Do not be alarmed if your carrier requests an APS—carriers will do so when they can't find any information as well as when they suspect something might be wrong with your health. When my wife and I applied for our first individual/family policy in 1999, the underwriter requested an APS for my wife because, as a student and a foreign-born citizen, she had no medical records in her MIB or with other insurance carriers.

After You Submit Your Application

It typically takes two to four weeks to receive a formal response on your application from the time you submit it. However, it could take three months if the underwriting process is delayed by a request for information from a medical provider or if it takes time to schedule a medical exam for an APS. Sometimes the insurance underwriting department may be backed up with many applications. Most insurance carriers will never rush the underwriting department to approve your application because of the enormous potential risk if they make a mistake—the general rule is, "If you need an answer right now, the answer is no."

Even though it might be easier to obtain, over the long term you do not want to own a health insurance policy from an insurance carrier with sloppy or hurried underwriters. As explained in Chapter 2, the biggest factor determining future increases in your individual/family insurance premium are claims from the group of the people in your state who purchased a similar policy from the same carrier in a given time frame. If you are accepted by a carrier that is strict in underwriting you, you should take comfort that this same carrier is probably strict with other applicants—since over the long term your annual premium will go up based on the medical claims of the other people in your underwriting group.

 TIP: If you need health insurance and can't wait weeks or months for an approval, you should consider purchasing a short-term major medical policy. These policies are instantly underwritten when you apply and can last for up to 6 to 12 months (see Chapter 13, "Short-Term Health Insurance"). While not a substitute for regular individual/family health insurance because of their short duration, these policies can offer $1 million or more in temporary protection while you take time to choose permanent coverage and go through the approval process. A typical premium for a 35-year-old male with a $2 million lifetime max, $1,000 deductible, short-term policy is only $55.19 per month, and you can cancel the policy at any time without penalty.[3]

After the underwriter reviews your application, the insurance carrier will respond in one of four ways:

1. Approved as submitted
2. Approved with uprating
3. Approved with exclusion(s)
4. Rejected

Application Approved as Submitted

While every state, insurance carrier, and applicant is different, about 60 percent of the applications for individual/family policies come back "approved as submitted." Even if you have sent in a check or authorized a debit from your bank account for the initial premium, you typically have 10 to 14 days after your coverage has started to review your plan documents and cancel—receiving a full refund of any premiums paid.

 TIP: If you have applied to more than one carrier, you may choose to accept coverage from the first carrier that approves as submitted while waiting to hear from another carrier— especially if your prior coverage was expensive COBRA or if you didn't have coverage. Virtually all health insurance policies may be canceled by the insured without penalty at any time, and you'll receive prorated refunds of premiums paid.

WARNING: Never cancel your existing coverage until you have written notification that your new policy is effective.

Application Approved with Uprating

About 15 percent of applications submitted come back "approved with uprating." In this case, you (or your agent) receive a letter stating that the carrier is ready to accept your application but at an uprated premium, typically 15 to 30 percent higher than the standard rate for which you applied. The letter may state the specific health issue or family member that is the reason for the uprating. You typically have 10 to 30 days to respond, or your application is withdrawn.

TIP: Even if you don't want the policy, you should always find out the specific reason for the uprating. There could be a mistake in your MIB, or a medical provider might have reported wrong information—and if so you want to have this information corrected as soon as possible.

> My experience has been that the percentage increase on
> approvals with upratings can sometimes be negotiated to a
> lower rate. If the underwriter thought that your family was a
> bad health risk, you would have been rejected. The approval
> with uprating says the carrier wants you as a paying policy-
> holder.

However, you should never directly challenge the integrity of insurance
carriers or underwriters by confrontationally asking for a lower rate and
accusing them of callously uprating you. Instead, begin a dialogue by
politely asking the specific reason for the uprating—which family member
and for what medical issue.

They might tell you, for example, that your premium is uprated 30 percent because your son Johnny had asthma two years ago and the concern
is that it could return. In this case you might reply: "Unfortunately, this
policy may not be competitive enough for my family with the uprating.
Why is the entire family premium for four people being uprated because
of one family member? Shouldn't just the prorated part of the premium
applied to Johnny be uprated [i.e., your family premium might be uprated
by only 7.5 percent]?"

TIP: This is the most common (and perhaps sometimes
deliberate) mistake made by insurance carriers when they
uprate a policy—they uprate the entire family premium by a
percentage that should apply only to the portion of the premium allocated to the family member who has the issue that
caused the uprating.

How I Negotiated a Better Deal with My Insurance Company

In December 2004 my family application for a new Blue Cross Blue
Shield policy was uprated 30 percent because of a medical issue I had in
February 2004. I politely asked why the entire family premium was
uprated instead of just that portion (roughly half) of the premium applicable to me. The underwriter agreed and immediately lowered the 30 percent uprating offer to 15 percent.

The 15 percent uprating raised our family premium from roughly
$400 a month to $460 a month. This $60 per month increase, as
explained in Chapter 2, would have cost us $31,242 over the expected
life of the policy.

> **TIP:** I asked the underwriter to immediately fax me a letter revising the written 30 percent uprating offer to 15 percent, which she did. Getting a carrier to modify a written offer is like chiseling ice—you should chisel off only one part at a time, document it, and then move on to your next issue. Don't be embarrassed by going back again with additional issues.

Once the revised offer had been documented, I called the underwriter again and told her I was ready to accept the uprated policy offer if she would write me a letter to the following effect, and she agreed:

- The 15 percent uprating charge was due solely to a specific health issue related to me individually.
- The carrier would remove the 15 percent uprating within 12 months without re-underwriting the entire family if I obtained health insurance coverage for just myself elsewhere.
- The underwriter would review the uprating applied to me on the anniversary of the medical issue that caused the uprating.

The medical issue that caused the uprating was a 15-minute visit to a doctor in February 2004 after I fell while snowboarding. My snowboarding companion insisted on taking me to his special back doctor—claiming I needed preventive care even if I no longer felt any pain. Before I knew it, I made the mistake of allowing this doctor to inject a steroid into my back to loosen my supposedly tight nerves. The doctor billed my insurance company $935 for this injection, calling it "surgery," and my local Blue Cross Blue Shield carrier paid him $463 even though I had a high-deductible policy (explained momentarily).

> **TIP:** You should always seek medical care when you need it. In cases where your choice to seek care might be optional, be aware of how it could affect a future application for health insurance—care you receive will probably end up in your file somewhere, and you are going to have to report it on a questionnaire for new health insurance. In my case, an unnecessary 15-minute visit to a pain doctor ended up almost costing my family $31,242 in increased health insurance premiums.

> **TIP:** Many high-deductible policies have a limited exception whereby they will pay the full amount, without a deductible,

in cases of an accident. In this case, my doctor checked "accident" as the cause of injury when he submitted the claim. As explained in Chapter 6, having first-dollar coverage for accidents is allowed under federal HSA rules.

In January 2005 I applied and was accepted for coverage from a different insurance carrier for just myself. The premium was actually considerably less than my portion of the non-uprated family premium from Blue Cross Blue Shield, but I didn't really want this policy because it had an inferior network. The new carrier didn't ask any questions about the steroid injection, although I had noted it on the application.

TIP: Many issues that are causes for rejection or uprating by one carrier are irrelevant to another carrier. This is why it is important to use a licensed health insurance agent who is familiar with the different carriers and their underwriting criteria (discussed later in the chapter).

Also in January 2005, I contacted the back doctor and told his office manager that I had been uprated for a health insurance policy because of my visit in February 2004. She checked, and sure enough, the doctor had reported to my insurance carrier that I had an "ongoing back issue" and needed more care. I called the underwriter at Blue Cross Blue Shield and asked for the exact language they would want to see in a letter from the doctor on the upcoming February anniversary of my back incident—and then I asked the doctor's office manager to write this exact language to Blue Cross Blue Shield, which she did, and the doctor signed the letter without examining me.

In February 2005, on the anniversary of the original accident, I submitted a request to have the uprating removed from our family policy, noting in the request that I had been individually approved for health insurance without uprating or exclusion by another carrier. Later that month our carrier removed the 15 percent ($60 per month) uprating charge from our family health insurance policy—saving us $31,242 over the life of the policy.

Application Approved with an Exclusionary Rider

About 5 percent of applications submitted come back "approved with an exclusionary rider," either for a specified period of time or for the life of the policy. An exclusionary rider is a rider to your policy excluding coverage for a specific illness or disease.* This 5 percent figure has been declin-

*Exclusionary riders are prohibited in Michigan and Indiana.

ing over the years in favor of total rejection, as underwriters have learned that people with one type of health issue often soon develop another health issue. Exclusionary riders are typically used today only for narrowly defined issues, like bad knees, that don't directly or indirectly lead to other medical problems.

If you have already been accepted with an exclusionary rider, you should do the following:

Find out everything you can about the reason for the exclusion and verify the accuracy of the supplied information.

Politely ask whether the carrier will agree in writing to terminate the exclusion after a period of time free of issues related to the exclusion.

Get an offer in writing for the same policy that does not include the family member who was the reason for the exclusion, and apply elsewhere for coverage for this member. (This is more fully described in Chapter 7.)

In addition, you should follow the preceding advice regarding uprated applications and the following advice regarding rejected applications (especially about withdrawing your application beforehand).

Application Rejected

The fourth possibility is to have your application come back "rejected." You never want to be rejected for individual/family health insurance, but not for the simple reason you might think. This also applies to being uprated or having exclusions placed on a policy.

Virtually every application for individual/family health insurance asks whether you or other family members have *ever* been rejected for health coverage, have been uprated, or have had an exclusion placed on an offer for a policy. If the answer is yes, you are asked to list the name of the insurance company, reason, and date.

This question has no time limit—once you are rejected, you and your family members are probably going to have some explaining to do for the rest of your life whenever you apply for health insurance.

Unless a mistake was made in the underwriting process, you will probably not be able to get the underwriter to change the decision. Therefore, the first thing you want to do after being rejected is to call the underwriter so you understand fully why you were rejected. You should also contact the Medical Information Bureau for a copy of your MIB report, which the bureau is required to provide to you for free under the Fair Credit Reporting Act if you have been rejected for health insurance.

TIP: When speaking to the underwriter about your rejection, do not argue. The only chance you have of reversing the decision is by showing that a mistake was made—hopefully by a third party rather than by the underwriter. Be very careful about what you say—conversations with an underwriter are often recorded and, as with telephone verification calls, anything you say will end up in their files forever and may end up in your MIB.

If your family application was rejected because of the health of one family member, see if you can get the insurance carrier to send you a modified offer excluding that family member from coverage. Even if you don't want the policy, this may help you lessen the damages when you have to explain to another carrier what happened on this application.

Licensed Independent Health Insurance Agents: Whether to Use One and How to Choose One

A health insurance agent or broker is an individual licensed by the state to sell health insurance. The terms *agent* and *broker* are used interchangeably—there is no difference between them. There is no charge to you for using the services of a licensed health insurance agent—the commission is entirely paid by the carrier. The carrier is prohibited from selling the policy any cheaper if you do not use an agent. Agents are prohibited from discounting their commissions or giving you any part of their commission—this is against the law in all states and is called *rebating*.

A good health insurance agent is able to intelligently discuss with you all of the information in this chapter and help you pick the right options and policy. Good agents know which carriers in your state are likely to accept or reject certain preexisting conditions, and they can advise you before you submit an application. Most of all, once your application is submitted, a good agent will follow your application through the underwriting process and try to withdraw your application or amend it before it gets formally rejected, uprated, or approved with an exclusionary rider.

Professional full-time health insurance agents have quality relationships with the major issuers of health insurance in your

state. Agents have special phone numbers to call carriers, and they are allowed to ask underwriters specific questions without identifying their client.

So, what's the catch? Why would you ever *not* use the services of a good health insurance agent?

There is no catch. You should always use a good health insurance agent when choosing and applying for health insurance. The only problem is finding a good health insurance agent who can represent you.

Almost all states offer a common licensing exam for "life and health," so most life insurance agents are licensed to sell health insurance and vice versa. However, very few "life and health" agents sell health insurance. The commission on a $500,000 universal life insurance policy is about $6,000—paid up front when the policy is sold. The commission on the same family's $300-a-month-premium health insurance policy might be only $18 to $60 a month.

In the United States there are approximately one million licensed life and health insurance agents. Only about 25,000 of these agents have ever sold a health insurance policy, and many of these 25,000 don't ever want to again. Aside from the much lower commissions for health insurance, the work involved to properly sell a health insurance policy exceeds the work involved in selling a life insurance policy to the same person.

Fortunately, every day there are more specialized firms and individual health insurance agents focusing on the exploding market for individual/family insurance.

Here are eight things to look for when picking an agent or agency to represent you or your employees in purchasing an individual/family health insurance policy:

1. *Shopping.* If you like to shop online, the agent should have an online web site where you enter your family information to get instant online price quotes on different policies offered by different carriers. This allows you to shop at your leisure until you are ready to make a decision.

TIP: Beware when shopping online for health insurance. The vast majority of health insurance quote web sites today request personal contact information and then don't deliver any online quotes—they sell your information to third parties along with your express permission to phone you, even if you have placed your phone number on the FTC Do Not Call list. A good online insurance web site will not ask for your name or contact information until you have seen quotes and are ready to choose a policy.

TIP: If you value your privacy or have placed your telephone number on the FTC Do Not Call list, use a cartoon pseudonym (e.g., "Daffy Duck") when you shop online until you are ready to make a purchase.

---

2. *Appointments.* Agents you contact should be appointed to sell health insurance from several or most of the major health insurance carriers in your state—and they or someone at their agency should have a professional relationship with the underwriters at each carrier.

3. *Knowledge.* The agent should know and be able to clearly explain all of the information contained in this chapter.

4. *Selecting a carrier.* Should you or a family member have or have had a health issue, the agent should know which carriers in your state may have a bias against certain preexisting conditions. Once a carrier is selected, the agent should be able to contact the carrier without mentioning your name and ask the underwriters whether your medical issue raises any red flags.

5. *Access.* You should be able to speak to the agent or a licensed associate on the telephone or via e-mail at your convenience, or to visit that individual in person. Your health information is personal and confidential, and you should feel secure when sharing it with someone.

6. *Monitoring.* The agent or agency should have a process in place to monitor your application once submitted and, after consulting with you, be able to withdraw your application or amend it before it gets formally rejected, uprated, or approved with an exclusionary rider.

7. *Negotiation.* The agent should have a personal style and communication ability that makes you feel comfortable—as he or she will be the one representing you to the underwriter if you have an issue with your application.

8. *Volume.* The agent or agency should be a significant producer of policies for the carrier selected. This will enable that person to better negotiate on your behalf during the underwriting process and to help you solve issues with the carrier at a future date.

There is a lot of information in this chapter, and you will probably want to refer to it again, particularly when you are submitting your application for health insurance. If you choose, as most people do, to use the services of a licensed online or in-person health insurance agent, you should still be familiar with the material here—to choose which agent you want to represent you and to understand how to select and apply for a policy.

If you are now ready to get your own individual/family health insurance policy, make sure you first read Chapter 6, "Health Savings Accounts," to help you decide whether this new option is for you. If you and/or your spouse currently receive health insurance from an employer, continue on to the next chapter to learn how to maximize your employee health benefits.

The Best Options for Employees with a Good Company Plan: High Deductibles, Disability, Cafeteria Plans, FSAs, and HRAs

Most employees today should have a Health Savings Account—
HSAs are so important that they are discussed
on their own, in Chapter 6.

If you work for the government or a large, profitable company with a good health benefits plan, your immediate financial risk is not that your employer might cancel or massively reduce health benefits. Your immediate financial risks are these:

Your employment might be terminated and you could lose your health benefits.

You may get a debilitating illness that leads to you being terminated because you can no longer work.

The only solution to losing your health benefits after termination is to forgo employer-sponsored health insurance in the first place. In this chapter I show you a new way to get your employer to reimburse you for the cost of an individual/family policy. If you choose to remain on your employer's plan, I explain how to get your spouse and dependents their own individual/family coverage for less than your employer may be charging you.

In this chapter we also examine long-term-disability insurance that you can probably obtain tax-free through your employer—insurance that pays you 50 to 75 percent of your wages until age 65 if you are no longer able to work in your chosen profession or job due to a debilitating illness.

The Crisis in Employer-Sponsored Health Insurance

Traditional employer-sponsored health insurance has been hit by soaring costs in recent years, making it less affordable for employers and employees. As shown in the table that follows, from 2001 to 2004, the annual premium that U.S. health insurance companies charged for employer-sponsored health benefits plans increased approximately 50 percent to approximately $10,000 per family and $3,700 per single.[1] The average employee contribution for family coverage increased 49 percent, and the average annual deductible for conventional family coverage increased 35 percent.

Employer-Sponsored Health Benefits 2001–2004

	2001	2004	Change
Total annual family premium	$6,666	$10,000	+50%
Total annual single premium	$2,500	$ 3,700	+48%
Average monthly employee contribution for family	$ 149	$ 222	+49%
Annual deductible (family)	$ 640	$ 861	+35%

During this period, many employers stopped providing health benefits entirely. The percent of jobs that included health benefits fell to 61 percent—6 percent (or 5 million) fewer U.S. jobs provided health benefits in 2004 versus 2001.[2]

The average cost of employer-sponsored health benefits is expected to have reached approximately $14,000 per family and $4,500 per single in 2006. On average, individual employees will be paying more and getting less in terms of higher deductibles, higher co-pays, higher out-of-pocket (OOP) maximums, and lower lifetime maximums. For example, since Microsoft began in 1979, the company has prided itself on giving employees and their dependents unlimited health benefits with no co-pays or deductibles. But in 2005, Microsoft stopped paying full price for brand-name pharmaceuticals—employees who choose a brand-name versus the generic alternative must now shell out a $40 co-pay. This change, which will save Microsoft $20 million a year, indicates a new trend for Microsoft: putting employee health benefits on the negotiating table.[3]

Average insurance costs are soaring, but averages can be misleading since almost no employee benefit plan fits the "average"—some plans are very good and some are terrible, depending mostly on the plan design and the health and age of the company's workforce. In 2004, when the average employer-sponsored benefit plan premium increased 11.2 percent, the premiums on 24 percent of employer plans increased less than 5 percent. In contrast, the premiums on 28 percent of employer plans increased 15 percent or more—probably due to having a higher-age workforce or more employees with catastrophic illnesses.

When it comes to choosing the best healthcare options from your employer, you cannot rely on averages—you must first analyze your family's healthcare requirements and then review each benefit option offered by your employer, as well as the quality and trends of your employer group. No two families and no two employers are alike.

Should You Get Your Own Individual/Family Health Insurance Policy?

If you do not have a family and work for a company that provides good health benefits, this is a difficult choice to make since it will probably end up costing you more money today—although it may save you money tomorrow.

Let's say that the total premium charged by a health insurance company to include you in your employer-sponsored group policy is $4,000 a year,

Group versus Individual Policy Monthly Premium, Sacramento, California

Age	25	35	45	55	60
Employer group policy[a]	$ 333	$ 333	$ 333	$333	$333
Individual policy[b]	$ 88	$ 124	$ 192	$298	$358
Monthly savings ($)	$ 245	$ 209	$ 141	$ 35	($ 25)
Annual savings ($)	$2,940	$2,508	$1,692	$420	($300)

[a]As explained in Chapter 2, the pro rata cost of an employer group policy is so much higher because, unlike individual/family carriers, employers must accept everyone and cannot charge different premiums for age or health status.
[b]Kaiser Permanente HMO, Sacramento, CA 95864, in 2005 with $30 co-pay, Rx coverage, $1,500 deductible, $3,500 OOP max, unlimited lifetime max.

or $333 a month. The cost to you to buy an individual policy (if you are a healthy male) with roughly the same benefits is considerably less, especially if you are younger.

However, in most cases today, your employer is paying 70 to 100 percent of the $333 a month cost to include you in its group employer plan. If your employer is paying for most of the cost, it will rarely be immediately economical for you to switch to an individual policy. Also, if you are unhealthy or nearing retirement age, the cost to buy your own individual policy may actually be higher than the prorated cost of your employer's group policy.

However, if you are under age 60, you are probably thinking: "How can I get my employer to give me the $333 a month, let me buy my own individual policy, and keep the difference?" I explain how to do this in the remainder of this chapter and in Part II.

In addition to the financial reasons, there are also intangible reasons to consider in deciding whether to buy your own individual policy:

- Are you planning on quitting soon and going into business for yourself? You may want to buy your own individual policy now just to guarantee you have affordable health insurance before you develop any expensive conditions.

- Are you concerned about developing an illness and not having enough coverage? The preceding individual policy has unlimited lifetime coverage, whereas a company policy from, say, Chevron/Texaco in California, has a $1.5 million lifetime maximum.

- Are there benefits you require that are not provided in your employer's plan, such as alternative medical providers? You may want to find an individual policy that gives you discounts and coverage for these providers.

Should You Keep Your Company Plan for Yourself but Get Your Spouse and Children Their Own Individual/Family Plan?

In the 1950s and 1960s, most employers paid the entire premium (or actual medical costs if self-insured) for employees *and* their dependents— with no employee contributions, co-pays, or other cost-sharing devices. In the next three decades medical costs dramatically increased, and many spouses began receiving their own benefits by joining the workforce. In response, employers started paying only a portion of the premium for the employee's spouse and dependents. Today, employers offering employee health benefits typically pay zero to 75 percent of the cost for an employee's spouse and dependents. Other than Microsoft, only a few employers today still pay 100 percent of the cost for spouses and dependents—most of these employers are government or municipal entities, where the decision makers are spending other people's money (e.g., taxpayers) instead of their own.

You are probably paying 25 to 100 percent of the cost of including your spouse and dependents on your company health plan—without realizing it, since it is automatically deducted from your pretax wages. Unlike the decision to get yourself your own individual policy, getting your spouse and dependents their own policy is an easier choice to make, since it will probably end up saving you money today in addition to saving you money tomorrow.

Let's say that the prorated additional cost for your family (healthy female spouse plus two children ages 5 and 8) in your employer-sponsored group policy is $8,000 a year, or $666 a month. The cost for a comparable family individual/family policy with roughly the same benefits is considerably less, especially if your spouse is younger.

Group versus Family Policy Premium/Month, Sacramento, California

Age (spouse)	25	35	45	55	60
Employer group policy	$ 666	$ 666	$ 666	$ 666	$ 666
Family policy[a]	$ 215	$ 264	$ 345	$ 467	$ 551
Monthly savings ($)	$ 451	$ 402	$ 321	$ 199	$ 115
Annual savings ($)	$5,412	$4,824	$3,852	$2,388	$1,380

[a]Kaiser Permanente HMO, applicant (F/35), children (M/8, F/5) from Sacramento, CA 95864, in 2005 with $30 co-pay, Rx coverage, $1,500 deductible, $3,500 OOP max, unlimited lifetime max.

However, unlike with your own health benefits that are paid mostly by your employer, you are probably paying 25 to 100 percent of the $666 per month pro rata cost to include your spouse and children in the employer's group plan. If your employer is taking the full $666 a month out of your paycheck, it will probably be economical for you to switch your spouse and children to their own individual policy. If your employer contributes

50 percent of the $666 a month cost, it may be immediately economical only if your spouse is less than 45 years old or if you can obtain a comparable individual/family policy for $333 a month or less.

In addition to saving money today, some of the intangible benefits of switching your family members to their own policy include the following:

■ *Job loss.* Your spouse and children maintain their health insurance even if you lose your job.

■ *Financial protection.* If your spouse or children are healthy today, getting them their own individual/family policy guarantees them affordable coverage even if one of them should develop a medical condition—since premiums cannot generally be increased because of illness on individual/family policies. If you wait to buy individual health insurance until someone in your family has a severe medical condition, it will be far more expensive.

■ *Medical providers.* You select which medical provider network and which type of coverage you desire for them (HMO, PPO, etc.).

■ *Early retirement.* If you choose to retire early, your family policy will be unaffected—guaranteeing your spouse and children medical coverage until your spouse turns 65 and your children reach adulthood.

 TIP: Employees who turn 65 and switch to Medicare often have a rude awakening if their spouse is under age 65—employers generally cannot allow an employee's spouse to remain in their group benefits plan unless the employee is also a participant. If you are approaching 65 and your spouse is younger, your spouse should get separate individual coverage before he or she develops a medical condition.

How to Buy Your Own Individual/Family Policy—Tax-Free

As you compare the costs and consider whether to switch members of your family to their own policy, you must also calculate the after-tax cost difference between your employer-sponsored policy and purchasing your own individual family policy.

If your employer allows you to fund your employee contribution of $666 a month with pretax dollars (with a Section 125 POP plan, explained subsequently), then your after-tax cost is 35 percent less than the full $666 amount (\$666 − 35% = \$433) that is withheld from your pretax wages (assuming 35 percent combined state and federal tax bracket). Most large employers offer this option to their employees.

However, you may be able to make the monthly premium you pay for your individual/family policy equally tax deductible—in which case you could directly compare this monthly premium to the \$666 pretax amount being withheld from your wages. The monthly premium of the policy you purchase for your spouse and children is deductible (or nontaxable) if:

■ Your spouse has self-employed income equal to at least the annual premium cost (e.g., \$8,000 per year). Since 2003, self-employed individuals are allowed a 100 percent deduction from their income for individual/family health insurance premiums, up to the amount of their self-employed income.

TIP: If you've been thinking about starting a home-based or family business, this might be the ideal time, since the first \$8,000 of income would effectively be tax-free if the business is in the name of your spouse.

■ Your employer allows you the option to switch your benefits to an HRA plan under which, in lieu of or in addition to your group benefits, you are reimbursed tax-free for out-of-pocket medical expenses, including individual/family insurance premiums (see HRAs discussion later in the chapter).

Should You Choose a High-Deductible Insurance Plan?

TIP: The best reason to choose a high-deductible plan is to qualify to open a Health Savings Account (HSA)—see Chapter 6.

The biggest change you may have noticed in your employer-sponsored health insurance plan is the size of the annual deductible, which has probably increased every year since you began working for your employer. Increasing the size of the annual deductible has been the easiest and best way for employers to lower the cost of their group employee benefit plans.

When an employer raises your annual deductible from, say, zero to \$1,000, they save much more than potentially just \$1,000 per employee.

An employee's first $1,000 is sometimes spent in 20 or more locations—at a pharmacy, at a doctor's office, or at a physical therapist. Each of these 20 individual transactions must be *adjudicated* (i.e., manually examined by the employer or a third party, approved, and then paid or reimbursed) at a cost of up to $50 per transaction. Your first $1,000 of medical spending may actually cost your employer $2,000 after processing, unless you already have a higher-deductible (i.e., greater than $1,000) benefits plan.

By raising your deductible $1,000, employers can save $1,000 in medical expenses plus up to another $1,000 in paperwork costs.

In addition to paying out less to medical providers and saving on transaction costs, employers also receive an intangible benefit from high-deductible plans—fewer doctor visits. Employees are more reluctant to visit a doctor when they are paying 100 percent of the cost, especially for an annual checkup when they feel fine. However, this can be bad for employers—since sometimes an annual physical detects a medical problem for which early treatment could save tens of thousands of dollars. Most good employer plans today pay 100 percent for an annual physical, or "wellness exam," even if the employee has not met the annual deductible requirement—you should always take advantage of this feature. As you will see in Chapter 6, "Health Savings Accounts," Congress wisely allows unlimited 100 percent employer-paid wellness doctor visits without violating the high-deductible requirements for HSA plans.

Most large employers today offer you a choice of a higher annual deductible in return for a lower employee premium contribution.

Just as with choosing an individual/family policy (see Chapter 4), the best financial choice from your employer plan is usually the option with the highest deductible— if you can afford the financial risk, especially in an emergency, of paying the first $1,000 to $5,000 of your medical expenses.

To choose the right annual deductible amount from your employer, along with other options such as co-pays, coinsurance, and out-of-pocket maximums, you must first make assumptions about your future healthcare costs under different scenarios. See Chapter 4 for specific instructions on how to analyze each of these components.

While raising the deductible has been the easiest and best way for employers to lower the cost of their group employer-sponsored benefit plans, it is often not the best way for employees on an after-tax basis. Premiums paid by employers or contributed by employees are almost always made with pretax dollars, while employee-paid amounts under the deductible, plus co-pays for doctor visits and pharmacy, are paid with precious after-tax dollars. Fortunately, you can make these amounts also tax deductible by using Flexible Spending Accounts (FSAs) as described next, or Health Savings Accounts (HSAs) as described in Chapter 6.

Flexible Spending Accounts (FSAs), Health Reimbursement Arrangements (HRAs), and Health Savings Accounts (HSAs), are all designed to help you fund your out-of-pocket medical expense with pretax dollars—saving you and your employer up to 50 percent on FICA and income taxes.

Long-Term-Disability Insurance—More Important than Life Insurance

No discussion of health benefits, and especially employer-sponsored health benefits, can be complete without a basic introduction to long-term-disability insurance.

Americans don't need protection against dying . . . they need protection against living disabled.

One hundred years ago, when men were generally the sole breadwinners for the family, the average employee's life expectancy was 46 years.[4] Workers needed life insurance to financially protect their family in case they died during their working lifetime. Today, the average employee's life expectancy is 77 years, yet most people still purchase life insurance before they even think about long-term-disability insurance and long-term-care insurance. They don't realize that employees today have a 300 percent greater chance of suffering a long-term disability before age 65 than of dying before age 65. Advances in medical science have converted yesterday's previous causes of death, like cancer and heart disease, into today's leading causes of long-term disability.

Most employees don't need more life insurance; they need long-term-disability insurance and long-term-care insurance.

Until age 65, you have a three times greater chance of suffering a long-term disability than of dying, and you have virtually a 100 percent chance of needing assisted-living care as you age.

Long-term-care insurance pays the cost of assisted-living care either in a nursing facility or in your own home. Almost every person will eventually require some type of long-term care, and about one-third of large employers offer long-term-care insurance to their employees. However, it is less important to employees than disability insurance, because people generally think more about today's risks than about tomorrow's. We discuss long-term-care insurance in Chapter 8.

Long-term-disability insurance pays you some percentage of your salary should you become disabled and unable to work, typically because of an illness. Every year about 12 percent of the under-65 U.S. population suffers a long-term disability. Depending on your age, you have about a one in three chance of suffering at least one long-term disability (defined as being unable to work for at least 90 days) before age 65, as shown in the following table.[5]

Probability of Disability for at Least 90 Days before Age 65

At Age	Chance of Being Disabled	Average Length of Disability
25	40.3%	2.4 years
30	38.5%	3.0 years
35	36.5%	3.5 years
40	34.0%	3.9 years
45	30.5%	4.3 years
50	26.2%	4.6 years
55	20.5%	5.0 years

Most people think that Social Security pays them disability if they become ill and unable to work. It does: The average Social Security disability payment to a single disabled worker is $815 per month, or $1,360 per month if he or she has a family.[6] In addition to being woefully inadequate, it is very difficult to qualify for Social Security disability—only about one-third of the applicants are accepted the first time around, and you must be medically unable to work for at least a year to apply. If your disability results from a work-related injury, your state workers' compensation board may also pay you disability compensation—typically about 50 percent of your salary, up to $150 per week, and for up to only 26 weeks.

To supplement these low government-sponsored amounts, some employers offer their employees both pretax and after-tax options for long-term-disability insurance. About 40 percent of large employers pay 100 percent of the cost for their employees of a limited-benefit disability policy.

Employers want every employee to have long-term-disability insurance. If you are a supervisor or manager, it can be very difficult to decide not to allow coworkers to return to work when their disability prevents them from properly performing their job, and it can be emotionally impossible to decide if you also know that your decision may bankrupt their family.

Long-term-disability insurance is very similar to health insurance. Employers can purchase *guaranteed-issue* group policies for their employees—that is, every employee is guaranteed the right to coverage at the same price (based on their age) regardless of their health. Employees can also purchase their own individual disability policies, which are medically underwritten—your monthly premium is based on your age and health at the time that you apply, and a disability resulting from a preexisting condition may be excluded from your policy.

The cost of group employer disability policies is surprisingly low. A typical employer plan that replaces 60 percent of income up to $5,000 a month until age 65 costs about $8 to $73 a month per employee based on their age, as shown in the following table.[7] Similar to employer-sponsored health insurance, this premium may be freely increased in future years, and your disability coverage terminates when you no longer work for the company. If you plan to stay with your current employer until age 65, or if you don't have a lot of money to spend on disability insurance, participating in the group employer disability policy could be an excellent decision—as long as you understand that you have no disability coverage if you leave before age 65.

Variable[a] Monthly Premium for Group Disability Insurance Policy[b]

At age	20	30	40	50	60
Monthly premium	$8	$14	$27	$56	$73

[a]*Variable* means the premium increases as you age.
[b]At 60 percent of salary up to $5,000 per month until age 65.

The premium for an individual disability policy that you purchase yourself is about six times more expensive depending on your age—*but you cannot directly compare an individual policy with a group policy.* Similar to an individual/family health insurance policy, with an individual disability policy the premium may typically never be increased and the policy may not be canceled. If you are self-employed or plan to go out on your own, you should consider getting an individual disability policy—the fixed monthly premium is based on your age when you apply, and your premium does *not* increase as you age, as shown in the following table.[8]

Fixed[a] Monthly Premium for Individual Disability Insurance Policy[b]

Your age when you apply	20	30	40	50	60
Fixed monthly premium until age 65	$82	$97	$150	$237	$338

[a]*Fixed* means premium does not increase as you age.
[b]At 60 percent of salary up to $5,000 per month until age 65.

Here are some factors to consider when purchasing a disability insurance policy, either through your employer or by yourself.

"Own occupation" or "any occupation." What is the definition of *disability* in your policy? Does it mean being able to work in the occupation in which you were engaged when you became disabled, or in any occupation? For example, if you are a surgeon who injures your hand and can no longer work as a surgeon, perhaps you could work as a teacher. The tighter the definition of disability, the higher the monthly premium.

Guaranteed renewable and noncancelable. Look specifically for these two clauses in any individual policy, and don't expect any guarantees past your plan year from an employer-sponsored group policy.

Tax-deductible premium or tax-free benefits. In general, if your premium is paid by your employer or yourself (with an FSA, discussed later in the chapter) with pretax dollars, disability benefits are taxed as income when you receive them. If your premium is paid with after-tax dollars, benefits are not taxed when you receive them. The conventional advice in the insurance industry is to pay your premium yourself or with an after-tax payroll deduction so disability benefits are not taxable income when you receive them, as that is when you will need the extra income the most.

 TIP: I strongly disagree with the conventional advice to pay your premium with after-tax dollars. There is less than a two-thirds likelihood that you will ever receive any disability benefits, so why pay extra income taxes today on benefits you may never receive? Second, most people are in a higher income tax bracket while working than they would be if they go on disability, so the best financial decision is to pay your income taxes after you go on disability, not before. *If you want a greater disability benefit, buy more disability insurance with less expensive pretax dollars rather than lose the valuable tax deduction today for your premium.*

Elimination period. This is the amount of time you must be disabled before benefits begin, typically 90 to 180 days, which is often covered by a short-term-disability policy. Some states have mandated state short-term-disability coverage, so check before you buy any—residents of California, Hawaii, New Jersey, New York, and Rhode Island are guaranteed their full after-tax salary (up to a reasonable maximum) for 6 weeks if they become disabled, then 50 to 60 percent for 20 more weeks.

Supplemental or overlapping coverage. Some policies guarantee you a fixed benefit, say $5,000 a month, reduced by any benefits you received from government entities like Social Security. This is usually a good option to lower your current premium, since it shifts the risk of ever obtaining government benefits onto your private disability carrier. Do not depend on Social Security or any government-mandated disability benefits when you calculate your disability requirements.

Premium waiver, partial disability, and so on. *Premium waiver* specifies that your premiums will be automatically paid when you are receiving benefits. *Partial disability* specifies your benefits in case of only partial disability. These and other terms should be reviewed with your benefits administrator or an insurance agent licensed to sell disability insurance.

I strongly recommend that you purchase long-term-disability insurance—some through your employer and some on your own (so that you will have some coverage if you leave your job). However, as with any insurance, don't let an insurance agent talk you into purchasing more than you need.

Individual disability insurance is expensive, and the current premium can affect your lifestyle today. You should purchase only the minimum coverage you will need to get by should you become disabled, perhaps just enough to cover your home mortgage and other fixed monthly payments.

How Your Employer's "Cafeteria Plan" (Section 125 Plan) Works

Employers are allowed to provide tax-free employee health benefits under what are commonly known as either "Section 125 plans" or "cafeteria plans." The term *cafeteria* refers to the recent development among larger employers of allowing employees to choose among a limited list of benefit options.

Here are the benefits allowed under Section 125:

Health benefits
Dental benefits
Vision benefits
Prescription drug benefits
Long-term-disability benefits (both pretax and after-tax)
Deposits to Flexible Spending Accounts (FSAs, discussed next)

Pretax and After-Tax Cost of $14,000 Health Insurance Benefit

100% Employer-Funded Example	
With Section 125 plan	
Net employee benefit	$14,000
Total employer cost	$14,000
Without Section 125 plan	
Employer cost (wages)	$21,538
Less: 35% (state and federal taxes)	$ 7,538
Net employee benefit	$14,000
Employer cost (wages)	$21,538
Additional employer FICA (7.65%)	$ 1,648
Total employer cost	$23,186
Net employer savings ($7,538 + $1,648)	$ 9,186
100% Employee-Funded Example	
Without Section 125 plan	
Net employee benefit	$14,000
Total employee cost	$14,000
With Section 125 plan	
Reduced employee wages	$14,000
Saving: 35% (state and federal taxes)	$ 4,900
Employee net cost	$ 9,100
Net employee tax savings	$ 4,900
($14,000 lower taxable income)	
Net employer (FICA) savings	$ 1,071
(7.65% × $14,000)	

Employers may offer these benefits as options to employees and contribute 0 to 100 percent (except for FSAs) of the cost for employees and their legal dependents. When properly administered with a Section 125 plan, the benefit cost is a tax-deductible expense to the employer and a nontaxable benefit to the employee.

The income tax savings, as described in Chapter 1, is the primary reason employer-sponsored health benefits exist in the first place. When an employer contributes 100 percent of a $14,000 annual family premium contribution, using a Section 125 plan saves the employer $9,186 in extra wages and FICA (Social Security and Medicare taxes) that would have been necessary to net the employee the same $14,000 benefit. When employees contribute 100 percent of the $14,000 premium themselves, using a Section 125 plan saves the employee $4,900 and additionally saves the employer $1,071 in FICA.

It is easy to see why most employers use a Section 125 Premium Only Plan (POP) for employer and employee contributions.

TIP: If your employer doesn't contribute anything to your employer-sponsored health benefits plan, ask the company to offer a zero-employer contribution Section 125 POP to allow workers to shift after-tax income to pretax dollars. Employer tax savings in FICA alone should exceed the POP setup fee.

TIP: In addition to reducing your taxable income, benefits paid under Section 125 plans also reduce your gross salary for purposes of calculating your Social Security and unemployment benefits. If you need to qualify for a higher level of these benefits, you can file a "Section 125 Waiver" with your employer asking to have your health contribution premiums funded on an after-tax basis.

Flexible Savings Accounts (FSAs)

In the 1960s and 1970s, employers instituted co-pays, deductibles, and coinsurance to have employees bear more of the cost for their medical benefits. Employees had to use precious after-tax dollars to fund these out-of-pocket medical expenses. In 1978, Congress created the Flexible Savings Account (FSA), which allows employees to shift part of their earned taxable income into pretax dollars to pay medical expenses other than health insurance premiums.

About 50 percent of employers with more than 50 employees offer FSAs, and about 36 percent of eligible employees participate. The average annual Medical FSA employee contribution is $1,136.[9]

> Because they have been around since 1978, FSAs are the most common tool offered by employers today to help employees fund their out-of-pocket and optional medical expenses with pretax dollars. But FSAs are outdated. FSAs encourage waste due to their IRS-mandated "use it or lose it" feature, and FSAs cannot be used to fund premiums for individual/family policies.

 TIP: In general, as explained in Chapter 6, you should almost always want to first contribute money to your Health Savings Account (HSA) up to the annual maximum before contributing to your FSA, because HSAs are "use it or keep it" and FSAs are not. Exceptions to this rule are for funding items not allowed by HSAs but allowed by FSAs (like dependent care expenses), or if you have fully funded your HSA but want additional tax deductions from an FSA.

There are two types of FSAs: Health Care Flexible Spending Accounts and Dependent Care Flexible Savings Accounts. Here's how they work.

During your enrollment period before the start of each plan year, typically in October for a calendar plan year beginning January 1, you tell your employer how much money to withhold from your pretax wages each month or each pay period to contribute to your FSA, say $400 a month to your Medical FSA. Then, beginning January 1 of the next year, you have a $4,800 allowance in your Medical FSA to spend on medical expenses allowable under Section 213 of the IRS Code. Each month, or when you incur a qualified medical expense, you submit the receipt to your employer's third-party administrator (TPA) for reimbursement.

If you are sure you are going to spend it, an FSA can be useful to fund your out-of-pocket medical and dependent care (day care) expenses, with pretax dollars—saving you about a third of the cost on these items. For example, assume you are sure in October that in the next year you will be spending at least $4,800 in out-of-pocket medical expenses plus $5,000 in day care expenses ($9,800 total). You would instruct your employer to withhold $816.66 per month ($9,800 for 12 months) from your paycheck and have this same amount available to reimburse you for medical and day care expenses—saving you $3,430 in state and federal income taxes (and saving your employer $750 in FICA).

FSA $2,400 Medical + $5,000 Dependent Care Example

Without FSA	
Net employee benefit	$9,800
Total employee cost	$9,800
With FSA	
Reduced employee wages	$9,800
Saving: 35% (state and federal taxes)	$3,430
Employee net cost	$6,370
Net employee tax savings	$3,430
($7,400 lower taxable income)	
Net employer (FICA) savings	$ 750
(7.65% × $9,800)	

Now, here's the catch for you. If by 2½ months following December 31 or the end of your plan year, you have not spent the full $4,800 in your Medical FSA and the full $5,000 in your Dependent Care (day care) FSA, you forfeit any unspent amounts in each FSA to your employer. Thus, you should never elect to contribute any amount to an FSA that you don't fore-see yourself spending in the coming year. This is typically called "use it or lose it."

Now, here's the catch for your employer. Your employer must allow you access to the full amount in your Medical FSA beginning January 1, even if you haven't yet made a single monthly contribution. If you spend the full amount of $4,800 in January and then quit before you've paid in your full $4,800 annual contribution, your employer is out the $4,800 (less any of your monthly contributions) and cannot seek restitution from you for the balance.

This might seem like a dirty trick when done deliberately, but you might feel justified using it when you consider that employers effectively get to keep unspent FSA balances.[10] For example, in October 2007 you elect to have $4,800 contributed to your Medical FSA in the next calendar year. In January 2008 you have LASIK surgery for $2,000 and dental work for $2,800, draining your entire $4,800 FSA before you've made a single contribution. You switch to a new employer in late January and your for-mer employer is out up to $4,800.

A few states, such as Pennsylvania, do not allow a state income tax deduction for contributions to a Medical FSA or a Dependent Care FSA, so your tax benefits may be slightly less in these states. You cannot claim both a deduction for a Dependent Care FSA and the dependent care tax credit, so check with a tax advisor to see which is more advantageous—in general, you are probably better off with the Dependent Care FSA if your taxable income is greater than $25,000 per annum.

Here are some recommendations and questions to help you decide how much of your pretax wages you should transfer to your FSA:

- Make a list of how much you spent last year on out-of-pocket medical expenses (e.g., doctor's visits, prescriptions, co-pays, certain over-the-counter medications, amounts under your deductible, coinsurance).

- Based on this list, how much do you expect to spend in the coming year?

- Do you anticipate any special items for your family (eyeglasses, contacts, braces, hearing aids, etc.)?

- Are you considering any major medical items (dental surgery, LASIK eye surgery) during the upcoming year?

- Do you anticipate spending any amounts for elderly care of a dependent?

- Do you anticipate spending any amounts on day care for children under 13?

Health Reimbursement Arrangements (HRAs): A Great New Way for Employers to Fund Employee Health Benefits

HRAs, along with HSAs, which are discussed in Chapter 6, represent the newest and most cutting-edge development in employer-sponsored health benefits. HRAs are sometimes called "Section 105 plans" after the IRS Code section that governs them.

HRAs are similar to FSAs, with three important distinctions:

1. HRAs must be 100 percent funded by employers and cannot be funded by employees through salary reduction.

2. HRAs can be either "use it or lose it" or "use it or keep it"—whichever the employer chooses to offer for each HRA.

3. HRAs can be used to cover generally everything an FSA can cover plus:

Individual/family health insurance premiums

Medicare and long-term-care insurance premiums

Preventive care such as weight loss and smoking cessation

A wider list of medical items like over-the-counter medicines

Since 2002, the IRS has added new features and benefits to HRAs. For example, beginning in 2006, unused balances in an HRA may be used to fund medical expenses after an employee retires, and when an employee retires, the employer may make a tax-free contribution to an employee's HRA equal to the value or a portion of the retiree's unused vacation and sick leave.[11]

Note that the *A* in HRA stands for "Arrangement," not "Account," as in Health Savings Account (HSA). Your HRA is technically just an accounting entry showing the amount of HRA funds you have available from your employer from which to apply for reimbursement. There is no actual account, and on job termination, employees typically forfeit their HRA balances (except in some cases starting in 2006 whereby the employer chooses to make unspent HRA funds available for retirement).

HRAs today are so new, and the rules have been changing so fast, that few employers currently are taking advantage of the many benefits they offer. Among employers that do offer HRAs, the two most common uses are:

1. Paying part of the employee's deductible medical expenses so that employees will choose employer health plan options with a higher deductible. For example, some employers offer a $5,000-deductible health insurance plan with a $2,000 "use it or keep it" HRA. Each year any unspent amounts in the employee's HRA may or may not be carried forward for future years.

2. Funding specialized employee benefit programs such as weight loss, maternity, or smoking cessation. The HRA is a relatively simple vehicle for employers to administer for a specialized or single-purpose benefit without recasting their entire group health benefits plans.

But the biggest use of HRAs tomorrow, as you will see throughout Part II of this book, will be for employers to provide tax-free reimbursement to employees for the premium on their own individual/family health insurance policies.

As shown in Part II, the ultimate employee benefit vehicle of the future, which some employers are offering today, consists of:

- A tax-free "use it or lose it" HRA to fund the premiums on your individual/family health insurance policy and long-term-disability insurance

- A tax-free "use it or keep it" HRA to pay some of the deductible medical expenses, now and during retirement

- A Health Savings Account (HSA) to accumulate hundreds of thousands or more for future medical expenses and retirement

Health Savings Accounts: Why You Should Fully Fund Your HSA before Putting Even $1 in Your IRA or 401(k) . . . and How to Build a $500,000+ HSA Nest Egg

HSAs are like an IRA on steroids.

—John Goodman, "father" of health savings accounts[1]

Health Savings Accounts (HSAs) represent the biggest change in health and retirement care since Social Security and Medicare. They allow you to save hundreds of thousands of dollars, tax-free, for your future medical expenses or retirement—while financially reforming the entire U.S. healthcare system.

When people say they have a "Health Savings Account," they typically mean that they have a high-deductible ($1,050 to $5,450) "HSA-qualified" health insurance policy, combined with an IRA-type savings account called an "HSA"—both components are discussed in this chapter. Employers setting up HSA programs for their employees should read this chapter and Chapter 12.

HSAs versus IRAs and 401(k)s

If you are like most readers of this book, you are probably planning to make a contribution this year to your IRA or your 401(k). Approximately 45 million U.S. households have IRAs, and 42 million individuals have 401(k)s. Although they began only about 20 years ago, IRAs and 401(k)s combined hold about $5.1 trillion, half of all U.S. retirement assets. The average-size IRA is about $71,000 and the average-size 401(k) is $45,000.

You should not contribute one more dollar to your traditional IRA, 401(k), or any other savings or brokerage account until you have first contributed 100 percent of the maximum amount allowed, up to $5,450 a year (in 2006), to your Health Savings Account (HSA).

If your employer makes contributions to your 401(k), you should ask your company instead to first contribute the maximum amount to your HSA.

 TIP: This advice assumes that you want to maximize your income tax deductions and have a traditional IRA or 401(k), as most working Americans do. It does not apply if you have a Roth IRA, which you should have only if you do not pay significant amounts of ordinary income taxes. (Taxpayers with Roth IRAs do not receive a deduction from their taxable income for contributions, but they do not have to pay taxes on qualified distributions from a Roth IRA.)

With a traditional IRA or 401(k), you receive a deduction from your taxable income for 100 percent of the contributions you make each year, but after age 65 you must pay state and federal taxes at high ordinary income tax rates on all distributions—even on capital gains in these accounts.*

---

*Traditional IRAs and 401(k)s have proven to be tax traps for millions of Americans because most of the money in IRAs or 401(k)s at retirement is from capital appreciation—which is then taxed at higher ordinary income tax rates instead of lower capital gains rates. Also, many seniors are not in lower tax brackets after retirement. Seniors dislike taking money out of their retirement accounts and paying ordinary income taxes so much that the Congress now requires Required Minimum Distributions (RMDs) beginning at age 70½ based on life expectancy for 100 percent taxable distribution. At death, unused IRA/401(k) balances are taxed at ordinary federal and state income rates, with the remainder subject to estate taxation.

In contrast, with a Health Savings Account (HSA), you receive all the same benefits you do with a traditional IRA or 401(k), except you *never* have to pay income taxes on distributions used for qualified medical expenses—and you can take these distributions without penalty anytime before or after age 65. HSA funds can also be withdrawn for any purpose other than qualified medical expenses—in which case they are treated as if they were withdrawn from your IRA or 401(k)—there is no penalty if you are over 65, though you do pay income tax.

HSAs have essentially the same benefits of traditional IRAs and 401(k)s—plus distributions from HSAs are allowed tax-free at any time for qualified medical expenses.

Traditional IRA/401(k)/HSA Contributions and Appreciation Until Age 65

Age at Beginning	Annual Contribution	Total Contributions	8% Annual Investment Growth[a]	After-Tax HSA Account Value at Age 65
25 (40 years)	$5,250	$210,000	$1,384,327	$1,594,327
35 (30 years)	$5,250	$157,500	$ 523,138	$ 680,638
45 (20 years)	$5,250	$105,000	$ 164,001	$ 269,001
55 (10 years)	$5,250	$ 52,500	$ 31,050	$ 83,550

[a]8.0 percent compounded daily (8.3 percent annual yield). From 1728 Software Systems home page, 2000, 1728 Software Systems, 6 May 2005, http://www.1728.com/annuity.htm.

After-Tax Value of Health Savings Account versus Traditional IRA or 401(k)

Age at Beginning	After-Tax HSA at Age 65	Income Taxes (35%)	After-Tax IRA/401(k)	HSA Value vs IRA/401(k)
25 (40 years)	$1,594,327	$558,014	$1,036,313	154%
35 (30 years)	$ 680,638	$238,223	$ 442,415	154%
45 (20 years)	$ 269,001	$ 94,150	$ 174,851	154%
55 (10 years)	$ 83,550	$ 29,243	$ 54,308	154%

Note: This assumes that all HSA funds can be used for qualified medical expenses—which, in addition to healthcare, include certain health insurance premiums, long-term-care insurance premiums, and preventive care (see text).

As illustrated in these tables, if you or your employer contribute the 2005 HSA maximum of $5,250 a year, in 20 years the $105,000 ($5,250 × 20) of contributions will have appreciated to $269,001—but it will be worth 154 percent of this amount after-tax with an HSA versus an IRA or

401(k) (and even more if your combined federal and state income tax bracket is above 35 percent).

These numbers are even better than they look, because the $5,250 2005 HSA maximum contribution amount automatically increases each year with inflation (it was $5,450 in 2006), and HSAs have many more immediate intangible benefits. For example, HSAs provide a safety net for today and tomorrow since HSA funds can be withdrawn without penalty at any age to pay health insurance premiums while you are unemployed.

HSAs have triple tax advantages:

1. Contributions are tax deductible going in.

2. Appreciation is tax-free.

3. Withdrawals are tax-free (when used for qualifying medical expenses).

An HSA is the only tax-advantaged investment vehicle that offers permanent rather than temporary escape from state and federal income taxes.[2]

Why HSAs Are So Important

Critics of HSAs have made the following allegations:

- HSAs shift healthcare costs from employers to employees since HSAs can be used only with high-deductible health insurance.

- HSAs are tax-saving vehicles for rich people to pay less taxes.

- HSAs will reduce benefits for people with health problems since only the healthy individuals will choose HSA-qualified high-deductible health insurance.

HSAs will do some of these things to some extent, but they offer significant benefits:

- HSAs make healthcare more affordable for tens of millions of Americans. As shown in Appendix A, HSA-qualified individual/family health insurance policies were available in 2006 at prices, on average, one-half to one-third less than for traditional policies. Millions of uninsured Americans can now afford health insurance (although most of them don't yet know that it has recently become affordable).

Average Monthly Premium for Individual/Family Health Insurance Policies (2005–2006)

	Traditional Policy, Lower Deductible	Health Savings Account Policy, Higher Deductible
Single	$173	$ 92
Family	$541	$272

Note: See Appendix A for details.

- HSAs reward consumers for making financially smart but medically sound choices—like choosing generic drugs over chemically identical name-brand ones.

- HSAs provide employees with the financial and health coverage buffer they need between jobs.

- HSAs significantly reduce the 28 percent ($560 billion) of the $2.0 trillion U.S. healthcare budget that goes to paperwork.

- HSAs help Medicare by ensuring that baby boomers have the necessary funds to supplement Medicare during their retirement.

- HSAs return entrepreneurial innovation to U.S. healthcare, since tens of millions of Americans with HSAs will be allowed to select the medical provider of their choice.

- HSAs promote proactive preventive care and wellness care instead of offering reactive "sickness medicine" provided by third parties who cannot make optimum long-term choices.

- In addition, HSAs do much, much more, as explained throughout this book.

A survey of the first 1 million HSA purchasers revealed the following:[3]

- The majority of HSA purchasers (52 percent) were 40 years of age or older.

- Nearly half of HSA purchasers (49 percent) were families with children.

- Two-fifths of HSA purchasers (41 percent) had incomes of $50,000 or less.

- Three of ten HSA purchasers (30 percent) had previously been uninsured.

The HSA Safety Net: How an HSA Can Help You between Jobs

HSAs are primarily known as tax-advantaged vehicles to protect your family from medical expenses during retirement. But the benefits of HSAs to protect you and your family during your working years are so great that they should be called Health "Safety" Accounts.

If you lose your job, the most obvious benefit of having an HSA is that you may use HSA funds to pay qualified medical expenses, just as you could when you were employed—without paying any penalty or income taxes on your withdrawals.

Assuming you follow the advice I give later in this chapter, and do not reimburse yourself for past medical expenses but keep records of your qualified medical expenses, you may be able to withdraw tens of thousands from your HSA for nonmedical purposes—without paying any penalty or income taxes on your withdrawal.

You may also make nonqualified HSA withdrawals to pay rent, buy food, or fund any other nonmedical expense by paying a 10 percent penalty on withdrawals for nonqualified medical expenses—10 percent may seem relatively meaningless if you are desperate for funds.

And finally, you can take advantage of a special safety net that Congress built into HSAs. Although the definition of "qualified medical expenses" for HSAs specifically excludes insurance premiums (except for long-term-care insurance), the definition is modified to include all health insurance premiums when you are collecting federal or state unemployment benefits or are on COBRA.

Your HSA is the ideal buffer to maintain your health insurance and pay out-of-pocket medical expenses between jobs.

HSA-Qualified High-Deductible Health Insurance

Now that you understand the benefits of HSAs, let's look at the details of how they work and how you can get one. A Health Savings Account is an IRA-like account that you open at a bank, credit union, brokerage firm, or other financial institution. To open an HSA and receive its tax benefits, you must have HSA-qualified high-deductible health insurance—either from a group plan sponsored by your employer or from an individual/family policy that you have purchased yourself from an insurance carrier.

TIP: The premiums for high-deductible HSA-qualified individual/family health insurance policies are often half the price of traditional co-pay policies—allowing you to save thousands each year that you can contribute tax-free to your HSA. Appendix A shows an example of how much you can save in your state with a high-deductible versus a traditional co-pay health insurance policy.

Requirements for your high-deductible health insurance to be HSA-qualified follow. If your health insurance should later fail to meet these requirements, you don't lose the money or any of the benefits of your Health Savings Account—you are prohibited only from making new contributions to your HSA until you once again obtain HSA-qualified health insurance.

Annual Deductible Requirements and OOP Maximums

For your health insurance to be HSA-qualified, the following conditions must apply:

For single persons. Your policy must have an annual deductible of at least $1,050 and no more than $5,250 in annual out-of-pocket expenses (including deductibles, co-pays, and coinsurance).

For families. Your policy must have an annual deductible of at least $2,100 and no more than $10,500 in annual out-of-pocket expenses (including deductibles, co-pays, and coinsurance).

These amounts are for calendar year 2006 and are indexed annually for inflation.

One of the main reasons Congress established HSAs was so consumers would be spending their own HSA money for the first $1,050 to $10,500 each year of their medical expenses, in the hope that consumers would spend their money wisely and seek less expensive treatments like generic drugs. However, Congress did not want consumers to rely solely on the balance in their HSA, so people who open HSAs are required to have health insurance covering their medical expenses above $2,100 to $10,500 per family ($1,050 to $5,250 single).

In calculating the maximum figure of $10,500 ($5,250 single), excluded are reasonable benefit design items such as annual or lifetime coverage limits, "usual, customary, and reasonable" payments to providers, precertification requirements, and limits on specific benefits (such as maternity hospital stays). For example, if you spend $2,000 at a medical facility and your insurer considers only $1,200 to be "usual, customary, and reasonable," only the $1,200 figure would count against your deductible and in computing your annual out-of-pocket maximum exposure.

 TIP: Don't assume just because you have an HSA-qualified health insurance policy that you are covered for all medical expenses above $10,500 ($5,250 single) per year (in 2006)— you should carefully understand your out-of-pocket maximum exposure, as explained in Chapter 4.

The amount of the annual deductible on your HSA-qualified policy is also the maximum amount up to $5,450 family ($2,700 single) that you and your employer combined may contribute each year to your HSA (in 2006). Most HSA-qualified health plans have annual deductibles of $2,100 to $5,450 per family ($1,050 to $2,700 per single).

 TIP: In choosing your HSA-qualified health plan, you should generally select the highest annual deductible that you feel you can afford. This will typically save you the most money on your premium and allow you to contribute the maximum amount each year to your HSA—up to $5,450 for a family or $2,700 for a single (in 2006). Remember to increase your deductible each year as inflation raises the maximum annual HSA contribution amount. Each additional $1,000 a year you contribute to your HSA will increase your HSA balance 30 years from now by $130,000.[4]

Checkups and Preventive Care May Be Fully Covered Regardless of Your Deductible

Having an annual deductible of at least $2,100 ($1,050 single) does not mean that your HSA-qualified health plan cannot provide full coverage for certain items. Congress was concerned that people with high-deductible coverage might be reluctant to spend their own money on preventive care or annual checkups. HSA-qualified health plans are allowed to provide unlimited first-dollar coverage for benefits outside of the minimum annual deductible amount, with or without co-pays.

Items Allowed Outside of Minimum High Deductible

Periodic health evaluations (e.g., annual physicals)

Screening services (e.g., mammograms)

Routine prenatal and well-child care

Child and adult immunizations

Tobacco cessation programs

Obesity and weight loss programs

Preventive care

Preventive care does not include treatment of an existing condition, but does include drugs and medications designed to prevent a disease that has not yet manifested itself or to prevent reoccurrence of a disease—such as cholesterol-lowering medication for people with high cholesterol.

TIP: Try to choose an HSA-qualified health insurance policy or employer group plan with 100 percent coverage for annual checkups, immunizations, and other important preventive items. In addition to encouraging you to use them, your health insurance provider can usually negotiate better prices for these items than you can get on your own.

You are also allowed to have other first-dollar health insurance coverage for specific diseases, accidents, disability, vision care, long-term care, and drug discount cards—without violating the HSA-qualified minimum high-deductible requirement.

TIP: Accident insurance programs are available that pay maximum benefits of $5,000 a year for about $25 per month. These programs are excellent supplements to high-deductible HSA coverage since they can protect your HSA balance. Visit www.zanebenefits.com for more information.

Combining HSAs with Your Employer's Section 125 (Cafeteria Plan) FSA or HRA

In general, you cannot have an HSA-qualified health plan combined with an FSA or HRA (see Chapters 4 and 5) providing zero-deductible "first-dollar" coverage unless your FSA/HRA:

Limits reimbursement to only the previously mentioned permitted benefits (e.g., vision, dental, preventive care)

Reimburses you only after you have met the annual minimum high-deductible requirement for your HSA

Provides you retirement benefits that do not violate the HSA-qualified coverage rules.

You are allowed to use your Section 125 employer salary reduction plan to make pretax contributions to your HSA. This is better than making contributions to your HSA with your own after-tax money and receiving a tax deduction, since you also save on FICA and FUTA by having your employer directly contribute part of your wages to your HSA.

 TIP: Some medical items, like long-term-care insurance premiums, may not be paid through FSAs but may be paid by HSAs. If you want to pay, say, a $980-per-year long-term-care insurance premium with tax-deductible funds, ask your employer to withhold an additional $980 from your salary and contribute it to your HSA, then use your HSA to fund your $980 long-term-care insurance premium.

Transition Relief Rules

The legislation allowing HSAs in 2004 was introduced and passed so quickly that it caught many states and large employers by surprise—they had conflicting laws or rules in place that would have limited HSAs in their state or workplace. To accommodate them, the IRS issued transition relief rules that temporarily suspended certain federal requirements for HSA-qualified health coverage until 2006.

For example, New Jersey has a rule requiring health plans to have first-dollar coverage for the treatment of lead poisoning. The IRS suspended such state-mandated coverage from disqualifying HSA-qualified plans until 2006 so that state legislatures could amend their laws—and most states have already done so or are doing so as of this writing. Similarly, some large employers had prescription drug benefit co-pay plans that would similarly have disqualified their employees from qualifying for an HSA—prescription drug rules were also temporarily suspended by the IRS until 2006.

Although the transition relief rules expired in 2006, the IRS may issue additional transition relief rules at any time. The U.S. government is determined to make the transition to Health Savings Accounts as smooth and as fast as possible, and thus they may issue more temporary suspensions of HSA requirements if they find such suspensions to be in the public interest.

The Treasury Department, the IRS, and Congress itself have bent over backward to make HSAs available to as many Americans as possible in the shortest possible time. HSAs are perceived on both sides of the aisle as good for employees, good for employers, and most important, as a critical tool to help control rising U.S. healthcare costs (see Chapter 1 and epilogue).

Once you have obtained your HSA-qualified high-deductible health insurance, you are allowed to open your Health Savings Account.[5]

Managing Your Health Savings Account

This section discusses choosing an HSA financial institution and making contributions to and withdrawals from your account.

Choosing a Depository Institution for Your HSA

Currently, hundreds of financial institutions offer HSAs; soon there will be thousands more. Federal regulations allow HSAs to be automatically offered by insured banks and credit unions, insurance companies, and any other institutions offering IRAs. Depending on the state in which you live, the bank or financial institution offering the HSA may be called either a *custodian* or *trustee*.

You may feel most comfortable opening your HSA at a local bank or credit union, but there is no need to do so. Unlike with a checking or savings account, you may never make a cash deposit or cash withdrawal from your HSA. Moreover, once the balance in your HSA has grown to more than a few thousand dollars, you will probably want to move most of your HSA funds to a money market fund, a financial advisory firm, or a brokerage firm that can help you invest for the maximum long-term return. Many financial institutions offer the same options for investing higher-balance HSAs that they offer for IRAs.

You should choose an HSA the same way you choose any other IRA or financial service account—paying particular attention to annual or monthly maintenance fees, withdrawal fees, debit card fees, and so on.

 TIP: Fees you pay to your financial institution are typically automatically deducted from your HSA—but you don't want them to be. You should contribute the maximum amount allowed each year to your HSA, and you are allowed to exclude from contributions reasonable banking-type fees paid with non-HSA funds. Some financial institutions allow you to

pay your HSA fees with a check from a separate account—
ask if you can do this.

Contrary to what many people think, you may have an unlimited number of different Health Savings Accounts at an
unlimited number of financial institutions—provided the
total contributions and withdrawals to all of them combined
do not exceed the IRS regulations for a single HSA.

TIP: Most financial institutions today charge annual fees of
$3 to $5 per month ($36 to $60 per year) to maintain an
HSA, and some waive this fee and pay higher interest if your
HSA balance is above $5,000 or $10,000—thus you may
want to keep just one HSA until your HSA balance reaches
the level to qualify for free service or higher interest rates.

You may freely transfer balances directly from one HSA
account to another—but you should never transfer money
from an HSA to a non-HSA account, because such transfers
could be deemed taxable withdrawals for nonmedical purposes.

Making Contributions to Your HSA

Your HSA is the best investment vehicle to save you money on taxes today
and earn tax-free interest and appreciation for tomorrow—even better than
an IRA or 401(k). You will not have to pay taxes on HSA withdrawals after
retirement if you use your HSA funds for qualified medical expenses for
you, your spouse, or your dependents. You should contribute the maximum
amount of money into your HSA each year as soon as possible.

You and your employer (combined) may contribute to a family HSA the
lesser of $5,450 per year ($2,700 single) or the annual deductible on your
HSA-qualified health insurance (in 2006). These figures are adjusted
annually for inflation. As explained previously, HSA banking fees may be
paid outside of your HSA without being counted as contributions.
Interest and capital appreciation inside your HSA are not counted toward
your maximum annual contribution amount.

The following four types of contributions may be made to HSAs.

1. *Employer contributions from employer-sponsored HSA plans.* These are sent directly from your employer to your designated HSA. During your enrollment period you select an HSA-qualified benefits option; in return for accepting the high-deductible HSA-qualified health benefits option, your employer agrees to contribute a set amount each month to your HSA. Employer contributions may be a fixed amount for all employees or a percentage of salary, and they are subject to ERISA nondiscrimination rules for employees in a given class (see Chapter 12 for more information on employer-sponsored HSA plans).

   Tax benefit: You get the money into your HSA and pay no income taxes or FICA on the employer's contribution, even if you take the money out and spend it the next day (on qualified medical expenses). Your employer gets a full income tax deduction for its contribution and does not have to pay FICA or FUTA on the contributed amount.

2. *Employer contributions in lieu of salary.* These are contributions made under a Section 125 plan (see Chapter 5) whereby you direct your employer to make contributions to your HSA as a reduction in your pretax salary.

   Tax benefit: You get the money in your HSA and pay no income taxes or FICA on your contribution—even if you take the money out and spend it the next day (on qualified medical expenses). Your employer gets a full deduction from its taxable income for its contribution, and both you and your company save 7.65 percent in FICA taxes. Since you effectively get the contribution tax-free, you do not get (or need) a separate deduction from your reported taxable income as you do with a self contribution.

TIP: If your employer allows you to contribute to your HSA under a Section 125 cafeteria plan, do it—this option saves you the most money on taxes, FICA, and FUTA, and you can be assured of making regular contributions.

TIP: If your employer's Section 125 plan doesn't allow this feature, speak to your benefits administrator about making it available. It costs almost nothing to administer, and your employer also saves 7.65 percent in matching FICA on every dollar you contribute to your HSA in this way.

3. *Self-contributions.* These are direct contributions made by you, or anyone else (e.g., relative) on your behalf, to your HSA. You may make a self-contribution anytime during the calendar year or up until April 15 (or whenever you file your tax return) of the following year.

Tax benefit: When you file your income tax return, you get an above-the-line deduction for 100 percent of your self-contributions—even if you do not itemize your deductions. If a relative makes the contribution for you, you (not your relative) get the income tax deduction, even if you take the money out and spend it the next day (on qualified medical expenses).

TIP: You should make the maximum allowed deposit to your HSA at the beginning of each year, on January 1, even though you are allowed to deposit up until April 15 of the following year (470 days later). Why? Because money in your HSA earns tax-free interest. If you contribute each year on January 1 instead of 470 days later, your HSA will earn an extra $727 each year (at 8 percent) on your $5,250 contribution in tax-free interest for 470 days. Over 20 years, just this extra $727 per year in interest will accumulate to $37,300, or to $94,250 over 30 years.

TIP: If your employer is contributing monthly to your HSA, or if you are contributing indirectly through a Section 125 plan, make an additional self-contribution as soon as possible to bring the total contributions up to the maximum level allowed.

Catch-up contributions. Individuals who establish HSAs early in their careers can save hundreds of thousands for medical expenses by the time they retire. To be fair to individuals now approaching retirement who didn't get this chance during most of their working years, Congress established "catch-up" contributions for people approaching retirement. In addition to the $5,450 (in 2006) annual contribution limit, individuals 55 and over can make additional contributions until they enroll in Medicare. These catch-up contributions are limited to $700 in 2006, $800 in 2007, $900 in 2008, and $1,000 in 2009 and thereafter.

TIP: If you and your spouse are both over 55 and each establish an HSA in your own name, you can make up to $10,000 ($1,000 per year for 10 years after 2009) in catch-up contributions ($20,000 total), which could save you $7,000 in income taxes (35 percent tax bracket), plus your $20,000 would appreciate tax-free in your HSA.

Although spouses are allowed to make catch-up contributions separately, if spouses are covered under each other's health insurance, the lower annual deductible applies to both. HSA contributions can be divided freely between two spouses provided the total does not exceed the family limit (e.g., $5,450 in 2006).

In addition to these four types of contributions, you may also contribute tax-free to an HSA the balance from a Medical Savings Account or any other HSA (*rollover contribution*). All contributions except rollovers must be made in cash.

The date on which you receive your HSA-qualified health insurance, not the date on which you open your HSA, is the operable date for prorating how much you can contribute to your HSA. For example, if you switch to an HSA-qualified health plan on June 30, you are eligible to contribute 50 percent of your HSA maximum annual contribution that year even if you don't open your HSA bank account until December 31, or even April 15, of the following year.

Making Withdrawals from Your HSA

In 1999, when I opened our family HSA (then called a Medical Savings Account, or MSA), I made the same mistake that most new HSA account holders make today—I withdrew money from my HSA to pay for medical expenses.

You are reading correctly. Before retirement, it is a mistake to use your HSA to pay for qualified medical expenses that you could otherwise afford to pay with non-HSA funds.

Although there is an exhaustive list of qualified medical expenses for which you can use your HSA funds, in most cases the correct financial decision is to not touch the funds in your HSA until you reach retirement.

You receive all of your HSA tax benefits by making contributions to your HSA, and you receive no additional tax benefits by withdrawing funds to pay for qualified medical expenses.

> **Moreover, the funds withdrawn from your HSA no longer accumulate tax-free interest and appreciation.**
>
> **Just as you should fully fund your HSA before putting $1 into your IRA or 401(k), you should also spend any nonretirement funds you have available for medical expenses before taking out even $1 of your HSA before retirement.**

Assume you have both an HSA and a normal savings or brokerage account (and assume an 8 percent long-term interest rate, age 35, and a 40 percent combined federal and state income tax bracket). Your family spends $2,000 a year on qualified medical expenses, which you could pay with either your HSA or your ordinary savings account. You could use your HSA and leave $2,000 in your savings account, where it would earn compound interest at the rate of 5.2 percent after taxes (8 percent less 40 percent in income taxes). After 30 years, this extra $2,000 a year would have appreciated to $139,016. However, if you left this same $2,000 in your HSA earning 8 percent without having to pay income taxes, in 30 years it would be worth $259,290, almost twice as much.

Here's the best deal of all when it comes to leaving money in your HSA. There is no time limit on how long you can wait to reimburse yourself with funds from your HSA as long as the medical expense was incurred after you opened your HSA. If you spent $2,000 of non-HSA money for qualified medical expenses for 30 years, and left this $60,000 in your HSA accumulating tax-free interest, in year 30, or anytime you wish, you could still reimburse yourself up to $60,000 tax-free—and spend this money on anything, including nonmedical items.

 TIP: Each year, make a list of your qualified medical expenses and receipts, but don't reimburse yourself from your HSA. If you ever want money from your HSA for a nonmedical expense, you can then make tax-free withdrawals for unreimbursed expenses all the way back to the first day you opened your HSA—even if it's 30 years or more later.

Sometimes you may not have the money available to pay your deductible medical expenses without touching your HSA, or you may not have enough money to make an annual contribution to your HSA. In such cases, you should still pay all of your qualified medical expenses outside of your HSA and then pass the reimbursement through your HSA to maximize your income tax savings.

For example, say you cannot afford to make any new HSA contributions this year. At the end of the year, or before April 15 when you file your tax return, you calculate that you have spent $3,800 for qualified out-of-pocket medical expenses. You should make a contribution of $3,800 to your HSA and simultaneously make a qualified withdrawal of $3,800 to reimburse yourself for these expenses. This way, you get a $3,800 above-the-line deduction from your income taxes for your medical expenses, even if you do not itemize your deductions, thus saving yourself $1,330 in income taxes (assuming a 35 percent combined state and federal tax bracket).

You are your own administrator of your HSA. The bank or financial institution where you keep your HSA will typically not ask you about contributions or withdrawals—you are solely responsible to the IRS to comply with HSA rules and regulations. If you make a mistake, and have evidence that it was a mistake, by withdrawing funds for a nonqualified expense, you are allowed to return these funds to your HSA without penalty up until April 15 of the following year. If you make a permanent withdrawal for nonqualified expenses, you must report such a withdrawal as taxable income and pay an additional 10 percent penalty on the withdrawn amount.

Similarly, if you contribute more than the legal annual maximum to your HSA, you are allowed to withdraw and return the excess contribution and any earnings on it without penalty up until April 15 of the following year. If you do not, you must pay a 6 percent excise tax on the excess contribution and its earnings and lower your contribution the following year by the amount of the excess contribution—and you must pay an additional 6 percent excise tax on the excess contribution and its earnings each year until you do so.

HSA-Qualified Medical Expenses

You are allowed tax-free withdrawals from HSAs at any time for qualified medical expenses. Before retirement, the best HSA strategy is to leave as much as possible inside your HSA, since you can take reimbursement at any time.

TIP: Certain qualified medical expenses, like premiums for long-term-care insurance, are much more economical if you begin purchasing them early. You should consider using your HSA funds for long-term-care premiums if you do not have other funds available. As explained in Chapter 8, long-term-care insurance is one item you should purchase long before retirement—since it is less expensive if bought earlier and ultimately protects your retirement. Note that there is an annual limit on the amount of long-term-care premiums that qualify for HSA withdrawals (e.g., $980 per year for ages 51 to 60, $490 per year for ages 41 to 50), so consult your accountant before funding your long-term-care premiums with your HSA.

How to Spend All Your HSA Money Tax-Free after Retirement

After retirement, or anytime you wish, you are allowed to withdraw money tax-free from your HSA for a long list of qualified medical expenses, including:

Prescriptions (including co-pays)

Doctor visits (including co-pays)

Dental

Chiropractic

X-rays and other medical procedures

Over-the-counter medications

Eyeglasses, contacts, LASIK, and other vision care

Hearing aids

Transportation to and from medical providers

Weight-loss programs (medically supervised)

Smoking cessation

Medicare premiums, including Part A, Part B, Medicare HMOs, and the new Medicare prescription drug insurance (see Chapter 8)

Long-term-care expenditures

Long-term-care insurance premiums

Hundreds of medical treatments and procedures that haven't yet been invented

At age 65, the average U.S. life expectancy is currently 85 years and increasing. Look again at the preceding list—it's easy to see that you will want and need all the money in your HSA and that you will most likely get to withdraw it all tax-free to spend on qualified medical expenses. Even a $300,000 HSA balance provides only $10,000 a year (excluding extra interest) over a 30-year retirement.

What if you pass away before you spend all the money in your HSA? Your HSA continues after you die and simply transfers to your spouse for his or her medical expenses. When your spouse dies, the HSA is treated like an IRA or any other retirement account and included in their estate.

The Future of HSAs

At the time of this writing, there are proposals in Congress to expand HSAs by:

- Making all health insurance premiums on HSA-qualified health plans tax deductible "above the line" regardless of how they are paid

- Giving families making less than $25,000 a $2,000 annual tax credit (not a deduction) for the premium on an HSA-qualified health plan, which would effectively guarantee most working families health insurance since they would simply deflect $2,000 they now pay in federal taxes to pay their health insurance premium

- Giving low-income families a $1,000 annual contribution to their HSA from the federal government

---

HSAs represent the biggest change in health benefits since 1945, when Franklin Roosevelt created the present system, and HSAs will improve healthcare and lower costs for all Americans.

More than 1 million American families opened HSAs in just the first 14 months after they became available.

HSAs usually save you money from day 1. However, in some cases your HSA options may not be the best short-term economic choice—for example, if you visit the doctor often and have a low $10 co-pay that otherwise might cost you $55 with high-deductible insurance. However, even in such cases, the long-term advantages of an HSA typically outweigh the additional few hundred dollars you might lose today with high-deductible insurance.

CHAPTER 7

What to Do if You or a Family Member Has a Major Health Problem

Every state has state-guaranteed coverage through state risk pools or their equivalents for people with health issues. See Appendix A for an example of this type of coverage in your state.

The best health insurance for most people under age 65 is their own affordable individual/family health insurance policy. Such policies are almost always "guaranteed renewable," which means that your policy cannot be canceled as long as you pay the premium, and your premium cannot be increased just because you have a major, expensive medical problem.*

You may be reading this chapter now because you or a family member has a health problem (*preexisting condition*), such as cancer, heart disease, or diabetes, that prevents you from qualifying for an affordable individual/ family policy in your state. You may have been rejected for health insurance or may have had a health insurance company agree to accept you only with an uprated (increased) premium or an exclusion for your preexisting condition. If so, you should talk to a good insurance agent who knows which companies offer better-priced health insurance in your state for people with preexisting conditions. You should also apply with other insurance companies, if you haven't already, but be sure to reread Chapter 4 first.

It sounds harsh to say it, but you would not have to be reading this chapter now if you had purchased an individual/family health insurance

---

*See also Chapters 3, 4, and 5. See Chapter 8 if the unhealthy family member is over age 55.

policy before your family member had developed his or her preexisting condition. You would have the same health insurance you originally purchased, without an increase in your premium because of the preexisting condition, and your policy would be guaranteed renewable until age 65.

This is why you should get the healthy members of your family their own individual/family policy now—so if one of them develops a preexisting condition they will still have affordable health insurance. In addition, the premium for your healthy family members will be much less if you do not include the family member with the preexisting condition.

Someone who cannot medically qualify for life or health insurance because of a preexisting condition is called an *uninsurable*. Do not let the name scare you off. Uninsurable does not mean that you cannot get health insurance—it means that you will have to pay a higher premium for health insurance until the preexisting condition goes away.

There are basically six options for you or your family member who is "uninsurable." In order of preference for most people, they are as follows:

1. Find a job with good health insurance benefits.
2. Get subsidized state-guaranteed health insurance (through a state risk pool or its equivalent) if you are not HIPAA-eligible.
3. Get state-guaranteed health insurance if you are HIPAA-eligible.
4. Qualify for Medicaid and other income-based programs.
5. Become eligible for someone else's health insurance or Medicaid.
6. Purchase a medical discount card.

Finding a Job with Good Health Insurance Benefits

The easiest way to get health insurance coverage for you or a family member with a preexisting condition is to get a job with a company that provides health benefits. Employers are prohibited from discriminating against employees or applicants based on their health or the health of a member of their family. Employers can exclude coverage for a preexisting condition only for 12 to 18 months, and generally they cannot exclude coverage for preexisting conditions if you were covered during the previous 12 months.

If you have an "uninsurable" family member, go back and read Chapter 3, paying particular attention to your HIPAA rights as a new employee and as an employee transferring between employers.

Once you have such coverage from an employer, if you lose your coverage you may become HIPAA-eligible, which is the best situation to be in if you have a preexisting condition that prevents you from getting private health insurance. Ten states offer you state-guaranteed coverage in their state risk pool only if you are HIPAA-eligible, and these states offer no other state-guaranteed option for uninsurables. See Appendix A for details on your state.

How to Become a "Friend of the Governor": State-Guaranteed Subsidized Insurance for Those Who Are Not HIPAA-Eligible

 TIP: State-guaranteed health insurance can be the bargain of a lifetime if you are very ill—an annual premium of $3,600 a year can get you $100,000 a year or more in health benefits. Unfortunately, for obvious financial reasons, states don't spend money advertising their state-guaranteed coverage—often, only people who know the governor or someone in state government get to take advantage of it. After reading this section, if you have a family member who is very ill, you will know your rights to state-guaranteed subsidized health insurance as a resident of your state—as if you were a "friend of the governor."

Every state provides some type of guaranteed subsidized health insurance to its citizens and residents who cannot get coverage for either of the following two reasons:

1. You are uninsurable (because of a preexisting condition) and cannot get coverage in the private market.

2. You are very poor, probably receiving welfare assistance, and cannot afford the premium for health insurance.

In this section we examine only uninsurable individuals. The inability to afford health insurance is discussed later, under Medicaid, in the context of how you or a family member can qualify for Medicaid.

This section is written as if you are the member of your family with the preexisting condition. The information is the same if your child, spouse, or dependent has the health issue. You should be seeking state-guaranteed coverage only for this family member, since it typically costs twice as much as a regular individual/family policy.

State-guaranteed coverage for uninsurables is much more expensive than private coverage for healthy individuals—you can get your healthy family members their own individual/family policy for a much lower premium.

State-guaranteed coverage, through state risk pools and their equivalents, is designed to help only those who cannot medically qualify for private health insurance—not those who cannot afford health insurance.

What Is a State Risk Pool?

A state risk pool, also called a *high-risk pool,* is typically a nonprofit entity that pays for the losses experienced by insurance carriers who provide individual/family health insurance to unhealthy individuals who qualify. (See Appendix A for specific information on the state risk pool in your state.)

State risk pools lose hundreds of millions of dollars every year. States subsidize their state risk pools (or equivalents) by charging insurance carriers a premium-based fee on health insurance policies sold in their state, through tobacco and other revenue taxes, and by using federal grants and matching federal funds.

State risk pools were started in 1976 to provide coverage to people who could afford individual/family policies but could not medically qualify for them. Today more than 250,000 people receive state-guaranteed coverage from a state risk pool or its equivalent.[1]

Approximately 33 states have state risk pools, and states without them have some type of substitute or equivalent state-guaranteed coverage for their unhealthy citizens. At a very minimum, states are required under federal law to guarantee health insurance coverage to "HIPAA-eligible" individuals (discussed in Chapter 3) regardless of their health status and without exclusions for preexisting conditions. At the time of this writing, 40 states offer state-guaranteed subsidized coverage to their unhealthy residents whether or not they are HIPAA-eligible; usually they offer even better deals for HIPAA-eligible individuals. (See Appendix A for information on your state.)

Eligibility

To qualify for state-guaranteed coverage, you cannot be eligible to participate in an employer's health benefits plan, cannot be eligible to receive COBRA benefits, and must satisfy at least one of the following three conditions:

1. You have been denied coverage by a private health insurance carrier for health reasons.
2. You have been offered coverage with an exclusion for a preexisting condition.
3. You have been offered coverage for an uprated premium.

In some states, such as Texas, you can satisfy one of these three conditions by obtaining a letter from a licensed health insurance agent stating that one of these conditions would occur if you were to apply for private health insurance. You can find phone numbers, web sites, and more information on state-guaranteed coverage in your state in Appendix A.

TIP: Ask the state-guaranteed coverage administrator if it will accept such a letter instead of making you apply to a carrier and get rejected. As explained in Chapter 4, once you are rejected, you and your family members are probably going to have some explaining to do whenever you apply for health insurance. While state-guaranteed coverage may be your only option today, hopefully you will soon become healthier and will obtain much less expensive health insurance from a private carrier.

In some states, such as South Dakota, all applicants must be HIPAA-eligible. South Dakota does not guarantee any coverage to unhealthy citizens who have not recently had health insurance.

TIP: If you are an employer, see Chapter 11 for how to make all of your employees instantly HIPAA-eligible so they can be guaranteed immediate coverage without any exclusions for preexisting conditions.

Cost

The premium for state-guaranteed coverage is legally set, typically at 200 percent of the average individual policy premium—although it seems higher because state risk pool managers often use the highest "average" they can find in setting rates. The table that follows shows some state risk pool health insurance premium rates in 2005 and a comparable traditional (nongovernment risk pool) policy (see Appendix A for your state):

Premiums for State Risk Pools: Male, Age 35, 2005

State Risk Pool[a]	Premium (per Month)	Annual Deductible	Comparable Healthy Premium/Deductible
Missouri	$270	$1,000	$124 / $1,000
Texas	$364	$1,000	$117 / $1,500
Maryland	$224	$ 500	$134 / $750
California	$356	$ 0	$204 / $1,500
Connecticut	$290	$1,500	$132 / $1,500
Kentucky	$249	$ 750	$ 79 / $1,000
Illinois	$257	$1,000	$ 98 / $1,000
New Jersey[b]	$411	$ 0	$411 / $0
Maine[b]	$445	$1,000	$445 / $1,000
Massachusetts[b]	$503	$ 250	$503 / $250

[a]See Appendix A for policy details.
[b]No state risk pool; every policy sold in New York, New Jersey, Massachusetts, Maine, and Vermont is effectively a state risk pool policy because all citizens must be accepted (*guaranteed issue*) at the same premium (*community-rated*) regardless of their health.

While these premiums may seem expensive, they are nonetheless a good deal for unhealthy citizens, and they are also good for employers with employees in a state risk pool who might otherwise be in the employer's group plan.

A participant in a state risk pool may be consuming $10,000, $100,000, or more in annual medical expenses while paying only $2,000 to $6,000 in annual premiums.

Most state risk pools accept only individual applicants. Because the premium is typically twice as expensive, you should choose such coverage only for the sole family member with the preexisting condition. However, you should always check to see whether your state risk pool has coverage available for other family members and at what cost. A few states (illogically) offer coverage for additional family members at rates cheaper than you would pay for private (nongovernment risk pool coverage). For example, if you qualify to buy health insurance through the state risk pool in Maryland ($224 premium for an unhealthy male, age 35), that state allows you to add five children for an additional $112 ($336 total premium)—much less than similar coverage for five children would cost from a private carrier.[2] In a case like this, if you have a large family, coverage from a state risk pool is much cheaper than coverage from the private market.

Benefits

The benefits from a state risk pool are quite good—the policy is often administered by the leading insurance carrier in your state, or you are given a choice of several major carriers. You use the same doctor and hospital networks that you would if you had an ordinary individual/family health insurance policy—which you do, except that you are paying about a 200 percent premium for it (and your state government is paying much more to subsidize your coverage). The one major difference in coverage from a state risk pool is that you typically have a lower lifetime maximum benefit of $1 to $2 million instead of the $3 to $5 million that is common with an ordinary individual/family policy.

Preexisting Conditions

Most state risk pools have a 12-month exclusionary period during which you are not covered for medical expenses resulting from a preexisting condition. If they didn't, because applications are guaranteed issue, applicants would wait until they were very ill or in the hospital before applying and paying their premium. This preexisting condition exclusion period is waived if you are HIPAA-eligible or can demonstrate that you have had 12 months of continuous coverage without a lapse of 63 days (see Chapter 3).

The Five Remaining States with Only State-Guaranteed Coverage instead of a Free Health Insurance Market

The five states of New York, New Jersey, Massachusetts, Maine, and Vermont have no need for state-guaranteed coverage since state law requires all individual/family policies sold in these states to be "guaranteed issue" and "community rated" (i.e., everyone applying for an individual/ family policy must be accepted and at the same premium rate). The entire individual/family insurance marketplace in these states is effectively a giant state risk pool—without any government subsidy for the unhealthy.

TIP: If you live in one of these five states, you might be thinking, "Why should I waste money on health insurance since I can always buy it after I become ill?" In fact, this was a good strategy until these states recently closed this loophole. New York and the other states now exclude preexisting conditions from coverage for 12 months when you purchase a new policy.

As shown in Appendix A, unhealthy individuals in these states pay about 150 percent of the state risk pool premium rate in other states, and healthy individuals pay 300 to 400 percent of the premium paid in other states.

The exception to this rule is individuals who are both unhealthy and older. In the Texas state risk pool, the monthly premium for an unhealthy individual age 35 is $364, but rises to $840 if the individual is age 64. In Massachusetts, however, the premium remains the same, $503, whether an individual (unhealthy or healthy) is age 35 or age 64.

Only people who are both older *and* unhealthy benefit in New York, New Jersey, Massachusetts, Maine, and Vermont, where everyone is guaranteed an individual/family policy at the same (extremely high) premium.

The theory behind state laws requiring health insurance to be guaranteed issue and community rated is flawed: Because of "adverse selection," only unhealthy individuals will choose to purchase health insurance when the price is four times the price of comparable coverage in other states. The state of Kentucky adopted guaranteed issue and community rating in 1994 and, as a result, 45 out of 47 carriers left the state.[3] Similar experiences happened during the 1990s in the states of Washington and New Hampshire. In the early 2000s, all three of these states abandoned guaranteed issue and community rating, and carriers have been returning to offer affordable policies in these states.

Other Substitutes or Equivalents to State Risk Pools

In lieu of a state risk pool, the state of Ohio mandates that the 14 largest insurance carriers offering individual/family policies in Ohio each have a 30-day period of "open enrollment" every year—a time when any Ohio citizen or resident may purchase an HMO policy regardless of health issues and with no exclusions for preexisting conditions. The insurance companies do not want you to know about these programs, but the company names and the dates of their 30-day open enrollment periods are available from the Ohio Department of Insurance (see Appendix A).

The individual U.S. states offer vastly different programs to their unhealthy citizens, and 10 states offer no health insurance options at all for uninsurables who are not HIPAA-eligible. You must have had health insurance for at least 18 months without a lapse in coverage of more than 63 days to be HIPAA-eligible.

TIP: If you are desperate for healthcare for yourself or a family member, or if you are in danger of medical-related bankruptcy, you might want to move to a state with favorable state-guaranteed coverage. In addition to checking out the benefits and waiting period before preexisting conditions become covered, check the residency requirement for eligibility in Appendix A. Texas requires 30 days of residency, California requires only an "intent to remain in California," and Alaska requires a full year of residency before you become eligible for state-guaranteed coverage. HIPAA-eligible individuals are not subject to state residency requirements. The right state for you depends on a great number of factors, so get all of the facts on each state and learn how they cover your condition before making your decision.

State-Guaranteed Health Insurance for HIPAA-Eligible Individuals

You generally become HIPAA-eligible after you lose your employer-sponsored health coverage and accept and use up your COBRA benefits.

All states are required under federal HIPAA law to guarantee you health insurance if you are HIPAA-eligible.

Chapter 3 describes ways to become HIPAA-eligible without necessarily paying for expensive COBRA for 18 to 36 months (e.g., work for a firm with 19 or fewer employees that doesn't offer COBRA).

How States Guarantee Coverage to Their HIPAA-Eligible Individuals

Each state handles its federal obligation to guarantee health insurance to HIPAA-eligible individuals differently, and some states offer multiple choices to HIPAA-eligibles. There are three main ways states handle this obligation:

1. *State risk pools.* Most states, like Texas, allow you to apply to the state risk pool and waive the normal 12-month exclusionary period for preexisting conditions. New York, which does not have a state risk pool, mandates that HIPAA-eligible individuals may not have any exclusions for preexisting conditions.

2. *Conversion coverage.* Some states like Florida, Ohio, and California mandate that the insurance carrier providing the group policy to your former employer, from which you may have accepted COBRA to become HIPAA-eligible, offer you an individual/family policy with no exclusions for preexisting conditions. The premium typically cannot exceed 200 percent of the normal rate in the state, and the policy benefits must be similar to those of your former group policy. This is a particularly good option if you are coming off of an expensive group employer-benefit plan, since you get to keep all your benefits without paying a lot more for them.

3. *Guaranteed-issue insurance from private carriers.* Some states, like California, mandate that you may apply to any insurance carrier offering individual insurance policies and that you must be offered at least two choices, a traditional low-deductible policy and a high-deductible policy. California also limits the premium charged to 200 percent of what healthy individuals are charged for similar policies.

Being HIPAA-eligible is the best situation to be in if you have an expensive preexisting condition that prevents you from getting affordable private health insurance and you don't have employer-sponsored insurance. All states must guarantee you an individual/family policy without exclusions for preexisting conditions if you are HIPAA-eligible.

If you are an employer, jump ahead to Chapter 11 to learn how to make all your employees instantly HIPAA-eligible without having them first go on COBRA.

Medicaid and Other Income-Based Programs

For those with low incomes, there are programs available that are strictly income-based.

Medicaid

Medicaid, which became law in 1965, is a federal/state program that pays for medical care for individuals and families with very low incomes, typically at or below the federal poverty line (FPL). The FPL today is approximately $10,000 for a single individual and $20,000 for a family. Approximately 38 million Americans today are on Medicaid (see Appendix B).

While each state sets its own eligibility requirements and benefits, each state must meet minimum federal guidelines in order to qualify for

Medicaid funds. States must cover individuals eligible for Aid to Families with Dependent Children (i.e., welfare), all children under 19 in families with incomes below the FPL, and certain working and disabled persons who would qualify for public assistance if they did not work.

The benefits of Medicaid vary from state to state and are generally quite good. In most states, Medicaid provides 100 percent of doctor visits, hospital services, and even full prescription drug coverage. This latter item has been a strong bone of contention for some middle-class Americans and Medicare recipients who pay hundreds of dollars a month for their own prescription drugs—they see their tax dollars providing a benefit to others that they often cannot afford to provide for themselves.

Newspaper stories appear often about U.S. families with a critically ill child who want to work, but cannot—if they earned more income they would become ineligible for Medicaid and thus unable to afford the thousands of dollars of prescription drugs their child requires each month to remain alive.

An estimated 6.5 million of the 43 million Medicare beneficiaries also receive Medicaid—mostly for prescription drug coverage. This is expected to end during the next few years when the new Medicare Prescription Drug Plan Part D becomes fully effective (see Chapter 8).

TIP: **There are many ways to qualify for Medicaid if your income is close to or below the FPL, or if you have a disability and income of up to 250 percent of the FPL. Contact the health insurance department in your state for questions about Medicaid eligibility and benefits (see Appendix A).**

Other Income-Based Programs

In addition to Medicaid, most states have other programs for people of moderate incomes who earn too much to qualify for Medicaid.

California has a program called "Healthy Families" for children and teens whose families earn too much to qualify for Medicaid. The premium is only $27 per month for all children under 19—a family of four qualifies if their family income is less than $48,000 a year.[4]

New York has a program called "Healthy New York," which is available only to people employed in the state for at least 12 months by an employer that does not offer employer-sponsored health insurance. The premium is approximately $177 per month for an individual and $510 per month for a family.[5] This is about 60 percent less than the premium for a comparable individual/family policy in New York shown in Appendix A. Singles may earn up to $23,800 and families up to $48,250 a year to be eligible for this program.

Contact your state health insurance department to learn about similar programs in your state (see Appendix A).

Becoming Eligible for Someone Else's Health Insurance or Medicaid

Every employer-sponsored health benefits plan, individual/family health insurance policy, and state Medicaid program has extensive eligibility requirements defining an eligible spouse or dependent. These definitions are not as confining as they traditionally have been.

If you have a relationship with an individual who has good health insurance from any source, you should explore what you can legally do to become eligible for coverage under that person's health insurance policy, as either a dependent or a domestic partner.

For example, the Summary of Plan Document (SPD) of many large employee-benefits plans is fairly liberal in defining "eligible domestic partner"—which is the same as a spouse for eligibility in an employer-sponsored group benefits plan. Some large companies, like Chevron/Texaco, heavily subsidize the cost of the spousal premium.

Chevron/Texaco requires only that an employee and his or her domestic partner of either sex sign a notarized statement certifying that they "have lived together for at least six months" and that "an intimate, committed relationship of mutual caring has existed and is expected to continue indefinitely." Once an employee signs this statement, the children of the domestic partner are also immediately eligible for participation in the employer's group plan, at rates heavily subsidized by the employer.[6]

Similarly, after consulting with an attorney in your state, there may be other legal ways to modify your family structure to get the person with the preexisting condition legally qualified as a dependent of someone else with good health insurance. In addition, your attorney may suggest ways to legally dismantle your family in order to have one spouse and/or child qualify for Medicaid and thus receive free medical care.

Modifying your family structure to become eligible for health insurance is a difficult process fraught with legal pitfalls and should be considered only with the aid of a good attorney in your state.

You should never do anything illegal to qualify for health insurance. In addition to criminal and civil penalties, there is no statute of limitations for fraud. As explained in Chapter 4, your health benefits could be canceled years from now retroactive to your initial date of application.

Purchase a Medical Discount Card or Join a PPO

Many private companies offer medical discount cards for fees ranging from $10 to $120 a month. These cards offer discounts of hundreds or thousands of dollars per year from your medical providers.

Some of these companies (e.g., Costco and Wal-Mart) are legitimate, and you may save many times the monthly fees in medical discounts from your providers. However, some of these discount cards are worthless, and their sponsors will refuse to issue a refund if your providers won't accept them. Medical discount cards have received a bad reputation from attorneys general in many states.

Some companies marketing these medical discount cards, either directly to the public or through a trade association, mislead consumers into thinking they are high-deductible insurance plans. Hundreds of consumers mistakenly believe they have health insurance—until it is too late. Some of these consumers could qualify for real individual/family health insurance policies for not much more than they pay for the discount cards. Providers of these cards have been sued for misleading consumers in almost every state, and health insurance departments are now requiring bold "this is not health insurance" disclaimers on all medical discount cards.

As illustrated in Chapter 4, medical providers typically inflate their stated prices 25 to 900 percent in order to give 20 to 90 percent discounts to health insurance companies and quality PPOs. Some of these cards may actually save you the money they promise if they are associated with a strong PPO.

TIP: If you cannot get health insurance and are considering a medical discount card, first ask all of your regular medical providers how much discount you will get with the card. You should also ask them if they would provide you this same discount from now on if you paid cash even without the card—you may be surprised to discover how much money you have been wasting by not asking sooner for such a cash discount.

TIP: You do not need a medical discount card if you have health insurance—virtually all health insurance policies include a PPO-network offering better discounts than a private medical discount card, even when you are paying cash under a high-deductible policy. Most medical discount cards also include a pharmacy discount card (see Chapter 9).

How to Get Affordable Medical Care When You Are Over 55: Early Retirement, Medicare, and Long-Term Care

In 2006, the new Medicare prescription drug insurance plan became available for a premium of only $37 a month. This program can save seniors thousands of dollars. Your premium is permanently increased 1 percent per month (12 percent a year) for every month you delay enrolling past age 65, so act now or call your parents today.

Most people think that their health insurance problems will be over when they turn 65 and become eligible for Medicare. Unfortunately, while Medicare is the best solution for most people over 65, and although it does cover most doctor visits and hospitalizations, the average senior with Medicare still spends about $4,000 a year (25 percent of their income) on the out-of-pocket medical items that Medicare does not cover. In this chapter you learn how to maximize your Medicare benefits, minimize your out-of-pocket expenses, and save thousands of dollars each year if you are over age 65. I also explain the new Medicare Prescription Drug Insurance program that began in 2006 and how to figure out if it is right for you.

Once you are on Medicare, your biggest financial expense shifts from medical care to long-term care—ranging from getting in-home assistance for the needs of daily living, to full-time nursing care in your later years. Traditionally, when aging parents lived with their children or down the street, no one needed expensive long-term care provided by strangers.

Today, few people can afford to take off work to care for an aging parent, and most seniors don't want their children to physically take care of them as they age. Seniors want to spend their golden years in their own homes or in a retirement community instead of a nursing facility. This chapter will teach you how to get long-term-care insurance for a life with dignity up until the very end—without bankrupting your estate or requiring your children to take care of you.

Health Insurance during Early Retirement—Ages 55 to 65

If you retire before age 65 when you become eligible for Medicare, you may face the most challenging health insurance period of your life.

Why Employers Are Cutting or Canceling Their Retiree Health Insurance Benefits

When employer-sponsored health insurance began, people often worked for the same employer for most of their lives—there was an unwritten contract between a corporation and its workers to provide health benefits, retirement benefits, and lifetime employment. This contract was shattered during the past two decades as globalization forced employers to lower their labor costs to remain in business. A few management teams tried to honor the unwritten contract with their lifetime employees—they failed. Managers were forced to switch to younger workers or overseas labor or else watch their company be taken over by a new management team that did not know or care that the unwritten contract ever existed. As a result, the number of large companies offering retiree medical coverage dropped from 40 percent in 1993 to 21 percent in 2003.[1] Most large companies that still provide retiree medical benefits today are obligated to do so under signed agreements with former (often unionized) employees.

> **If you currently work for one of the few companies that provide retiree health benefits, don't expect your company to still be providing them when you retire. If you are currently receiving retiree benefits, don't count on these benefits continuing unless your former employer is bound by an ironclad contract.**

Even if your former employer is bound by a contract, unless the company is exceptionally strong, your retiree health benefits may be terminated through bankruptcy court. ERISA law protects pensions, but not retiree health benefits, against corporate bankruptcy. No company can stay in business today if it pays out more to former employees than to current ones.

TIP: If you are age 61 to 64 and receiving retiree health benefits, or are still working, watch out for your spouse's health benefits when you turn 65 and switch to Medicare. Most employer-sponsored group health plans do not allow spouses or dependents to participate unless the primary employee is currently enrolled, so your younger spouse could end up without coverage when you turn 65.

It's easy to see why retiree health benefits are so expensive. As illustrated in Chapter 2, individuals age 54 to 65 spend three times as much on healthcare as do individuals age 35 to 44. If the total cost of your employer-sponsored group health policy is about $4,500 per year per employee, the average age 54 to 65 employee or retiree could be costing the company two to three times this average amount, $9,000 to $13,500, in medical expenses.

Some companies allow retirees to receive coverage only if they pay the full premium themselves, which is similar to COBRA but without the 2 percent administration fee. This can be extremely expensive for employers but a very good deal for employees retiring before age 65. ERISA law does not allow age discrimination, so older, retiring employees may end up paying $4,500 versus the $9,000 to $13,500 in medical expenses they, on average, actually consume.

Before I tell you what to do if you are under age 65 and retired, or contemplating retiring before age 65, I need to tell you who is getting outstanding lifetime retiree health benefits at your expense. You may want to join them.

The Government Retiree Healthcare Crisis for Taxpayers: How You Are Paying for the Health Insurance Deal of the Century

In the 1980s I wrote a book, *Other People's Money*, predicting the then-coming $200 billion savings and loan crisis—the crisis was hidden by accounting rules that made it difficult to see the fraud until it was too late. Today an even larger crisis hidden by accounting rules is looming over this country . . . and over your wallet. This crisis is the hundreds of billions in lifetime retiree health benefits given to government employees, and your local and state officials have perpetrated the deception by hiding the actual cost from taxpayers.

Today less than 10 percent of private employers provide retiree health benefits, but 48 out of 50 states and half of our cities still do—and not just to "retirees." In North Carolina, a state employee becomes eligible to receive lifetime retiree health benefits after only five years of service—an 18- to 23-year-old can work for the state, leave for a 32-year career in the private sector, and then retire at age 55 with lifetime retiree health benefits paid for by taxpayers. It's even worse for local school districts and municipalities that may not have the resources available to an entire state. *Fortune* magazine estimates that California's largest school districts alone already owe $17 billion in unfunded retiree health benefits—money that comes directly out of the classroom. The city of Buffalo now spends more on healthcare for retirees than it spends on healthcare for active workers.[2]

One of the most frustrating things about this crisis is that the states, cities, and school districts don't even know how much they have given away, but they, and we, are about to find out. New accounting rules took effect in 2006 that force government entities to disclose their retiree healthcare obligations.

If you work for a state or local government entity that provides free retiree health benefits, you might get to keep them. But I wouldn't count on getting any more such benefits once the taxpayers learn how they have been deceived into paying for something that they don't get themselves.

If you or a spouse work for a school district or are contemplating taking a teaching or government job for a few years, you should look into what type of retiree health benefits they offer, as this could be the health insurance deal of the century . . . for as long as it lasts.

Health Insurance Solutions for Early Retirees—Ages 55 to 64

Getting health insurance coverage after retirement is the biggest issue facing workers today who have saved enough money to retire early. If you are very healthy, or if you already have an individual/family policy, you are in luck. No matter how many medical issues you have had, if you were healthy when you first applied, you are probably still paying the basic premium for a healthy individual of your age. Basic premiums on HSA-qualified health plans range from $158 to $252 a month from top name-brand carriers.

Premiums for HSA-Qualified Policies: Healthy Female, Age 60

State[a]	Premium	Deductible	Carrier
Ohio	$158	$3,500	United Healthcare
Texas	$208	$2,600	Unicare
Florida	$270	$2,500	Humana
California	$214	$2,500	HealthNet
Connecticut	$222	$2,650	Golden Rule
Pennsylvania	$202	$2,600	American Medical
Illinois	$215	$2,250	Blue Cross Blue Shield

[a]Ohio—United Healthcare Single HSA Saver; Columbus, OH 43085; quoted 5.02.05.
Texas—UniCare HSA Compatible Plan 2; Austin, TX 78701; quoted 5.02.05.
Florida—HumanaOne Individual Health Plan; Tallahassee, FL 32301; quoted 5.02.05.
California—Health Net SmartChoice HSA; Sacramento, CA 95814; quoted 5.02.05.
Connecticut—Golden Rule Single HSA 100 Plan; Hartford, CT 06101; quoted 5.02.05.
Pennsylvania—American Medical Security; Harrisburg, PA 17101; quoted 5.02.05.
Illinois—BCBS of IL High Ded. Health Plan $2250; Springfield, IL 62701; quoted 5.02.05.

If you have already retired early and have no health insurance, or if you plan to retire before 65 but not right away, you should immediately apply for individual/family health insurance. The longer you wait the greater the chance you could develop a preexisting condition that might make you medically ineligible. Based on your age alone, you are in one of the highest risk groups, and it is likely at your age that you have had at least one medical issue that could get you uprated or rejected—so carefully follow the instructions in both Chapter 4 and Chapter 7 before you apply.

You should expect to pay a much higher premium based on your age. As shown in Appendix A, in California, an HSA-qualified high-deductible policy for a 35-year-old single male costs only $97 per month, but the same policy jumps to $323 per month at age 61. Similarly, the traditional co-pay policy shown in Appendix A costs $204 per month at age 35, but jumps to $678 per month at age 61. (There are better policies for older ages; see the chart above.) Fortunately, you need to pay these rates only until age 65, when you switch to Medicare.

 TIP: If you are over 50 and seeking individual/family health insurance, it might be better to separate your family when you apply, especially if your spouse is younger. Health insurance for couples and families is sometimes based on the age of the oldest individual, and different carriers have different age-rating bands—one might be 55 to 59 and another 56 to 60—so shop around and try different combinations of family members to find the best deal. If you choose a family policy, put the policy in the name of the younger spouse so that person still has coverage when the older spouse switches to Medicare.

 TIP: Premiums for individuals age 55 to 64 are so high that in some cases it may actually be cheaper to get state-guaranteed health insurance from a state risk pool as if you were unhealthy—check out the rates in your state. As explained in Chapter 7, to become eligible for a state risk pool you typically have to first apply and get rejected or uprated by a private carrier, although many state risk pools may accept you with just a letter from a licensed agent stating you would have been uprated or rejected if you had applied.

If you are approaching age 65 and/or are unhealthy, this is one of the few times you are probably better off living in a community-rated state like New York, New Jersey, Maine, Massachusetts, or Vermont. These states do not allow premiums to be based on age or health, so even though the average policy sold there is very expensive—$340 a month in New Jersey in 2004[3]—it may save you money compared to what a policy could cost you in a state like California or Florida.

Negotiating with Your Employer for Early Retirement Health Insurance Expenses

You are probably not the only one age 55 to 64 who would like to retire early and leave your employer-sponsored group health benefits plan—your employer and your coworkers have a great financial incentive for you to do this. Even if you are not consuming a single dollar in annual medical expenses, based on your age alone, the premium for you is about three times the price of the premium for younger workers—with the excess price paid by your employer and younger employees (ERISA law prohibits employees from being charged different amounts based on their age).

The total premium for an employer-sponsored group health plan is based on an annual census of the employees, with the premium for an older worker typically three times the premium for a younger one—even if they are both healthy.

Thus, you may have some bargaining power with your employer who will save a significant amount of money if you leave the company's group plan.

TIP: Never ask your employer to do something for you alone related to its ERISA-governed employee benefits plan— employers are not allowed to do anything for you without offering the same benefit to everyone else. However, there are ways to ask for what you want without violating ERISA. For example, suppose you are 62, want to retire early, and want your employer to pay the $250 per month premium on your individual policy until age 65. Go to your employer and offer to quit in return for a $9,000 termination bonus. Don't mention that you want the money to pay your healthcare premium or anything connected with the fact that you are getting a special deal for retirement.

 TIP: Ask your benefits administrator whether your company will soon be offering a retiree medical Health Reimbursement Arrangement (HRA) (see Chapter 13 for details)—and if not, ask for one. Beginning at age 40, employers should be giving employees financial incentives to opt out of the employer-sponsored group plan and purchase their own individual/ family health insurance—with the employer reimbursing each employee's premium through an HRA. In addition to guaranteeing retiree health benefits, your employer and coworkers save by shifting the cost of aging employees to a third-party insurance carrier or state government. There is also the added benefit of being able to pay a retiree's unused vacation and sick leave on a deferred basis, tax-free.

Medicare—Federally Subsidized Health Insurance for Seniors

Medicare is the federal health insurance program for people age 65 or older.[4] Because it is heavily subsidized by the government, Medicare is the best health insurance deal for most seniors. Approximately 42 million people are enrolled in Medicare at an annual total cost of about $325 billion ($7,738 per enrollee). Net federal spending (after enrollee premiums) on Medicare is estimated to have been $290 billion in 2005 and is expected to rise 53 percent to $444 billion by 2010.[5]

Medicare is divided into four parts, plus private supplemental insurance called "Medigap," which covers the gaps in Medicare.

Part of Medicare	Pays For	Cost (2005)
Part A Hospital insurance	Inpatient hospital, nursing facility, and hospice care	Included free with Social Security
Part B Doctor visit insurance	Physicians, outpatient, and preventive services	$78.20/month
Part C Medicare advantage	HMO/PPO-type private insurance plans	See text
Part D Prescriptions (beginning 2006)	Prescription drugs (2006 estimate)	$37.37/month
Medigap Supplemental insurance (Plans A–J)	Out-of-pocket expenses for Parts A and B	$100–$300/month

Many people have a rude awakening when they turn 65 and find out that Medicare Part A (hospital insurance) and Medicare Part B (doctor visit insurance) do not cover all of their medical expenses—the average senior on Medicare spends about $4,000 a year out of pocket, including supplemental insurance premiums, to cover the items that Medicare does not cover. People on Medicare get supplemental coverage in three basic ways: 35 percent have retiree health benefits, 22 percent have Medigap (explained later in the chapter), and 14 percent have Medicaid (see Chapter 7).[6]

Most medical items not covered by Medicare, including out-of-pocket deductibles, coinsurance, co-payments, Parts A and B premiums, and long-term-care insurance premiums, are considered "qualified medical expenses." This means that money to pay for these items can be withdrawn tax-free from a Health Savings Account. Only Medigap premiums are not qualified medical expenses.[7]

In preparing for Medicare, starting at age 55, you should have an HSA, and you and your spouse should contribute the maximum $20,000 in total catch-up contributions before age 65 (see Chapter 6).

Medicare Part A, Hospital Insurance: Hospitals, Skilled Nursing Facilities

Medicare Part A (hospital insurance) pays for inpatient hospital, skilled nursing facility, and hospice care. Virtually everyone who is eligible to receive Social Security benefits is automatically enrolled in Part A when they turn 65. There is usually no monthly premium for people eligible for Social Security benefits.

TIP: You do not have to pay a premium for Medicare Part A (hospital insurance) if you or a spouse has worked for at least 10 years in Medicare-covered employment. If not, you will have to pay a premium of $206 to $375 per month. To find out exactly how much, and to enroll in Medicare, contact the Social Security Administration at 1-800-772-1213 or your local Social Security office.

Medicare Part A (hospital insurance) accounts for about 45 percent of Medicare total costs and is currently funded by a tax of 2.9 percent of earnings paid by employers and employees (1.45 percent each). Because of the aging baby boomers in the U.S. population, the funding for Part A is expected to go into the red in 2012, and fund reserves are expected to be exhausted in 2020 (similar to Social Security).

Medicare Part A (hospital insurance) has annual and lifetime deductibles and requires that you make coinsurance payments that can be financially devastating if you need frequent or long-term hospitalization. In 2005, you would have had to pay a $912 deductible for a hospital stay of 1 to 60 days, then lifetime coinsurance of $228 per day for days 61 to 90, $456 per day for days 91 to 150, and all costs beyond 150 days.

Medicare Part A (Hospital Insurance) Out-of-Pocket Costs

Days in Hospital	Hospital Cost ($1,500/day)	Your Deductible/ Coinsurance Payment
30	$ 45,000	$ 912
150	$225,000	$ 35,112
180	$270,000	$ 80,112
360	$540,000	$350,112

Note that the days in hospital are cumulative over your lifetime, not just within a single year. If you spent a total of 360 days in hospitals past age 65, your noncovered hospital costs alone would be $350,112, unless you had supplemental insurance for Medicare Part A like Medigap.

Many people spend two weeks or less in a hospital, but then go to a skilled nursing facility. Medicare Part A pays for skilled nursing facilities for up to 21 days, but then requires you to pay coinsurance of $114 a day for the next 100 days. If you spent 100 days in a nursing home after a hospital stay you would be responsible for $9,006 in coinsurance payments for just the stay in the nursing home.

Medicare Part A (hospital insurance) has deductibles and coinsurance that could cost you tens or even hundreds of thousands of dollars. Everyone on Part A should purchase supplemental insurance, called Medigap, unless they feel very comfortable that their retiree health coverage or HMO (Part C) will cover these gaps.

Medicare Part B, Doctor Visit Insurance: Doctors, Outpatient Services

Part B (doctor visit insurance) pays for physicians, outpatient care, preventive services and some other medical services that Part A (hospital insurance) does not cover, including physical therapy and some home healthcare. Part B also covers many incidental items that could add up to thousands of dollars, such as vision care, chiropractic, and ambulance services.

Almost everyone in Part A (hospital insurance) elects to enroll in Part B (doctor visit insurance) unless they have other private coverage or choose Medicare Advantage (Part C). The monthly premium for Part B was $78.20 per month in 2005 and is increased every year. It is typically deducted from your monthly Social Security check.

Part B (doctor visit insurance) accounts for about 35 percent of Medicare's total cost and is funded 75 percent by the federal government and 25 percent by premiums paid by enrollees. Since the premium covers only 25 percent of the actual costs, Part B is almost always a good deal and you should enroll unless you feel very comfortable with your other coverage.

TIP: Starting in 2007, Medicare recipients with incomes above $80,000 will pay a higher monthly premium for Part B (doctor visit insurance) based on their income. This signifies a long-term trend for Medicare away from an insurance-based pay-in-pay-out system toward a more socialistic need-based system. Medicare is funded primarily with a payroll tax, so workers with higher incomes who have paid more will now get less.

You may enroll in Part B (doctor visit insurance) during a six-month period that begins three months before the month in which you turn 65. If you wait, you can enroll only between January 1 and March 31 (the "General Enrollment Period") of each subsequent year, and your premium will forever be increased 10 percent for each 12-month period that you could have been enrolled.

 TIP: Unless you are still employed, you should enroll in Part B (doctor visit insurance) as soon as you become eligible. If you wait for three years you will pay the monthly premium ($78.20 in 2005) plus 30 percent ($23.46 in 2005)

every month for the rest of your life. By delaying, you would have saved $2,815 ($78.20 × 36 months) in premiums over the first three years if you had no claims, but then you would pay $5,630 in additional premiums ($23.46 × 240 months) over the next 20 years.[8]

TIP: If you are still working (or if your spouse is) and keeping your group healthcare coverage, you may generally delay enrolling in Part B (doctor visit insurance) without paying a premium increase—provided that you enroll in Part B while you are still covered by your employer or within eight months following the termination of your employment or group coverage (whichever is first).

Part B (doctor visit insurance) requires you to pay a $110 (in 2005) annual deductible plus a 20 percent coinsurance or co-payment of the Medicare-approved amount for each service—assuming that your doctor or medical provider signs a waiver, called "assignment."

Assignment means that your medical provider agrees to accept the Medicare-approved amount as "payment in full"—paid 80 percent by Medicare and 20 percent by you (or your supplemental insurance provider). If your doctor does not accept assignment, then you must pay the "excess charges" between the Medicare-approved amount and the amount your medical provider charges for the service.

Everyone on Medicare Part B (doctor visit insurance) should have or purchase some type of supplemental insurance coverage like Medigap.

Part C, Medicare Advantage: The Alternative to Medicare Parts A and B and Supplemental Coverage

Medicare Part A (hospital insurance) and Part B (doctor visit insurance) are automatically available nationwide since you choose your physician or medical provider and they are reimbursed by Medicare a fixed amount for each service. Parts A and B are often called "the original Medicare plan," "traditional Medicare," or "fee-for-service plans." Traditional Medicare has coinsurance, co-payments, and deductibles for which you should purchase Medigap.

Over the past few years, HMO and PPO alternatives to traditional

Medicare have become available in many areas similar to those alternatives in private health insurance systems. These are called Medicare Advantage Plans and include Medicare Managed Care Plans (HMOs), Medicare Preferred Provider Organization Plans (PPO), Medicare Private Fee-for-Service Plans, and Medicare Specialty Plans.

The main reason people choose Medicare Advantage Plans is to save on Medigap (supplemental Medicare coverage), which typically costs $100 to $300 a month.

In 2000, approximately 6.3 million (16 percent) of all Medicare enrollees had chosen Medicare Advantage Plans (then called Medicare + Choice) as their alternative to traditional fee-for-service Medicare. These types of plans declined in popularity to 4.8 million (12 percent) in 2004, but are now expected to gain in popularity as the private companies running them are adding services like prescription drug coverage and lowering their cost. The U.S. government estimates that 16 to 30 percent of Medicare enrollees will choose Medicare Advantage Plans by 2013.[9]

Basically, when you join a Medicare Advantage Plan, you disenroll from traditional Medicare and receive a healthcare card similar to what you would receive from a private insurance carrier's plan or employer-sponsored plan. Your Medicare Advantage Plan provides you with a list of doctors and/or benefits similar to private PPOs or HMOs, and many of the plans include a prescription drug benefit. Medicare Advantage Plans usually cover the items not covered by the gaps in Medicare Part A (hospital insurance) and Part B (doctor visit insurance), so you won't need Medigap coverage.

 TIP: Although you disenroll from traditional Medicare when you choose a Medicare Advantage Plan, out-of-network physicians are still required to provide you emergency services and then get reimbursed from your Medicare Advantage Plan provider.

To join a Medicare Advantage Plan, you must be enrolled in both Medicare Part A and Part B, and you may have to pay a monthly premium to your Medicare Advantage Plan provider depending on the level of services you choose.

 TIP: Choosing the right Medicare Advantage Plan is similar to choosing your own individual/family insurance policy— you must first estimate your requirements and then analyze each plan as explained in Chapter 4. In general, you should not choose a Medicare Advantage Plan unless there is a particularly good local HMO or PPO that you want to join or you cannot afford Medigap.

Medigap—Supplemental Insurance for the Gaps in Medicare Parts A (Hospital Insurance) and B (Doctor Visit Insurance)

Unless you have chosen a Medicare Advantage Plan or have similar retiree medical coverage, you should purchase a Medigap supplemental insurance plan.

A Medigap insurance policy covers the gaps in Medicare Parts A and B. Under Part A, these coverage gaps start with the $912 deductible per hospitalization and rise to $540,000 if you spend 360 cumulative days in the hospital over your lifetime. Under Part B, these coverage gaps could run into thousands of dollars, with you paying 20 percent coinsurance for your doctors and other nonhospital medical services.

> **All Medigap policies cover at least 100 percent of (1) the Medicare Part A hospital deductible and coinsurance for the first 360 days of hospitalization, plus up to 365 more days of hospitalization, and (2) the Medicare Part B 20 percent coinsurance or co-payment if your doctor accepts "assignment."**

You almost always must have Medicare Parts A (hospital insurance) and B (doctor visit insurance) to purchase a Medigap policy. Medigap policies are "guaranteed renewable"— that is, they cannot be canceled nor can their price be increased based on your claims history for as long as you pay the premium.[10] Like Medicare itself, you and your spouse must each purchase your own Medigap policy.

 TIP: Some carriers, like Blue Shield of California, offer discounts if you and your spouse simultaneously enroll in the same Medigap plan type.

There are 10 standardized Medigap plans, A through J, that follow both federal and state laws in the state in which they are sold. Generally, Medigap Plan A offers the fewest benefits for the lowest cost, and Medigap Plan J offers the most benefits for the highest cost. The difference in benefits between the same-letter policies sold by different insurance companies in the same state is the cost. Medigap Plans A, C, and F are the popular plans (see chart later in this section).

TIP: In general, you should select the best policy you can afford (Medigap Plan F), since the price difference between the Medigap plans is not that great, and you are guaranteed issuance of Medigap without underwriting only once in your life.

Medigap Plans H, I, and J used to cover prescription drugs and were not allowed to be sold after January 1, 2006, when Medicare Part D (prescription drug coverage) began.

TIP: You can save money by purchasing a Medigap SELECT policy which, for each of the 10 standardized plans, is the same, except that you must use in-network hospitals and doctors to get full coverage (except in emergencies).

No Medigap policy covers long-term care, vision or dental care, hearing aids, private nurses, or unlimited outpatient prescriptions.

Similar to purchasing an individual/family health insurance policy, when you apply for Medigap, insurance companies will medically underwrite you and can deny you coverage, uprate your premium, and exclude or impose a waiting period for preexisting conditions. However, there is one major exception.

The one exception is that all insurance companies in all states must accept your Medigap application without uprating or exclusions for preexisting conditions if you apply during "open enrollment"—the first six months in which you are both age 65 or older *and* enrolled in Part B.

You should almost always apply for Medigap within six months of enrolling in Part B after your sixty-fifth birthday. The only case in which it might not make sense for you is if you have good private coverage from a former employer or are enrolled in Medicare Advantage.

Insurance companies may offer discounts off the basic premiums to females, nonsmokers, and married persons. You may also switch between

Medigap policies and, if you have had your policy for six months, your new policy must cover preexisting conditions.

You should shop carefully for Medigap policies, because the prices vary greatly between insurance companies and between states for virtually the same policies. Three basic criteria are used to set the price on Medigap policies:

1. *Community-rated pricing.* The price is the same for all people, regardless of their age, and typically can be raised only with inflation. Some states require community-rated policies (Massachusetts, Maine, New Jersey, New York, and Vermont). These policies are typically the most expensive unless you are very old and/or in ill health.

2. *Issue-age pricing.* The price is based on the age at which you are first issued the policy and typically can be raised only with inflation. These policies offer the most protection and are better values if you live a long time after you buy them.

3. *Current-age pricing.* The price increases as you get older. These policies are the least expensive to purchase initially but become more expensive as you age. These are also called *attained-age* policies.

Following are the premiums in 2005 for three popular types of Medigap insurance from Blue Shield of California in Los Angeles, California.

Medigap Monthly Rates—Individual, California[a]

Age	Plan A Major Benefit: Basic Coverage	Plan C Major Benefit: Skilled Nursing Facility Coverage	Plan F Major Benefit: Coverage for Excess Charges
65–66	$ 93	$110	$118
67–69	$ 94	$112	$123
70–74	$120	$156	$162
75–79	$160	$185	$208
80+	$166	$199	$226

[a]Blue Shield of California home page, 2005, Blue Shield of California—Medicare Supplement Plan Monthly Rates—Individual, 6 May 2005, www.mylifepath.com/bsc/findaplan/medicare/look/supp/rates.jhtml.

The major difference between Plans A and C is that C covers the $114 per day co-payment required under Part A for days 22 to 100 in a nursing facility and the $100 deductible for Part B. The major difference between plans C and F is that F covers the "excess charges" under Part B—the difference between the Medicare-approved amount and the amount your medical provider charges for the service.

To begin shopping for a Medigap plan, contact your state's insurance department (see Appendix A). You will probably also want to work with a licensed agent familiar with the laws of your state. For example, while Plan F pays "excess charges" above the Medicare-approved amount for a service, this benefit is worthless in certain states like Ohio, where "excess charges" to Medicare patients are prohibited. See Chapter 4 for information on selecting a good agent.

TIP: Unlike with buying other types of insurance, you may want to choose a lower-priced policy from a less-than-top-rated carrier. If your Medigap carrier goes bankrupt, you have the right within 63 days to purchase Plans A, B, C, or F from any carrier in your state, without medical underwriting, at their lowest premium price available.

Medicare Part D, Prescription Drug Insurance: A Great Deal for Everyone on Medicare

New Medicare prescription drug plans (Part D) became available in 2006. These plans are very different from the Medicare-approved drug discount cards currently available, which are described in Chapter 9. Medicare-approved drug discount cards were phased out of Medicare in 2006.

Medicare Part D (prescription drug insurance) saves $714 per year for a typical senior taking $150 per month in prescriptions—and far more for seniors spending $5,000 per month or more in prescriptions. However, it is such a good deal for the low $37 per month cost that everyone in Medicare should enroll, especially because the cost is permanently increased for each month you delay. You should enroll in Part D for the insurance protection alone (unless you have other prescription drug coverage) even if you currently are not taking prescriptions.

TIP: Visit the web site for this book, www.TNHIS.com (*TheNewHealthInsuranceSolution.com*), for the latest information on the new Part D prescription drug benefit plans.

Medicare Part D prescription drug plans are a huge benefit to retirees on Medicare, but they are expected to have cost the federal government

$37 billion in 2006 and to rise to $109 billion in 2015. The government estimates that 29 million of an estimated 43 million Medicare enrollees enrolled in Part D in 2006.[11] Similar to Part B (doctor visit insurance), the premium for Part D will be set at 25 percent of the cost of the benefits, so Part D should be a good deal for all Medicare enrollees. You should plan on enrolling in Part D unless you feel very comfortable with your other coverage.

> **TIP:** If you receive a prescription drug benefit from a former employer, you should wait before dropping it for Part D (prescription drug insurance). Medicare will be providing billions of dollars to retiree benefits plans that offer equal or better coverage to Part D to keep them from dropping their prescription drug coverage.

The premium for Part D plans is about $37 per month in 2006. You must have Medicare Parts A and B to enroll. There will also be Medicare prescription drug plans that work with Medicare Advantage Plans (HMOs, PPOs).

Individuals should enroll when they initially become eligible. Similar to waiting to enroll in Part B, if you wait past initial eligibility, you will pay a lifetime premium penalty equal to 1 percent of the base premium for each month you delay enrollment. The enrollment period to join or change plans is between November 15 and December 31 each year.

> **TIP:** Unless you are still receiving good prescription drug coverage, you should enroll in Part D (prescription drug insurance) as soon as you become eligible. If you wait 48 months, until 2010, you will pay the estimated base premium of $49 per month in 2010 plus 48 percent extra ($23.52) every month for the rest of your life. By delaying, you would have saved roughly $2,064 ($43 per month average × 48 months) in premiums over the first four years if you had no claims, but then would pay $5,645 in additional premiums ($23.52 × 240 months) over the next 20 years.

There is a standard benefits plan design recommended by Medicare.

- The standard Part D plan design requires $250 annual deductible.
- Then Part D pays 75 percent of the next $2,000 (until $2,250 total).
- Then Part D pays 0 percent of the next $2,850 (the "hole in the doughnut").
- Thereafter, Part D pays 95 percent (above $5,100).

All numbers are increased annually by Medicare, pegged to inflation. These plans have become known as *doughnuts* because of the missing $2,850 of coverage in the middle. Plan providers are allowed and expected to offer alternative plans that are actuarially equivalent and do not increase the $250 per year standard deductible and $5,100 per year catastrophic threshold.

Here's how the Medicare Part D standard plan looks for individuals with different prescription costs. A typical senior currently consumes $150 per month ($1,800 per year) in prescription drugs (some take no prescriptions and a few consume as much as $5,000 a month or more).

How Much Could Medicare Part D, Prescription Drug Insurance, Save You?

Annual Prescription Costs	$1,000	$1,800	$5,100	$10,000	$60,000
(a) Annual deductible	$ 250	$ 250	$ 250	$ 250	$ 250
(b) 25% of next $2,000	$ 188	$ 388	$ 500	$ 500	$ 500
(c) 100% of next $2,850	—	—	$2,850	$ 2,850	$ 2,850
(d) 5% of anything over $5,100	—	—	—	$ 245	$ 2,745
Patient drug cost (a + b + c + d)	$ 438	$ 638	$3,600	$ 3,845	$ 6,345
Annual premium cost	$ 448	$ 448	$ 448	$ 448	$ 448
Total patient cost (drug cost + annual premium)	$ 886	$1,086	$4,048	$ 4,293	$ 6,793
Net benefit to patient (annual prescription costs versus total patient cost)	$ 114	$ 714	$1,052	$ 5,707	$53,207

Part D prescription drug plan providers are expected to produce overall savings by negotiating price discounts with drug companies and by offering multiple drugs in each therapeutic category (see Chapter 9).

In addition to just running the numbers on each plan offered under Part D, you will need to evaluate each plan offered similarly to the way you evaluate the cost of prescription drug coverage on an individual/family policy (see Chapters 4 and 9). You should pay careful attention to following:

■ Formulary (the list of prescription drugs covered by the plan)

■ Available therapeutic substitutions (different, cheaper drugs than prescribed that are still effective in treating your illness, as discussed in Chapter 9)

■ Participating pharmacies—retail and mail order

■ Additional levels of coverage—providers are expected to offer more coverage than the standard in return for higher premiums

Long-Term-Care, Assisted Living, and Nursing Home Insurance

After you make it through retirement and into Medicare, your greatest financial health-related risk is long-term care. *Long-term care* includes a variety of services to meet health and personal needs in your old age, or at any age, should you suffer an illness and need time to recuperate.

Most long-term care is simply assistance with the activities of daily living: dressing, bathing, using the bathroom, and the like. Long-term care can be provided in any of the following places:

Your home. This may include skilled nurses, health aides, personal care aides, and home repair people (to install grab bars, nonskid tub aids, ramps, handrails, etc.).

Community centers. These can be senior centers and adult centers that provide day care, transportation, meals on wheels, and so forth.

Retirement communities. Residents often enter as fully functioning adults and then move on to increasing levels of assistance, including an on-site nursing home.

Assisted living communities. Here residents typically live in their own apartments but receive help with daily living activities like eating, bathing, using the bathroom, and transportation. Typical costs range from $2,000 to $5,000 per month per person.

Nursing homes. These are for people who cannot be cared for at home or in a community environment. Medicare does not cover this type of care except for a limited number of days following an illness.

The list of long-term-care options and requirements grows every day as our baby boom generation ages and life expectancy increases.

Unfortunately, long-term-care insurance is expensive, and you may never receive its benefits. You should evaluate your long-term-care insurance requirements as part of your overall retirement and estate planning and purchase only the amount of coverage you can afford today and may need tomorrow to supplement your other financial assets in case you need long-term care.

Approximately 10 million Americans need and receive long-term care today—about 65 percent of them are elderly, and about 35 percent are people with lifetime needs (e.g., those who have birth defects or who have suffered traumatic injuries).

Approximately $200 billion a year is spent on long-term care, with about 40 percent paid by Medicaid. The remaining 60 percent is provided mostly by individuals themselves ($50 billion), by Medicare ($36 billion) mostly for short periods of time, and by private long-term-care insurance ($20 billion).

Medicaid-Funded Long-Term Care—Not Desirable

Medicaid is a welfare program providing medical and long-term care to individuals with very low incomes (see Chapter 7).

Generally, nursing home residents who qualify for Medicaid must first apply all of their income and assets toward the cost of their care. When a spouse begins to require long-term care, the other spouse and their children often want to make the spouse requiring care "poor enough" to qualify for Medicaid through transfers of family assets. However, individuals who apply for Medicaid today are subject to a "look-back" period of three to five years for transfers of assets, and there are several proposals in Congress to even further tighten these requirements.

In addition, states typically do not allow Medicaid funds to be supplemented by third parties who desire to place their loved one in a better or more expensive facility.

Medicaid is not an acceptable or viable option for the long-term-care requirements of most people reading this book. Most people reading this book should either get long-term-care insurance or plan on spending most of their assets on long-term care if and when they need it.

Without a financial plan for long-term care, you could end up on Medicaid and in a nursing home not of your choosing when you run out of money.

How Much Long-Term Care Do You Need?

Unfortunately, there is no way to predict how much long-term care you will need. It depends entirely on how long you live, your health as you age, and especially your health in the last few years and months of your life. If you expect to live a long time, you should expect to have virtually an endless need for long-term care.

Here is what long-term care can cost:

- The average nursing home today costs $82,500 a year and is projected to exceed $200,000 a year by 2020.[12]

- Having someone come into your home just to help with bathing, dressing, meals, and household chores costs $20,800 a year at only $400 per week.

- If you ever require round-the-clock care, a home health aide could cost $18 an hour or more for 168 hours per week—that's $157,248 in labor alone. Double that to more than $300,000 a year for care by a nurse.[13]

How You Can Finance Your Long-Term Care

There are four basic ways to finance your long-term care:

1. *Family support and caregiving.* This is the way long-term care has been provided for generations. While all of us like the idea of taking care of our parents as they age or being taken care of by our children, this is simply not a viable option for most Americans today who have jobs and/or children of their own.

2. *Personal savings.* This is not a viable option for most people because they do not have millions of dollars available, nor do they know how much long-term care they will need. It is also selfish if your estate will be needed to support your spouse or children after you are gone.

3. *Home equity options.* This is an increasingly popular method, particularly with the advent of reverse mortgages, but it has the same limitations as personal savings. In addition, most people would prefer to live out their later years in a place other than a full-size home (e.g., in a retirement community).

4. *Private long-term-care insurance.* This is my favorite choice for financing long-term care. Insurance is the ideal method to finance unknown risks that can be predicted in the aggregate using actuarial information.

The Long-Term-Care Insurance Market

The long-term-care insurance marketplace is one of the worst marketplaces for insurance in the United States. Fortunately, it has improved every year since it started in the mid-1980s, and particularly since HIPAA established long-term-care insurance qualifications in 1996.

A recent study by *Consumer Reports* concluded that for most people, long-term-care insurance is risky and too expensive—mostly for the following reasons.[14]

- If you stop paying the premium, you stand to lose the coverage and everything you have paid so far.

- Many policies are difficult to understand, and some are packed with catches that can keep you from collecting.

- Many carriers have weak balance sheets and may not be around when you need your benefits, and few states have the same financial checks and balances in place that they do to protect purchasers of life or health policies.

However, the same study by *Consumer Reports* correctly concluded that while many long-term-care insurance policies "may be a lousy deal . . . right now (they are) just about the only deal."

Insurance agents will tell you to purchase long-term-care insurance when you are in your 30s or 40s because you may not pass medical underwriting at a later age. In general, unless you are concerned about your health, you should wait until your 50s or 60s. You can usually get a much better deal by purchasing a policy earlier, but you take a greater risk that the carrier you choose may not be in business by the time you need long-term care.

The inefficiencies in the evolving long-term-care insurance market can work for you as well as against you. Due to occasional underwriting mistakes on the part of insurance companies, people who would not qualify for an affordable life or health insurance policy can sometimes get long-term-care insurance.

If you are among the 59 million Americans with diabetes or prediabetes, or if you are chronically overweight, I recommend that you purchase long-term-care insurance at any age you can get it, as long as you can find a top-rated carrier to accept you.

If you have a medical problem, you may not be accepted by a financially strong carrier like GE Financial, John Hancock, or UnumProvident— these companies have A+ ratings precisely because they accept only healthy applicants who may not soon require long-term care.

Choose "HIPAA-Qualified" Long-Term-Care Insurance

With one important exception, the important things to know about choosing a long-term-care insurance policy are similar to those in choosing a long-term-disability policy (see "Long-Term Disability" in Chapter 5).

The important exception is the tax treatment of a long-term-care policy. Under HIPAA law, a "qualified" long-term-care insurance policy is treated as a health insurance policy for purposes of taxation: Employers may deduct premiums from taxable income and exclude benefits from taxable income.

HIPAA did far more for long-term-care insurance than just establish the tax-deductible criteria—HIPAA created a standard of qualifications for long-term-care insurance policies that have set the industry on a steady course. The following list of HIPAA qualifications for a policy to be classified as "qualified," in addition to the criteria in Chapter 5, should be on your shopping list in evaluating a policy.[15]

- The policy must be guaranteed renewable—which means it can be canceled only for the nonpayment of premiums, and the premium can be increased only on a group or class (not an individual) basis.

- To receive a benefit, the policyholder must be certified as "chronically ill" within the prior 12 months and must have a written plan of care provided by a licensed healthcare practitioner.

- To receive a benefit, the need for long-term-care assistance must be expected to last for at least 90 days.

- The chronically ill certification must be based on one or both of the following criteria:

  1. The inability to perform, without substantial assistance, at least two of six activities of daily living (ADLs). The ADLs are bathing, dressing, eating, toileting, transferring, and continence

  2. The need for substantial supervision to protect the individual from threats to health and safety due to a severe cognitive impairment

- Nonforfeiture benefits and benefit increase options (inflation protection) must be offered to the applicant at the time of sale, but they are not required as part of the policy.

- Benefits under a qualified long-term-care insurance policy cannot duplicate Medicare benefits.

I strongly recommend that you purchase long-term-care insurance, but don't let an insurance agent talk you into purchasing more than you need—you never need more insurance than you can comfortably afford.

You may use your HSA for the payment of long-term-care insurance premiums up to the following maximum annual amounts: age 40 or under, $260; age 41 to 50, $490; age 51 to 60, $980; age 61 to 70, $2,600; and age 71 or over, $3,250.

CHAPTER 9

How to Save 10 to 75 Percent on Your Prescription Drugs

Approximately 131 million people in the United States, about 66 percent of all adults, use prescription drugs. If you are like most people and have health insurance coverage with an annual deductible of more than a few hundred dollars, you have a big incentive to be smart about the way you buy prescription drugs. This is especially true if you have HSA-qualified high-deductible health insurance. All the money you save on prescription drugs stays in your pocket or keeps growing in your Health Savings Account (HSA). If you begin at age 35, each $50 a month you save in healthcare expenses means an additional $20,000 a year in your HSA when you retire.

Here are the top five ways to save money on prescription drugs:

1. Get a drug discount card.
2. Choose the right drug plan from your health insurer.
3. Shop overseas pharmacies.
4. Substitute generic drugs.
5. Use a different drug that has similar effects.

Not so long ago, you didn't need to worry about the cost of your prescription drugs; your prescription drug costs were all paid by your employer, or you made a small co-pay of $5 or $10 per prescription. Doctors didn't worry about drug costs either, since their patients weren't paying much, if anything, for the drugs they prescribed. In fact, doctors often closely followed the advice of pharmaceutical sales representatives (who, by the way, typically rewarded them with trips to Hawaii and other perks).

Today, people are more aware of how expensive drugs are since they have to pay for them. They are so expensive that roughly 25 percent of the prescriptions written in the United States are not filled, primarily because of price. For many seniors, prescription drugs are their largest monthly expense—costs of $300 a month or more per senior are not unusual. Medicare pays for doctor visits but doesn't currently pay for prescriptions, and many seniors have to make the terrible choice between buying their lifesaving medicines or their food.* Fortunately, as explained in Chapter 8, this should change for many seniors during the next few years when more seniors purchase Medicare Prescription Drug Insurance.

Get a Drug Discount Card and Save 10 to 25 Percent

If you have either employer-sponsored health insurance or a good individual/family plan, you probably already have a decent drug discount card. However, if you don't get a good card through your health insurance you should get a drug discount card.

For $0 to $50 a year you can obtain a drug discount card that will save you 10 to 25 percent on your prescriptions.

There are about 70 drug discount cards on the market now, and while they typically required an annual fee when they were first introduced, today most are free.

TIP: Watch the fine print when signing up for any drug discount card, particularly one that is free. Some charge high rates for shipping and handling, some charge extra fees to add family members, and some appear to be "free," but when you try to use them you're charged an "activation fee" of $15 or more.

---

*Seniors on Medicare should sign up for Medicare Part D prescription drug insurance for about $37 per month. This new insurance will save a senior who pays $150 a month for prescriptions about $60 a month; a senior paying $833 per month for prescriptions will save about $500 a month (see Chapter 8 for more details).

You are probably asking yourself, how can anything be good if it's free? Sponsors of drug discount cards are typically paid a $1 to $3 fee by the pharmacy each time you use the card, and they also receive rebates and other kickbacks from the pharmaceutical companies when you buy specific prescriptions. The pharmacies hate drug discount cards but are forced to accept them because they know you will take your pharmacy business, and your regular grocery shopping, elsewhere if the pharmacy in their store doesn't accept your drug discount card.

TIP: You should obtain every card you can that is free, and use the one that gives you the best discount for each individual prescription—different cards have different discounts for each drug, so no one card is universally the best. Always ask your pharmacist whether any rebates are associated with your prescription and whether you can get these rebates yourself instead of having the pharmacy or the drug discount card company keep them.

Most people think that when they use the drug discount card that comes with their health insurance, their insurance carrier or employer pays part of the cost of their prescription. Actually, the opposite is true. In most cases, the provider of the drug discount card is actually paid a $1 to $3 "prescription fee" from the pharmacy that accepted the card.

Drug discount cards are typically accepted at almost every retail pharmacy chain and at some mail-order pharmacies. The size of the discount, and the drug price itself, varies widely between different retail pharmacies and sometimes even between stores in the same retail chain. The following table shows that you could save $72 to $372 a year with a typical drug discount card on any one of six popular medications.

Sample Savings with an AARP Drug Discount Card versus CVS Mail Order

Drug Name[a]	CVS[b] Monthly	AARP Card[c] Monthly	Monthly Savings	Annual Savings
Lipitor[d]	$ 71	$ 64	$ 7	$ 84
Zocor[e]	$ 82	$ 65	$17	$204
Nexium[f]	$147	$116	$31	$372
Prevacid[g]	$142	$120	$22	$264
Zoloft[h]	$ 91	$ 71	$20	$240
Viagra[i]	$ 41	$ 35	$ 6	$ 72

[a]Dosage source: U.S. National Library of Medicine, Medline.
[b]CVS/pharmacy prices effective April 18, 2005. Does not include $1.95 shipping cost per order.
[c]AARP Prescription Drug Card managed by United Healthcare Insurance Company, $19.95 annual enrollment fee + $12.50 annual AARP membership. Free standard shipping.
[d]Lipitor: 10 mg once daily prorated on 90-day supply.
[e]Zocor: 10 mg once daily prorated on 90-day supply for Canada.
[f]Nexium: 40 mg once daily prorated on 90-day supply for Canada.
[g]Prevacid: 15 mg once a day prorated on 90-day supply.
[h]Zoloft: 50 mg once a day for 90-day supply.
[i]Viagra: 50 mg taken four times a month based on 10-day supply at CVS, 60-day supply at AARP, and 4-day supply in Canada.

In this example, the AARP drug discount card saves you money on all six drugs. In addition, if you spend more than $50 using the AARP card, shipping is free. The CVS mail-order price does not include a $1.95 shipping fee per order. Both the AARP and CVS cards offer local pharmacy service, and the AARP card is honored at CVS pharmacies. For both cards, the in-store prices are higher than those listed here for mail order.

 TIP: The retail prices quoted by many pharmacists, even when using a drug discount card, are "soft"—meaning the pharmacist often has discretion to lower the price even more if you ask (sometimes by entering the code number from a different drug discount card than the one you presented). You should always ask, "Is this the lowest price available, and is there anything I can do to get a lower price?"

How to Choose a Drug Discount Card

In the preceding example, the AARP drug discount card was Medicare-approved and cost $19.95 a year (plus $12.50 a year for membership in

AARP). Many organizations, like the Automobile Association of America (AAA), offer high-quality free drug discount cards to their paying members—if you are a member of AAA, you can download your card for free from AAA's web site (www.aaa.com). In some cases, free cards offer about the same or sometimes greater discounts than name-brand drug discount cards from organizations such as the AARP.

The following table shows a comparison between the AARP card, which costs $32.45 a year (including AARP membership), and a totally free card from a popular online provider, www.DestinationRx.com.

AARP Drug Card Discount versus Free Card Discount (DestinationRx)[a]

Drug Name	CVS Monthly	AARP Card[c] Monthly	Free Card Savings	Free Card Advantage
Lipitor	$ 71	$ 64	$ 62	+$ 2
Zocor	$ 82	$ 65	$ 66	–$ 1
Nexium	$147	$116	$127	–$11
Prevacid	$142	$120	$118	+$ 2
Zoloft	$ 91	$ 71	$ 70	+$ 1
Viagra	$ 41	$ 35	$ 37	–$ 2

[a]Note: All footnotes in preceding table are applicable.

In this table, note that in three cases, Lipitor, Prevacid, and Zoloft, the free card is cheaper. When you factor in the $32.45 in AARP annual fees, AARP loses its advantage altogether.

TIP: In considering which drug discount card to purchase, the annual fee should be secondary compared to how much each card potentially saves you on the exact prescriptions you use. Also, the card that saves you the most today may not be the best card for you tomorrow, so before you buy, ask if you can return the card for a rebate on unused months if you find it no longer fits your needs.

You can choose the best card for you by making a list of the prescriptions your family needs regularly and the prices you now pay. Then use the Internet or your telephone to research the discounts available for each of your drugs with each card.

Your Insurance Company's Drug Plan Could Save You Thousands

Most health insurance plans come with either a prescription drug benefit or an option to add one. In general, unless you have HSA-qualified health insurance, you probably want this option. As explained in Chapter 6, to open a Health Savings Account you must have qualifying health insurance, which requires you to spend out of pocket the first $1,000 to $2,000 per year of your health costs, and virtually any prescription co-pay or insurance program (other than a drug discount plan) would disqualify your health insurance from allowing you to qualify for a Health Savings Account.*

Chapter 4 explains how to estimate your future prescription drug costs and analyze and choose among different prescription drug plans offered by your health insurance company.

Assuming you are healthy, a typical prescription drug plan option for an individual/family health insurance policy might cost an additional $40 per month ($480 per year) and give you the following benefits:

- $5 for generic drugs on a list of approved, discounted drugs called a *formulary*
- $10 for name-brand drugs on the formulary
- 75 percent off drugs not on the formulary

Here's what this benefit would provide for the six popular drugs in our preceding examples, which are all on the formulary. (For purposes of illustration, the drugs are listed as both on and off the formulary.)

From the following table you can see that paying $40 per month for

---

*HSA transition rules allowed early HSA-qualified plans to have prescription drug coverage until 2006 (see Chapter 6).

prescription drug coverage is almost always a great deal if you take a popular prescription drug.

Monthly Prices Paid under Typical Drug Plan for Name-Brand Drugs[a]

Prescription Drug Name	Retail Price (30-day supply)	Co-pay on Formulary	Co-pay Not on Formulary	Savings on Formulary
Lipitor	$ 71	$10	$18	$ 61
Zocor	$ 82	$10	$21	$ 72
Nexium	$147	$10	$37	$137
Prevacid	$142	$10	$36	$132
Zoloft	$ 91	$10	$23	$ 81
Viagra	$ 41	$10	$10	$ 31

[a]Note: All footnotes in table on page 154 are applicable.

Here's an even better example. If you have a child with diabetes, your monthly bill for insulin alone could cost $350 per month. Paying $40 per month would save you $310 per month ($3,720 a year) on insulin alone!

So, what's the catch? Why would you not almost always want prescription drug coverage added to your health insurance for about $40 per month? The catch is that if you currently need prescription drug coverage at the time you apply for individual/family health insurance, you are not going to get it. Your application will be either rejected, uprated, or accepted with an exclusion for any drugs or care related to the disease for which you are currently taking prescription drugs (see Chapter 4).

When applying for individual/family health insurance, if your insurance carrier offers a real prescription drug benefit option, take it. After a few months or at the end of the year, you should reevaluate whether you want to keep it. In general, if you call your carrier to lower your benefits in return for a reduced premium, it will accept your request over the telephone. But if you call your carrier asking to add a benefit, like prescription drug coverage, it will underwrite your request and possibly raise your premium. It may even use your request as an excuse to try to re-underwrite your entire policy.

This happened to me at the end of 2004 when my out-of-pocket costs were more than $300 per year for each of my four children ($1,200 per year total) for required immunizations and pediatric wellness visits. These costs were eligible to be covered by my insurance carrier for an additional $40 per month ($480 per year) premium, so I applied to my insurance carrier to add this $40 per month benefit to my policy. The company used my request as an opportunity to re-underwrite (medically reevaluate) the entire family in an attempt to uprate (raise) my premium by $120 per month ($1,440 per year) in addition to the $40 per month increase I had requested.

When applying for individual/family health insurance, if you have any doubts about getting prescription drug coverage, take it—you can always cancel it later and get a prorated refund of any unused additional premium paid.

This advice does not apply if you have employer-provided health insurance—employers are not allowed to discriminate between employees based on their health status. Employers must treat all employees requesting prescription drug coverage equally, regardless of how many prescriptions they are already taking.

 TIP: If you or a family member is taking expensive medications, you should probably accept prescription drug coverage offered by your employer even if doing so disqualifies you from being able to open a Health Savings Account. If you already have a Health Savings Account, being disqualified does not mean you lose your HSA—it means only that you cannot make further contributions to your HSA until your health insurance again qualifies you to do so (see Chapter 6).

If you don't have an HSA and you work for a company that has a Section 125 "cafeteria" plan or a Flexible Spending Account (FSA), you should almost always elect to have withheld from your pretax salary the premium for prescription drug coverage, along with an allowance covering what you expect to spend out of pocket for prescriptions. Paying for your prescription drugs with pretax dollars can save you 25 to 50 percent in taxes and save your employer an additional 7.65 percent in FICA and FUTA contributions. Remember that with an FSA you have to estimate your prescription drug costs a full year in advance, since any money you don't spend during the next plan year is forfeited. See Chapter 5 for more details.

Shop Overseas Pharmacies

Another way to save big on prescription drugs is to buy them from other countries—some countries have pharmaceutical-quality standards equal to or better than the standards in the United States.

Sample Prices for Six of the Most Popular Name-Brand Drugs Overseas

Drug Name[a]	CVS Mail Order (U.S.)	Monthly Canada	Monthly Savings	Annual Savings
Lipitor	$ 71	$42	$29	$348
Zocor	$ 82	$46	$36	$432
Nexium	$147	$79	$68	$816
Prevacid	$142	$60	$82	$984
Zoloft	$ 91	$34	$57	$684
Viagra	$ 41	$45	$(4)	$(48)

[a]Note: Prices have been compiled via Pharmacychecker.com on 5/7/2005. Prices include shipping to U.S. destinations. Dosages are the same as in the preceding tables.

PharmacyChecker.com is one of the best web sites for checking out prices from quality pharmacies overseas, as well as the quality of an individual pharmacy itself. Tod Cooperman, M.D., who founded PharmacyChecker.com, has the following tips for shopping overseas for prescription drugs:

Shop from Canada. As long as the pharmacy is licensed in Canada, there should be no concerns about the quality of the drugs. They are as good as what you would purchase from a U.S. pharmacy, and in fact many are manufactured here.

Look beyond Canada. High-quality prescription drugs are also available from Australia, the EU countries, Israel, and New Zealand. These countries have drug regulations equal to or better than those in the United States.

Use Pharmacychecker.com to monitor the quality of foreign pharmacies. The site is free to explore and paid memberships are available for more in-depth information. The web site does not accept funding from pharmaceutical companies, but pharmacies do pay to be rated voluntarily. Pharmacychecker.com does not receive any money on sales.

Be secure. Read the fine print on any web site before you enter your confidential information—the general rules for privacy in the United States do not apply to overseas pharmacies.

Avoid buying drugs advertised in spam e-mails and pop-up ads. Cooperman says these companies are impossible to trace.

Don't expect to save on generic drugs from other countries. Generic drugs are actually cheaper in the United States than in Canada, since

Canada sets its prices on generics from a two-competitor system, whereas the United States has a free-market system with as many as 12 companies selling generics.

Watch for counterfeit drugs. If you're dealing with a reputable pharmacy, counterfeits should not be a problem. However, examine your pills when they first arrive to see whether they look different from those you normally get. If they crumble or if the consistency seems different, take it as a warning.

 TIP: There are fake prescription drugs on the market in the United States as well as overseas. If at any time you are not getting the expected results from your pharmaceuticals, you should question whether you have purchased fake drugs.

Remember to calculate shipping costs. To save on shipping, buy larger quantities, such as a 90- versus a 30-day supply, if you expect to be on the drug for at least that long.

Ask for Generic Drugs

A generic drug is a chemical copy of a brand-name drug. It has the same dosage, safety, and strength. It is intended for the same use as a brand-name drug, is taken the same way, is of the same quality, and has the same efficacy. Generic drugs are available for about 90 percent of all prescriptions, and you should always ask your doctor to prescribe a generic version if one is available.

In some cases, switching from a name-brand drug to a generic can actually be medically better for you—because many patients are taking outdated name-brand drugs prescribed years ago when they first developed a medical condition. When you ask your doctor for a generic prescription, you may actually receive a prescription for a better, newer version of the drug you have been taking, at a much lower cost.

Generic drugs are sometimes safer or better than the brand-name products they replace because they have been prescribed more recently and thus contain improved formulas.

Sample Savings Using a Generic Drug Instead of Name Brand

Brand Drug Name[a]	Retail Monthly Cost	Generic Drug Name	Generic Monthly Cost	Monthly Savings	Annual Savings
Lipitor	$ 71	Atorvastatin	$22	$ 49	$ 588
Zocor	$ 82	Simvastatin	$39	$ 43	$ 516
Nexium	$147	Esomeprazole	$31	$116	$1,392
Prevacid	$142	Lansoprazole	$42	$100	$1,200
Zoloft	$ 91	Sertraline	$34	$ 57	$ 684
Viagra		Not available			

[a]Note: Generic prices from **XL Pharmacy.com** in effect on April 18, 2005. Add $9.50 for medical fees and shipping. Dosages are the same as in the preceding tables.

Generics are also made for over-the-counter medicines. For example, in most drugstores, Tylenol, a product to relieve pain and reduce fever, is sold in a generic form as acetaminophen. It costs much less, but is essentially the same. According to the Congressional Budget Office, generic drugs save consumers an estimated $8 to $10 billion a year at retail pharmacies.

If your doctor starts to scribble "DAW" (Dispense as Written) on your prescription, ask why. Regardless of the reason, request a generic equivalent.

Use a Different Drug That Has Similar Effects

If no generic version of your prescribed drug is available, you can still save money by asking your doctor to prescribe a cheaper drug that has the same or similar effect. This is known as *therapeutic substitution,* or *category shifting.*

Toby Rogers, president of Rxaminer.com, runs one of the best web sites to help people learn about therapeutic substitution. His father, a cardiologist, practically invented the technique when he became alarmed that many of his older patients weren't taking their prescriptions—primarily because they were so expensive.

See www.rxaminer.com to determine what drug could effectively be substituted for the expensive drug you are currently taking, and then discuss the options with your doctor.

Also, before your doctor writes a prescription for you, ask the following questions:

If no generic version is available, are there other drugs in the same class? For almost every condition that is treatable, there is more than one drug that can successfully be used to attack the problem. The second and third competing drugs put on the market are sometimes called "me-too" drugs, and they often sell at a lower price.

Are there older, cheaper drugs available that are just as effective? Doctors often prescribe new drugs that are more expensive than older ones. Rxaminer.com lists comparable drugs side by side and provides cost comparisons. You can also save by asking for an older version of your expensive prescription drug. Once a prescription drug goes off patent, drug companies usually change the formula slightly and heavily promote the new formula. Sometimes the older version is still on the market and is as effective, but available for a much lower price.

Other Ways to Save

There are plenty of other ways you can reduce your pharmacy bill. The Cost Containment Research Institute (www.institutedc.org) has compiled a list of 17, some of which we have just discussed. Here are a few more ideas for you to consider:

Shop around by phone. Make a list of your medications, including strength and number taken daily, and call at least six pharmacies to compare prices, keeping in mind whether the pharmacies are on your plan.

Use a pill splitter (but do your research first). Many drugs are cheaper if you buy them in larger doses, then cut them in half. Ask your pharmacist or doctor first, though, since many drugs cannot be split without reducing their effectiveness. Most pharmacists say you should split only pills that are scored (i.e., those with a predesigned break-off line). However, Toby Rogers from Rxaminer says, "We split a lot of pills that aren't scored; you should be able to split pills that aren't a 'long acting' type or encapsulated."

Save by buying a 90- versus a 30-day supply. Most pharmacies offer higher savings if you buy a larger supply. In addition, people with insurance prescription coverage may save even more by getting a larger-day supply.

Over-the-counter drugs may be as effective as the prescription drugs. Most prescription cold medications average $20 to $60 for a one-month supply and contain the same decongestant that is available over the counter for less than $2. Some doctors still prescribe 20-milligram Pepcid to their patients, which can cost $60 for a one-month supply. Pepcid AC comes over the counter in 10-milligram strength; taking double the dose costs approximately $23.

You may be able to pay for over-the-counter drugs with pretax funds, saving yourself 25 to 50 percent of their cost. Many over-the-counter drugs are now qualified medical expenses for Health Savings Accounts and for reimbursement from HRAs (see Chapters 5 and 6).

Stop using drugs you no longer need. You should review all your prescriptions with your doctor at each visit. You may be taking drugs you no longer need. Also, report any side effects and ask questions about possible drug interactions. Don't hesitate to ask your pharmacist questions; it's free and can often save you money.

Take only those drugs you really need. When your doctor prescribes medication for you, make sure you understand exactly what it's meant to do and for how long. If you are prescribed two drugs for the same symptom, ask whether you really need both; if you develop new symptoms ask your doctor if the prescribed medicine could be causing it.

You may qualify for a free drug program. There are over 1,100 drugs that are made by 100 manufacturers that have free drug programs. Most major drug companies provide free medications but rarely, if ever, publicize their programs. An estimated $2 billion worth of free medication is given away annually. You can get a complete list of drugs and manufacturers' programs at www.institutedc.org.

Veterans have their own drug benefits. Recent laws grant veterans medical benefits for certain illnesses, like diabetes and hypertension, provided the veteran is subject to qualifying conditions such as Agent Orange exposure. Check with the Veteran's Administration to see whether you qualify for benefits.

Buy home test kits. Kits for determining ovulation, pregnancy, and colorectal cancer can be purchased as home tests at half the price of similar kits from your doctor's office.

Look for special deals by local governments. You can save on prescription drugs through special deals offered by state and local governments and even religious organizations. The states of Illinois, Kansas, Missouri, Vermont, and Wisconsin have initiated a web site where residents can buy 100 commonly used drugs from Canada, Britain, and Ireland at a discount of anywhere from 25 to 50 percent. The address for the site is www.i-saverx.net.

One of the main reasons prescription drugs are so expensive is because, until now, consumers have had few incentives to make economic choices about which drugs to take and where to buy them. In most areas of our economy other than medical care, informed consumers increasingly demand and receive (1) better products for less money and (2) cheaper and more convenient methods of distribution for the products and services they have chosen. Medical care, starting with the prescription drugs you choose and how you obtain them, is about to join the rest of the U.S. economy.

However, there is a better way to save on prescription drugs than to get a drug discount card, choose the right health plan, shop overseas, substitute generics, or use therapeutic substitution. The best way to save on prescription drugs is to work with your doctor to stop taking drugs altogether—as explained in the next chapter.

CHAPTER 10

How to Be a Smart Healthcare Shopper, Stay Healthy, and Keep the Savings

B y now you may have discovered you can save thousands of dollars each year by purchasing your own individual/family health policy, or you may be ready to switch to high-deductible health insurance, or you may have opened a Health Savings Account (HSA)—or hopefully all of these. Once you do, your healthcare paradigm shifts:

You now want to cut down on your healthcare spending since each dollar you save you get to keep—and over the years these dollars could add up to hundreds of thousands of dollars in your HSA.

You must learn to balance your new financial incentive to save on healthcare costs against the legitimate healthcare needs of your family.

You have a new incentive to eat better, exercise more, and invest in wellness care to improve your health—since staying healthy is the best way to save on your healthcare costs.

In this chapter we examine four things you should do to save on your healthcare costs:

1. Stop taking "maintenance drugs."

2. Change your lifestyle (diet and exercise) before it's too late.

3. Shift from sickness care to wellness care.

4. Ask your doctors to spend your money as if it were their money.

Stop Taking "Maintenance Drugs" That Treat Symptoms, Not Causes

There is one very important idea missing from Chapter 9, *How to Save 10 to 75 Percent on Your Prescription Drugs*. The idea is that you can save 100 percent on your "maintenance drugs" (heartburn medicine like Prilosec, antidepressants like Zoloft, heart disease drugs like Lipitor, etc.). These drugs treat your symptoms, not the causes of your illness, which in many cases, can be traced to diet, lifestyle, and exercise. The only way to save 100 percent on these drugs is to stop taking them altogether—by finding a doctor or other medical professional who understands the dangers of prescription drugs and will work with you to change your diet or lifestyle.

The prescription drug business was founded by people like Dr. Jonas Salk, who developed the first vaccine for polio, and Dr. Alexander Fleming, who discovered penicillin. The products these dedicated doctors developed prevented diseases from developing in the first place or cured diseases over a relatively short period of time.

Sadly, as healthcare moved away from the work of medical professionals and became the most profitable sector of our economy, the prescription drug industry shifted from making products that prevented or cured diseases to making products that merely treated the symptoms of diseases.

Today about 95 percent of the prescription drugs sold are *maintenance drugs*—drugs that treat only the symptoms of a disease and that you are expected to take for the rest of your life.

From an economic/business perspective, at least, it's easy to understand why this is so, and you need to understand this if you are taking any prescription drugs on a regular basis. I'll put the answer in the form of a question: If you were the CEO of a major pharmaceutical firm, would you spend your R&D dollars to make a pill that a consumer would only take once (e.g., a vaccine) or for only a short period of time (e.g., an antibiotic), or would you spend your R&D dollars on creating products that consumers would take every day, or two or three times a day, for the rest of their lives?

For the past three decades, the majority of private R&D dollars in the pharmaceutical industry have been spent on products that treat merely the symptoms of disease rather than cure or prevent disease—thus creating "customers for life."

If you were a businessperson developing a new health product to sell to your customers, wouldn't you like to have all Americans indirectly pay a tax subsidizing 50 percent of your retail price, even if they had no interest in taking your product? If drugs like Viagra or Levitra were sold over the counter, employers would have to give employees almost $2 in order for those employees to have $1 left after FICA and income taxes to buy the drugs—but because these drugs are "prescription only," employers are forced to pay 100 percent of the cost through their group health plans as a tax-free benefit to employees.

Today many of the prescription drugs sold do not have a strong legitimate reason to be prescriptions—they are not addictive or controlled substances like morphine. They are issued in prescription form partly to get all Americans to subsidize 50 percent of their cost through medical tax deductions and partly to force employers to pay for them.

More important than the fact that many prescription drugs were designed to make you a customer for life, and more important than the fact that all Americans end up subsidizing 50 percent of the price of other people's drugs, is the fact that many prescription drugs are indirectly dangerous, over the long run, to your life and health.

I am an economist and businessman, not a medical doctor; however, in conducting the extensive research for my last book, *The Wellness Revolution*, I concluded that few of the tens of millions of people taking maintenance drugs should be taking them. Instead, most people taking maintenance drugs should be working with a medical professional to cure the underlying disease—for example, changing their diet instead of taking Nexium for life (to counteract heartburn), losing weight instead of taking Lipitor for life (to lower cholesterol). I apologize to my medically oriented readers who may find these claims offensive—no offense is intended—but I would be less than honest if I did not share with you this conclusion.

In addition to preventing you from focusing on the causes of your illness rather than on the symptoms, the prescription medicines you take are the number one reason your application for individual/family health insurance could be rejected or your premium increased (uprated).

Let's go back and examine more closely the world's five top-selling prescription drugs discussed in Chapter 9—Lipitor, Zocor, Nexium, Prevacid, and Zoloft—which account for more than $25 billion in sales in the United States alone. These drugs have the following things in common for most people taking them:

- They do not prevent a disease.
- They treat only the symptoms of a disease.
- They are designed to be taken for the rest of your life.
- They are not narcotic or controlled substances and thus should not be prescription versus over-the-counter medicines.
- They would have less chance of being sold directly to consumers as real products without first co-opting trusted physicians as sales agents.
- They are dangerous to your long-term health, because by treating only the symptoms of a deadly disease, they prevent you from modifying your behavior to cure the disease.

Lipitor: Lipitor, the number one selling prescription drug in the world, is prescribed to lower your cholesterol. Every health and medical professional will tell you that the best way to lower your cholesterol is to change your diet and to exercise, which we will examine in a moment. Instead, millions of Americans take this drug for their entire lives—which is dangerous because it prevents them from making the lifestyle changes that they sorely need.

Zocor: Zocor, the number two selling drug in the United States, is functionally the same as Lipitor. It is truly amazing that Americans spend more than $10 billion a year for these two drugs when generics are available for both for about one-third the price (see Chapter 9).

Nexium: Nexium, designed to treat heartburn, is the latest trick perpetrated on consumers by the pharmaceutical companies. The majority of people who have heartburn have it because of what they eat, not because they are genetically disposed to acid reflux disease. A bad diet can cause depression, heart disease, cancer, and heartburn. Yet when their body screams out in pain for help, millions of people take this "little purple pill" to stop their body's natural alarm system (i.e., heartburn) from functioning so they can keep eating unhealthy foods.

Prevacid: Prevacid is functionally the same as Nexium. If Prevacid and Nexium were over-the-counter medicines instead of prescriptions, their advertising would have to inform consumers that the best way to cure heartburn is to stop eating the food that is causing the heartburn. But because they are prescriptions, in addition to getting a 50 percent medical tax subsidy, their national, direct-to-the-public advertising is exempt from normal truth-in-advertising regulations. Prescription drug advertising targeted to consumers should be prohibited since, in the real world, "ask your doctor" often means "change your doctor" if he or she won't give you whatever prescription drug you request.

Zoloft: Zoloft is the number one selling drug in the world for depression and anxiety—more than 28 million Americans (1 in 10) have taken Zoloft or its functional equivalents Prozac and Paxil. According to its own web site (www.zoloft.com), one of the major side effects of taking Zoloft, Prozac, and Paxil is that 2 to 4 percent of people under 18 taking these drugs have suicidal thoughts.[1] In addition to being expensive, drugs for depression are dangerous because they prevent people from dealing with the causes of their depression (including their diets). In psychiatric cases requiring chemical intervention, there are much cheaper alternatives like St. John's wort, which outsells Prozac 25 to 1 in Germany. According to a recent study at Harvard Medical School, antidepressant drugs should not be used in 75 percent of the cases where they are prescribed.[2]

If you take any prescription drugs on a regular basis, find a medical professional and develop a plan to get off your prescriptions as soon as possible: *Do not attempt to do this without the advice of a medical professional.*

 TIP: To find a medical professional to help you, start by telling your current doctor: "I currently take [prescription drug] on a regular basis and am looking for a medical professional to work with me to stop." If your doctor can't help you, he or she may be able to recommend a wellness-oriented MD who can, or refer you to a wellness health professional such as an osteopath (DO), naturopath (ND), or chiropractor

(DC). (There are tips later in the chapter for how to find one
yourself.)

The best way to develop a plan to stop taking prescription drugs is to
find an MD-type medical professional who works together with a wellness
health professional. For example, in Dover, Ohio, a cardiologist noticed
that two of her patients with high cholesterol had good results after
attending a Creating Wellness center run by chiropractor Dr. Shawn
Kapper. The cardiologist was so impressed that she sent 40 of her
patients with heart disease to Dr. Kapper, and the two doctors (chiropractor and cardiologist) developed a nondrug program to lower cholesterol for the betterment of their mutual patients.

Change Your Lifestyle (Diet and Exercise) to Dramatically Cut Your Lifetime Healthcare Expenses—Before It's Too Late

There's a lot you can do to improve your health and cut your healthcare
costs, but first let's look at why we spend so much on healthcare.

Why Americans Spend So Much on Healthcare

The United States spends far more per person on healthcare than any
other country—about twice as much as other developed nations. Yet people in the United States don't appear to be getting their money's worth.
The United States lags far behind other developed countries on almost
every important medical statistic—life expectancy, infant mortality, cancer, diabetes, heart disease, and so forth.

So, what is the problem with American healthcare?

Is it our inefficient medical bureaucracy, where 2 to 3 million
Americans are employed by medical providers and insurance carriers—
not to deliver healthcare, but merely to pass the buck for that care to
someone else?[3]

Is it the cost of medical malpractice insurance, which adds more than
$27 billion a year to the cost of providing healthcare—enough to pay
annually a high-deductible insurance premium for more than half of the
45 million Americans without health insurance?[4]

Is it our employer-based system, whereby the ultimate providers of
healthcare for most people (employers) have little incentive to spend even
$1 today on wellness and preventive care in order to save $100 tomorrow—because the odds are that the employee will be long gone or receiving

Medicare by the time serious diseases like cancer and heart disease develop?

The partial answer is yes to all of these questions, but the main reason Americans spend two times what they should on healthcare is not because of something wrong with American healthcare.

The main reason Americans spend two times what they should on healthcare is because Americans (along with Australians and Britons) are two times more unhealthy than people in most other nations, primarily because of their diet and a lack of exercise.

Today, more than 61 percent of Americans are overweight or medically obese—a figure that has doubled since the 1980s. Being overweight is just one of the symptoms of having a terrible diet—most Americans are also deficient in the basic vitamins and minerals necessary to keep their minds sharp and avoid major diseases like cancer.

If you are overweight or obese, please get immediate help in changing your lifestyle. Already, 59 million Americans have diabetes or prediabetes, mostly due to being overweight—if you are one of them, you have a 65 percent chance of dying from heart disease or stroke. Moreover, before you die, if you are obese, you will likely consume much of your estate in medical expenses and will needlessly and selfishly be torturing those you love the most.

The Effect of Diet and Exercise on Your Prescription Drugs

Refer back to the list of the five most popular prescription drugs. Most people taking these drugs can eliminate or reduce their consumption through diet and/or exercise. The primary cause of high cholesterol (Lipitor, Zocor) is your diet and lack of exercise. The primary cause of heartburn (Nexium, Prevacid) is also the foods you eat—although many people do have a genetic predisposition to acid reflex disease requiring long-term medication. And, when it comes to depression (Zoloft), I am convinced that diet and/or lack of exercise is a cause of depression and that a lifestyle change can yield amazing results, particularly for young people.

 TIP: If you have a child experiencing either depression or hyperactive behavior, try changing his or her diet—specifically, eliminate fast foods and processed foods containing preservatives and salt, cut down on dairy products, and add large quantities of fruits and vegetables. As a parent of four and as a teacher of college freshmen for 21 years, I have seen amazing improvements in behavior from changes in lifestyle, diet, and exercise.

Shift from Sickness Care to Wellness Care

Americans have the opportunity to make a sea change in their attitude and approach to healthcare.

Joining the Wellness Revolution

Consider the following definitions:

Sickness industry: Products and services provided reactively to people after they contract an illness, ranging from a common cold to cancerous tumors. These products and services seek to either treat the symptoms of a disease or eliminate the disease.[5]

Wellness industry: Products and services provided proactively to healthy people (those without an existing disease) to make them feel even healthier and look better, to slow the effects of aging, or to prevent diseases from developing in the first place.[6]

Most of the entire $2 trillion we currently spend on healthcare, one-sixth of the U.S. economy, has very little to do with health—defined in the dictionary as "being sound in body, mind, or spirit."[7] Doctors, hospitals, and drug companies are mostly part of the "sickness industry" because, until recently, most scientists and public policy leaders viewed wellness or preventive care as quackery. Today, numerous scientific studies have validated what a few million Americans seem to have known all along:

There are hundreds or thousands of efficacious treatments to make people feel healthier, to slow the effects of aging, or to prevent diseases from developing in the first place.

However, until you first experience one of these treatments working for you or a member of your family, you are probably going to remain a skeptic and miss out on improving the quality of your life and on reducing your long-term healthcare costs.

I stumbled onto the wellness industry in the 1990s. For 10 years I put off getting expensive knee surgery, against medical advice. Finally, I started taking a dietary supplement called glucosamine—within a year the cartilage was repaired and I no longer needed the operation. The surgeon was positively amazed when he examined my X-rays. This piqued my interest in finding out what else my surgeon, and my other medical providers, didn't know. I also noticed that people were spending more on new things like exercise programs, vitamins, organic foods, and alternative medicine. When I researched what was going on, I discovered wellness industry sales were $200 billion in 2001, and I wrote a book (*The Wellness Revolution*) predicting a $1 trillion wellness industry by 2010.[8]

Until recently, there has been one important component missing from the wellness revolution in the United States—the money for consumers to pay for it. One of the reasons I wanted to write this book is because *The New Health Insurance Solution* is ultimately as much about financing wellness as it is about health insurance.

When you are healthy, you save thousands of dollars on your health insurance premiums and out-of-pocket expenses, money that you can continue to invest in your future health through an HSA.

When you continue to invest in your health, you reap financial as well as quality-of-life rewards—giving you even more money to invest in your health.

HSAs, HRAs, and other vehicles discussed in this book provide tax advantages for wellness, preventive, and alternative care that were previously available only for sickness care.

Alternative Medical Providers

Until my late 40s I thought I was "healthy"—other than my knee problem; I saw a doctor only for an annual checkup. Today I visit my "doctor" every week—although it is a different type of doctor than I would have imagined seeing only a few years ago.

While doing the research for *The Wellness Revolution*, I became friends with several outstanding alternative medical providers. Two that stand out are Dr. Fabrizio Mancini, president of Parker College of Chiropractic, and Dr. Patrick Gentempo, president of Creating Wellness.

For years Drs. Mancini and Gentempo prodded me to start regular chiropractic care, but I resisted. I felt terrific. My snowboarding and mountain biking were improving. So why should I see a doctor? Finally, I agreed to see one of Dr. Mancini's graduates, Dr. E. J. Raven, in Park City, Utah. After I began a series of chiropractic "wellness visits," my wife, who is a scientifically minded, UCLA-trained biologist, was very pleased with my results—so pleased that for the past 12 months she has taken herself and our four children to Dr. Raven for a weekly "adjustment." We attribute our wellness care to eliminating the regular colds that come from living in a ski town with four small children, but there are simply no words to describe how much "better than healthy" we feel since adding quality alternative wellness care to our lives.

 TIP: You owe it to yourself to check out the various wellness practitioners in your area. Under the new tax laws, chiropractic, osteopathic, and naturopathic care are finally treated the same as care from MDs—you can use your HRA, HSA, or almost any other financial vehicle to pay for your alternative care.

Osteopaths are usually more wellness-oriented than traditional MDs—my wife switched her ob-gyn care to an osteopath, Dr. Stephanie Singer, who delivered our last two children. You can locate an osteopath in your area by contacting the American Osteopathic Association.[9] Similarly, you can find a local naturopathic doctor by contacting the American Association of Naturopathic Physicians.[10]

Speak to Your Doctor about Spending Your Money as if It Were His or Her Own Money

I've found that in many cases, doctors already know how to spend your money as if it were their money. They are just too busy to take the time to do so, or they may be prohibited from doing so by the owners of their medical practice or by their malpractice insurance carriers. Here's how to get them to do it.

Prescriptions

Ever since our family switched our health insurance in 1999, when a doctor writes out a prescription, I say: "We have high-deductible insurance." Twice, I've seen the doctor rip up the prescription and write a new one stating, "This drug is cheaper and is really the same thing anyway."

 TIP: Don't wait for your doctor to prescribe something and then ask for a cheaper equivalent—tell your doctor up front that you have a Health Savings Account and high-deductible

health insurance. You'll be surprised how many doctors already know about HSAs and how to save money on health-care.

One reason doctors don't prescribe cheaper equivalent drugs is that doctors and their medical practices have enormous financial incentives to prescribe certain brands of drugs. The pharmaceutical companies have armies of lawyers figuring out the latest "barely legal" way to compensate medical doctors who prescribe their brand-name products.

Many times doctors don't prescribe cheaper equivalent generics or therapeutic substitutes out of ignorance. As explained in Chapter 9, there are equivalent generics or therapeutic substitutes for almost all popular drugs. When you politely tell them, most doctors are pleased to learn about less expensive equivalent therapies. They don't teach economics in medical school, and you should not expect doctors to know the price of the things they prescribe. Unlike you, they rarely see the inside of a pharmacy. Doctors get many of their own prescriptions for free, as samples from pharmaceutical representatives.

Medical Tests

Unnecessary medical tests are another area where doctors can waste hundreds or thousands of your dollars. There are obviously some medical tests you should never skip—like having an annual mammogram or taking a biopsy of an unusual growth. But many tests are simply a waste of money. When doctors tell you they want to send you, or a sample of your fluids, for a medical test, here are some questions you should ask them:

- Why do you want this test?

- What are the likely results from the test, and what is the recommended action for each outcome?

- If the therapy is the same regardless of the result, could we skip the test and just begin the therapy?

- Are there any different tests that we should consider?

- How much does the test cost, and is there any way to get it done less expensively?

- If you were spending your own money, would you take this test?

You may be surprised by the responses you get, particularly to the last question. Many tests and medical procedures are not even sanctioned by the doctors who prescribe them—they are forced to do so for liability reasons by their medical malpractice insurance carriers. Ask again, "Would you take this test with your own money?" If the candid answer is no, ask whether you can sign a waiver instead, stating that your doctor advised you to take the test but that you refused against medical advice (AMA).

Surgery

Check your wallet when a doctor starts talking about surgery—then get a second or third opinion. Make sure you receive advice from at least one doctor who is not a candidate to perform the surgery. Doctors often have an enormous financial conflict of interest when it comes to recommending a surgery they might perform themselves. Be particularly careful when your doctor has already leased or purchased expensive equipment (e.g., LASIK tools) that they need to keep busy. Do not hesitate to ask, "What do you get personally if I choose to do, or not to do, the surgery?" Doctors are not subject to the same conflict-of-interest standards that have become commonplace for lawyers, public officials, and other professionals.

In this chapter we have explored just four of the things you can do to save money and improve your health—which in itself should be an entire book. Each time you speak with your doctor about reducing your prescriptions, changing your lifestyle, getting wellness care, or spending your money more wisely, you and your doctor become better educated about the most important social and economic challenge facing us today—improving our health and reducing the cost of healthcare.

PART TWO

How Businesses Can Fix Their Health Insurance Nightmare and Still Hire Great Employees

How Employers Can Save 50 Percent by Giving Employees Tax-Free Dollars to Buy Their Own Health Insurance: Defined Contribution Health Benefits

B ecause of recent changes in the law and in the health insurance industry described in this book, defined contribution health insurance plans, along with HSAs, have become the most dramatic change to employee health benefits since employers were first allowed to provide tax-free health benefits during World War II.

If your company is among the 60 percent of employers with an employer-sponsored group health insurance plan, you and your employees can save 50 percent* by switching to a *defined contribution* insurance plan. You can do this by canceling your group health insurance plan and giving the money directly to your employees through a Health Reimbursement Arrangement (HRA) so they can buy their own individual/family health insurance. You will be relieved to be out of the health insurance business, and most of your employees will be able to buy better insurance on their own for less than half of what you are currently paying for their health insurance. In addition, they can keep the savings in their own Health Savings Accounts.

*Savings are less in New York, New Jersey, Massachusetts, Maine, and Vermont because these states still are "community-rated, guaranteed issue"—meaning they do not allow health insurance companies to sell policies at lower rates to healthy people.

If you use many independent contractors or part-time employees who don't qualify for health insurance, or if you are among the 40 percent of employers who don't offer group health insurance because it's too expensive, you can now give your employees the individual/family coverage they really need, funded with pretax salary contributions. Your employees will pay far less than the cost of traditional group health insurance for similar coverage; through a Health Reimbursement Arrangement, you can contribute tax-free as much of the cost as you can afford.

If you are a business owner or manager, you probably knew the problems with employer-sponsored group health insurance before you read this book. What you probably didn't know was that there is now an affordable solution—canceling your group plan and giving your employees tax-free money to buy their own individual/family policies. This is called a *defined contribution* health insurance plan versus the *defined benefit* insurance plan you probably have today.

To better understand the problems with your traditional group health insurance plan, you may want to review Chapter 1, "You Are One Serious Illness Away from Bankruptcy: The Huge Gaps in Your Employer's Health Insurance Plan," only this time read it from the perspective of an employer, not an employee.

Traditional Defined Benefit Health Insurance versus New Defined Contribution Health Insurance

Traditional defined benefit plan: You provide your employees with a defined healthcare benefit—doctor visits, hospitalization, pharmacy and so on—at uncertain annual cost. The benefit is administered through your limited-choice employer-sponsored group health benefits plan.

New defined contribution plan: You provide your employees with a tax-free allowance or "contribution" to spend on their own healthcare— at an annual cost that you control. Employees use this allowance to pay the premiums for their own individual/family health insurance policy, to pay out-of-pocket medical expenses, and to make contributions to their Health Savings Account.

Everyone Benefits, but Healthy and Younger Employees Benefit the Most

As shown in Chapter 2, in 2006 the annual average cost of traditional defined benefit employer-sponsored health insurance was approximately $14,000 per family and $4,500 per individual. Nationally, a defined contribution program costs less than half this price for comparable health insurance for the roughly 80 percent of your employees who are healthy. (In a moment, I will show you how a defined contribution program also helps the 20 percent or so of your employees who are unhealthy.)

TIP: To be conservative, I am assuming that the health and age of your employees is roughly equivalent to the general population that currently applies for individual/family policies—of which about 80 percent are accepted. If your employees are younger or healthier, as many working individuals are, this 80 percent figure may be closer to 90 or 95 percent.

Interestingly, when given the choice to purchase their own individual/family health insurance policies, many of your healthy employees will not want to buy a low-deductible/co-pay policy similar to the one you are now providing them—even though it will cost them half of what you are currently paying. Instead, they will want a high-deductible HSA-qualified health insurance policy for one-fourth the price of your group plan, and they will want you to contribute the cost savings to their Health Savings Account.

Later in this chapter I explain how to present a new defined contribution plan to your employees in a way that addresses their natural fears that their benefits are being cut and highlights the financial advantages they will enjoy with a defined contribution plan.

Cost Savings on Individual/Family Health Insurance versus Traditional Employer Group Insurance for the 80+ Percent of Your Employees Who Are Healthy

	Single	Family
Employer-sponsored group insurance (2006)	$4,500	$14,000
Individual/family co-pay (low-deductible) insurance	$2,076	$ 6,492
Individual/family HSA (high-deductible) insurance	$1,104	$ 3,192

Note: See Chapter 2 and Appendix A for details: male, age 35, or family of four.

These numbers assume an average age of 35 for your employees. As explained in Chapter 5, in some states like California, the monthly premium for a 55-year-old single individual is about twice the premium for a 35-year-old. Older employees will not benefit as much financially from a defined contribution plan (unless your company sets a higher level of HRA reimbursement for older employees), but they will greatly benefit from getting permanent, guaranteed-renewable health insurance that they will not lose when they lose their job. Moreover, the financial risk of an older employee developing an illness is now borne by an insurance carrier or the state versus the employees themselves, your company, and your other employees.

Unhealthy Employees Also Save Money and Get Safer Coverage

What about the other up to 20 percent of your employees who are not healthy or who have an unhealthy family member—some of these employees may not medically qualify for affordable private individual/family health insurance. These 20 percent of your employees will not benefit as much financially as your healthy employees (unless your company sets a higher level of HRA reimbursement for unhealthy employees); however, they too will be much better off with a defined contribution plan—because they will now have guaranteed renewable health insurance independent of their employment. As highlighted in Chapter 1, three-fourths of the millions of Americans who have filed medical bankruptcy had health insurance from an employer when they first became ill—health insurance they lost when they became too sick to continue their job.

Here are the four options for your unhealthy employees or employees with an unhealthy family member:

1. Buy individual/family health insurance coverage from private carriers at uprated premiums 25 to 50 percent higher than for your healthy employees. For a family, only the portion of the premium allocated to the unhealthy family member will be subject to uprating (see Chapters 4 and 7).

2. Join the employer plan of their spouse—but still get money from your defined contribution program, which they can use for co-pays, put into an HSA, or pay for the cost of participating in their spouse's health insurance.

3. In some states such as Ohio or California, if you cancel your employer-sponsored group health insurance plan, they can apply as a HIPAA-eligible individual to any private insurance carrier and receive a state-subsidized, guaranteed-issue individual/family policy at about twice the premium paid by healthy employees (see Chapters 3 and 7 for information on how they can qualify for state-guaranteed coverage).

TIP: Consult with your benefits counsel before directly advising your unhealthy employees about state-guaranteed coverage—some states have regulations prohibiting employers with group health plans from actively encouraging their unhealthy employees to get state-guaranteed coverage, and these regulations could apply to your HRA program under certain circumstances.

4. In other states, such as Texas or Illinois, if you cancel your employer group health insurance plan, your employees will instantly qualify for subsidized state-guaranteed insurance with no exclusions for preexisting conditions—receiving virtually identical coverage as healthy employees from the leading carrier in their state (e.g., Blue Cross Blue Shield of Texas or Illinois). This coverage will cost about twice the premium paid by healthy individuals (see Chapter 7).

Since older or unhealthy employees require much more medical care than most employees, it is understandable (but nevertheless unfortunate) that they have to pay significantly more for their health insurance under a defined contribution insurance plan. However, even in the worst financial cases, items 3 and 4 in the preceding list, the higher premium that employees will pay for state-guaranteed coverage is still usually less than the average employer-sponsored cost—and this higher premium applies only to the one unhealthy member of their family. The rest of their family members qualify to save thousands of dollars based on the insurance rates for the healthy 80 percent of employees.

Typical Worst-Case Annual Individual Health Insurance Costs for Unhealthy Employees Who Qualify for State-Guaranteed Coverage

	Single
Employer-sponsored (2006)	$4,500
Missouri	$3,240
Texas	$4,368
Maryland	$2,688
California	$4,272
Connecticut	$3,480
Kentucky	$2,988
Illinois	$3,084
New Jersey	$4,932
New York	$3,624

Note: These state-guaranteed insurance prices are from Appendix A. New Jersey and New York prices are the same as for healthy individuals, since New Jersey, New York, Massachusetts, Maine, and Vermont are guaranteed-issue and community-rated regardless of health (see Chapter 7).

You should not switch to a defined contribution program for just the obvious financial reasons. In addition to saving lots of money, all your employees, including those who get state-guaranteed coverage, receive the numerous benefits of individual/family policies described throughout this book.

Unlike your employer group plan in which the premium will rise significantly in the year following any major medical claims from employees, your employees' individual health insurance premiums cannot be increased due to a major illness or any expensive claim. Their policy cannot be canceled for as long as they pay the premium—even if they no longer work for your company.

The thousands you save each year can be contributed to their Health Savings Accounts—eventually creating a nest egg of several hundred thousand dollars for their future medical expenses and their retirement.

Your employees will thank you for helping them get individual/family policies and Health Savings Accounts for the rest of their lives—especially those employees with unhealthy family members who previously lived in dire fear of losing their employer-sponsored health benefits.

TIP: **These great benefits to your employees assume that your company contributes all or most of the immediate premium savings from switching to a defined contribution plan to your employees for their HSA or HRA. Most employers are not switching to defined contribution plans to save money today—they are trying to get better, safer coverage for their employees and to put a cap on future health benefits cost increases.**

Your Company Benefits As Much As Your Employees Do

Your company and the U.S. economy are also much better off by switching to defined contribution healthcare. With a defined contribution healthcare program, you and your business associates are able to:

■ Concentrate on your business and your customers instead of managing the complexities and spiraling costs of your health insurance benefits. The true cost of employer-sponsored health benefits is the immeasurable productivity toll it takes on management.

■ Remain in business. The cost of health benefits now exceeds profits for most companies and is increasing faster than profits. If you don't do something now, in a few years your stockholders may decide they are better off not owning shares in your company.

■ Save by redirecting the time and in-house personnel you now devote to health benefits to improving your products and service to customers.

■ Stop wasting people and money on COBRA administration. Ex-employees no longer need COBRA since they now have permanent portable health insurance for half the cost, and your company has no continuing obligation to provide COBRA.

How Much Will Your Organization Save with a Defined Contribution Plan?

The numbers used in this chapter are mostly national averages based on employees age 35. In health insurance, no one state, and no one employer-sponsored group benefits plan, is "average"—premiums vary as much as 300 percent between states and between employee groups for the same coverage. Here's how to estimate how much you and your employees can save with a defined contribution healthcare program in your state.

Calculate the Cost of Your Existing Defined Benefit Program

First calculate the total cost of your existing employer-sponsored health benefits program—both the company-paid amount and the employee contribution amount. This will include your total group health insurance premium, administration personnel costs, and other health benefits programs like employer matching contributions to a Section 125 plan.

Let's say that your company currently pays 100 percent of the annual cost for each employee ($4,000), and 50 percent of the total $10,000 additional cost for an employee to add their family to the group plan. The total cost of your employer group plan is $1 million per year for 100 employees ($700,000 paid by your company and $300,000 by employees who have added their families to the plan).

Sample Worksheet for Calculating the Annual Cost of Your Employer-Sponsored Group Plan

	Employee Contribution	Employer Contribution	Total Plan Cost
100 employees	$ 0	$400,000	$ 400,000
60 families	$300,000	$300,000	$ 600,000
Total plan cost	$300,000	$700,000	$1,000,000
Per single employee	$ 0	$ 4,000	$ 4,000
Per family (incl. employee)	$ 5,000	$ 9,000	$ 14,000

Estimate the Cost of a New Defined Contribution Program

Refer to Appendix A and locate sample health insurance premiums for traditional (low-deductible) individual/family policies in your state comparable to your group plan.

TIP: The figures in Appendix A are for employees age 35 and families of four—premiums vary based on age, health, and family size. Go online to www.ehealthinsurance.com or www.zaneben.com, or visit the web site for this book, www.TNHIS.com, to get prices for individual/family health insurance based on the average age and family size of your employee group.

Let's assume your employees live in Illinois where a typical traditional (low-deductible/co-pay) individual/family Blue Cross Blue Shield policy costs $4,176 a year ($348 per month) for a healthy family of four, and $1,176 a year ($98 per month) for a healthy single employee. These figures for Illinois are 40 percent less than the national averages—because the national averages include New York, New Jersey, Massachusetts, Maine, and Vermont, where premiums are three times the price of other states. Individual/family policies in these five states are "guaranteed issue" and "community rated"—meaning everyone is accepted at the same premium, regardless of their health status or age (see Chapter 7).

TIP: Defined contribution programs work everywhere, but are especially cost-advantageous in the 46 states (including Washington, D.C.) where carriers are allowed to sell discounted policies to healthy people (see Appendix A).

Now you need to estimate what percent of your employees are not going to medically qualify for individual/family health insurance. You can find out by asking your group health insurance benefits consultant or insurance carrier. Under HIPAA law, they are prohibited from telling you the names of employees with health issues, but they can tell you "de-identified" information, such as how many employees have specific health issues in their families that would prevent them from getting individual health insurance.

TIP: Skip this step if your employees live in New York, New Jersey, Massachusetts, Maine, and Vermont, since individual/family policies in those states are guaranteed issue and community rated.

Let's assume that 15 percent have health issues and that (worst case) all 15 percent of these employees will end up getting state-guaranteed Blue Cross Blue Shield coverage at an annual average cost of $3,084 per unhealthy member (see Appendix A).

Sample Worksheet for Estimating the Annual Cost Savings, Per Employee, of a Defined Contribution Plan (Illinois)

	Single	Family
Healthy 85 percent of employees	$1,176	$ 4,176
Unhealthy 15 percent of employees	$3,084	$ 6,216[a]
100 percent of employees (weighted average)	$1,462	$ 4,482
Existing employer group plan (defined benefit plan)	$4,000	$14,000
Potential savings per employee (w/ defined contribution plan)	$2,538	$ 9,518

[a]One unhealthy family member costing $3,084, plus three healthy family members costing roughly 75 percent times $4,176.

Now let's examine the same chart for New York, where all employees must be accepted by carriers regardless of their age or their health status. Let's further assume that you have an older workforce and 35 percent of your employees have health issues, although it doesn't matter in New York since everyone pays the same premium.

Sample Worksheet for Estimating the Annual Cost Savings, Per Employee, of a Defined Contribution Plan (New York)

	Single	Family
Healthy 65 percent employees	$3,624[a]	$ 8,808[a]
Unhealthy 35 percent employees	$3,624	$ 8,808
100 percent employees (weighted average)	$3,624	$ 8,808
Existing employer group plan (defined benefit plan)	$4,000	$14,000
Potential savings, per employee (w/ defined contribution plan)	$ 376	$ 5,192

[a]See Appendix A.

As you can see, in Illinois, New York, or virtually any other state, your company and your employees can save money and get better coverage by switching to a defined contribution plan—savings range from 33 percent of your $1 million existing defined benefit plan cost in a state like New York to 67 percent in a state like Illinois.

Total Annual Cost Savings: Defined Contribution Plan versus Defined Benefit Plan

	Illinois Per Employee	Total	New York Per Employee	Total
40 single employees	$1,462	$ 58,480	$3,624	$144,960
60 families (incl. employee)	$4,482	$268,920	$8,808	$528,480
Total health insurance cost (defined contribution plan)	$327,400		$ 673,440	
Total employer plan cost (defined benefits plan)	$1,000,000[a] (70% employer-paid)		$1,000,000[a] (70% employer-paid)	
Potential savings (w/ defined contribution plan)	$ 672,600		$326,560	

[a]The company is contributing $700,000 and the employees are contributing $300,000.

Designing Your Defined Contribution Health Benefits Plan

Once you calculate the available potential savings, you must make the following three decisions:

1. How should these savings be divided between the company and its employees?
2. How much of a monthly healthcare allowance should be allotted to each single employee and each employee with a family?
3. What, if any, amounts should be additionally made available for unhealthy employees, older employees, or employees with special needs (e.g., pregnancy)?

Dividing the Savings between Employer and Employees

Most companies are so pleased to get rid of their employer-sponsored group health benefits plan that they don't want a dime of the savings—they give 100 percent of it to their employees. In this scenario, your company would give the full $700,000 of its prior health plan cost to employees through Health Reimbursement Arrangements (HRAs)—representing, on average, a $7,000/year HRA to each of your 100 employees. Most of your employees will be amazed and delighted that you are giving them so much money to spend directly on their own healthcare, because they have no idea how much you are currently spending on their group health plan.

TIP: Carefully read Chapter 13 (HRAs) for examples of the many different tax-free health, retirement, and wellness programs you can give employees with the savings from a defined contribution plan.

Some companies' group health insurance costs are currently so high that they are threatening their survival, and they will have to keep some of the savings from a defined contribution plan to stay in business. In this case, your company might give $500,000 of its former $700,000 in contributions as healthcare allowances—representing, on average, $5,000/year to each employee in an HRA.

To smooth the transition to a defined contribution plan, some companies want to give additional temporary or permanent healthcare allowances to unhealthy employees (who will have higher individual/family insurance premiums and spend more on out-of-pocket medical expenses)—just as their current employer-sponsored defined benefit group plan implicitly spends more on unhealthy employees. In this case, your company might give, on average, a $6,000 allowance to all 100 employees ($600,000 total) and an additional $5,000 to your 20 (or 20 percent) of employees with health issues ($100,000 total)—representing, on average, $6,000 to each employee in an HRA and an additional $5,000 in a separate HRA for employees with health issues. (HRAs are allowed for specific diseases or treatments, like smoking cessation or weight loss, even though this technically "discriminates" against nonsmokers or normal-weight employees.)

Special-Purpose HRA Program(s) for Singles, Families, and Unhealthy Individuals

There is no limit to the amount of special-purpose HRAs your company can establish. (See Chapter 5 for details of how HRAs work, and read Chapter 13 for more on how to set one up for your company.) You may want to incorporate everything into one HRA plan document, or you can set up a separate HRA for single employees, employees with families, and employees with health issues ("unhealthy employees"). Setting up separate HRAs provides the most flexibility, as illustrated in the following table.

Sample HRA Programs for a Defined Contribution Plan (Illinois)

	#	Annual HRA Allowance	Employer Cost	Average Insurance Premium	Add'l Benefit
Single employees	40	$3,600	$144,000	$1,176	$2,424
Employees w/ family	60	$7,600	$456,000	$4,176	$8,424[a]
Unhealthy employees	20	$5,000	$100,000	?[b]	$5,000
Total employer cost			$700,000		

[a]Employees with families receive $8,424 in additional benefits versus just $3,424, because they formerly contributed $5,000 of the premium for their group employer-sponsored plan.
[b]See Appendix A.

HRA for single employees. In this plan, single employees would receive $3,600 per year in annual healthcare allowance; after buying their own individual health insurance policy for an average of $1,176 per year in Illinois, a single healthy employee would have $2,424 left over to spend on out-of-pocket medical expenses or to save for future medical expenses. An employee in New York would pay an annual premium of $3,192 and have $308 left over to spend or to save.

HRA for employees with families. Employees with families would receive $7,600 per year in annual healthcare allowance; after paying an average of $4,176 for a family health insurance policy in Illinois, an employee with a family would have $3,424 left over for out-of-pocket medical expenses or to save for future medical expenses. Employees in New York would, on average, pay an $8,108 annual premium—but would actually still be ahead $4,492 per year because they would no longer be paying the $5,000 it was costing them to add their families to the old group employer-sponsored plan.

HRA for employees with health issues. Employees with preexisting health problems would receive $5,000 per year in additional healthcare allowances; in addition to paying medical expenses, these extra funds could be used for disease management, prescription co-pays, weight loss, smoking cessation programs, and maternity.

TIP: The one major difference between all group employer-sponsored plans and most individual/family plans is pregnancy coverage—HIPAA requires employer plans to cover maternity, whereas most individual/family plans cover maternity with a separate $5,000 annual deductible for maternity expenses. To ease the transition from group plans to individual/family, it is recommended to have a "maternity HRA" to cover this $5,000 deductible for at least the first few years—some employees may have been counting on having their pregnancy fully covered by their employer.

Implementing Your Defined Contribution Health Benefits Plan

Once you have estimated the cost of your defined contribution health benefits plan and figured out what HRAs you want to set up, it's time to sharpen your pencil and make sure your estimates are correct and that every one of your employees gets a good individual/family policy, or else is covered through their spouse's plan.

For illustration and analysis purposes, this section assumes that you are canceling your group plan and giving employees, on average, a $7,000 annual allowance to spend on their healthcare. While this is theoretically a good idea, no employer should do this so directly or so immediately. Employees are very defensive about "their" benefits, and the transition from a defined benefit plan to a defined contribution plan must be handled delicately.

There are two basic ways to handle the transition: (1) Implement defined contribution with a specific class of your employees. (2) Implement defined contribution as an option for employees in lieu of participating in the group defined benefit plan.

Starting with a Defined Contribution Plan for Independent Contractors or Another Class of Employees

In this case, you would define a group of employees that meet the definition of a separate class under group health insurance rules—such as independent contractors, employees who began working after a certain date, who work for a specific subdivision of your company, who work in a different state, or who are hourly versus salaried employees. Under HIPAA nondiscrimination rules, you are legally allowed to give different benefits to different employees, provided that all employees in the same "class" are treated equally.

Then, you should convert just this class of employees from defined benefit to defined contribution as explained here, working closely with an outside benefits consultant who explains the program to each employee and ensures that every employee in the group gets good individual/family coverage.

Your objective is to make certain that everyone in this defined class of employees has a positive experience with your defined contribution plan, and that word of this spreads to your other employees. Soon they will demand their own defined contribution plan.

Defined Contribution as an Optional Choice for Employees

Alternatively, you may want to allow employees in your regular group health insurance defined benefit plan to opt out and choose defined contribution benefits. If your defined contribution plan is designed and priced correctly, both healthy and unhealthy employees should desire to switch to individual/family coverage.

Healthy employees will obviously choose defined contribution for the enormous financial savings and the contributions you will make to their HRAs and HSAs. Unhealthy employees should choose to opt for your defined contribution plan, because (1) the cost of even state-guaranteed coverage saves them some money over their existing defined benefit plan, and/or (2) they get the benefit of guaranteed health insurance for life even if they are no longer able to work—which can be a priceless benefit to an unhealthy employee or even to a healthy employee considering early retirement.

TIP: Before offering defined contribution as an option to any employees in a group health plan, carefully review the terms of your group health insurance policy. Most group policies require a minimum participation of, typically, 75 percent of eligible employees. Once a number of employees choose the defined contribution option, your company may automatically find itself without a group plan—which may or may not be desirable.

Perform a Census of Your Employees (or a Class of Employees) When You Are Ready to Cancel Their Group Defined Benefits Plan

To get more accurate information, you need to perform a census of every employee and their family in your group plan or in the class of employees you are considering converting to defined contribution. You should work with a third-party health benefits consultant and prepare a "de-identified" census of each employee. This census lists each employee by a number (not a name) and their family's basic health information. Your health benefits consultant or a licensed health insurance agent should then locate a good individual/family health insurance policy for each employee.

 TIP: While health insurance agents typically work only on commission, you should consider paying a $100 per employee fee for this service so they find the best policy for each employee instead of the policy with the highest commission— and make this fiduciary obligation part of the agreement you sign with them.

Census Worksheet for a Defined Contribution Plan

	Family Details, Health Issues	Individual/Family Insurance Premium
Employee 1 (age, state)	Health status, spouse and children information	$356, Blue Shield Blue Cross, written quote
Employee 2 (age, state)	Health status, spouse and children information	$187, Golden Rule, offer pending
Employee 3 (age, state)	Health status, spouse and children information	$302, state-guaranteed coverage
Employee 100 (age, state)	Health status, spouse and children information	$654

Terminating Your Group Plan and Making (Almost) Everybody HIPAA-Eligible for State-Guaranteed Insurance

In Chapters 3 and 7 you learned about the rights of an employee who has become HIPAA-eligible—all states are required by the federal government to guarantee HIPAA-eligible individuals the extremely valuable right to purchase individual health insurance coverage with no exclusions for preexisting conditions.

When an employee loses coverage from a group employer-sponsored health benefits plan, they must accept and use up their COBRA benefits to become HIPAA-eligible—provided COBRA is offered.

> If the group plan is terminated, no COBRA will be offered, and all employees will become instantly HIPAA-eligible for state-guaranteed health insurance.

There is one exception: According to HIPAA law, company executives cannot make themselves HIPAA-eligible. If you are the head of employee benefits and you make a decision with other executives or the president of the company to terminate the group plan, everyone in the company is HIPAA-eligible except those who were involved in making the decision. This will have no impact on you and the other decision makers if no one in your families has a preexisting medical problem. But if a decision maker or a family member is unhealthy, it will make that person ineligible for their HIPAA right to buy individual health insurance with no exclusions for preexisting conditions.

> **TIP:** If you are healthy, you don't need or want to be HIPAA-eligible, since such coverage is typically twice the price of coverage for a healthy individual. But you never know who in your company may have a medical condition or an unhealthy family member for whom becoming HIPAA-eligible could be a lifesaver. When you analyze and decide to switch to a defined contribution health benefits plan, consult only with the minimum number of executives you need to, and before you do, ask whether they or a family member has any history of health problems or preexisting conditions—you may be doing someone a great favor by keeping them out of the loop until the final decision is announced.

Once your group plan is terminated and everyone (except the decision-making executives) becomes HIPAA-eligible, each employee has a 63-day opportunity to buy health insurance from a state risk pool or a private insurance carrier (or both) with no exclusions for preexisting conditions.

Implementation Timetable for Defined Contribution Plan

0–120 days before implementation	Complete the census of all employees; have your licensed agent or benefits consultant find good policies for all eligible employees effective day 1. Make sure every employee understands their options and the benefits of individual/family coverage.
Day 1: Implementation	Employees purchase policies, and each employee transfers from the group plan to the HRA defined contribution plan when their individual/family policy becomes effective.
Between day 1 and day 180	Cancel the group plan, or the plan may automatically be canceled when a certain percentage of eligible employees are no longer participants. All employees remaining in the plan now become HIPAA-eligible for the next 63 days.
Next 63 days	File applications for the remaining employees who need HIPAA-eligible status to get coverage.
Thereafter	Employees manage their own individual/family health insurance policies and submit proof of medical expenses to your third-party administrator (TPA) for monthly or quarterly reimbursement from HRAs.

Other Considerations

You want to gain some experience with defined contribution health benefits plans before implementing them with your core employees. Consider offering a defined contribution plan to your part-timers or independent contractors. These previously ineligible-for-benefits employees will be extremely grateful and become more loyal to your company, and your core employees should soon demand you implement a defined contribution plan for them once they see others receiving better benefits than they have at less cost.

TIP: Many companies set up a defined contribution plan for just their independent contractors. Since these are not techni-

cally employees, the HIPAA nondiscrimination and other federal regulations do not apply—giving employers much more flexibility in designing HRA (equivalents) for their independent contractors.

In this chapter I have explained defined contribution health plans—perhaps the most dramatic change in employee health benefits since employers were first allowed to provide tax-free health benefits during World War II. In the next chapter you learn about Health Savings Accounts for employers and how you can fund HSAs with your defined contribution health benefits plan. Finally, in Chapter 13, I further discuss HRAs and how to use them to the betterment of all your employees. Chapters 11, 12, and 13 should be carefully read together before implementing any of the suggestions contained in any one of them.

HSA Plans for Employers: Why Every Employer Should Encourage Tax-Free Employee Contributions to HSAs

This chapter is written for employers as a supplement to Chapter 6. You may want to reread Chapter 6, Health Savings Accounts (for individuals), before reading this chapter.

Health Savings Accounts (HSAs) are IRA-type savings accounts owned by individuals. Employers and employees are allowed to make annual tax-deductible contributions to an individual's HSA up to $5,450 combined in 2006 (increased annually). To qualify to open an HSA, a person must have high-deductible HSA-qualified health insurance—through either their employer's group policy or an individual/family policy that they purchase themselves.

HSAs are almost always the best choice to fund employee healthcare expenses, but because they cannot be used by employees to pay for individual/family health insurance, many employers should also use Health Reimbursement Arrangements (HRAs) to ensure that their employees pay no tax on their individual/family health insurance premiums. (Chapter 13 explains how to integrate HRAs with HSAs.)

More than 1 million families obtained HSA-qualified health insurance in the first 14 months they became legal. Seventy percent of the Fortune 500 are offering, or are about to offer, HSAs to their employees. The debate over whether your business should offer HSAs is over—the question now is how you should offer them. In the near future, employers without an HSA program will find it difficult to hire and retain top employees.

HSAs immediately save employers thousands per employee in taxes and premiums for health insurance—on both employer-sponsored group plans and individual/family policies. Many businesses that could not previously afford to offer health benefits may be able to do so with high-deductible HSA plans, because they cost 50 to 75 percent less than traditional employer group health insurance.

Annual Average Health Insurance Cost for Healthy Employees, 2005–2006

	Single	Family
Individual/family HSA/high-deductible policy	$1,104	$ 3,192
Individual/family low-deductible/co-pay policy	$2,076	$ 6,492
Traditional employer-sponsored group policy (2006)	$4,500	$14,000

Note: See Chapter 2 and Appendix A, for details.

But there is much more to Health Savings Accounts than just saving money on taxes and health insurance premiums.

■ HSAs provide your employees the best in healthcare today because they are not locked into the one PPO or HMO network your company chooses for them. They have an unlimited choice of medical providers, including dentists and alternative care providers like chiropractors, osteopaths, and naturopaths.

■ HSAs give each employee financial incentives to make wise decisions about healthcare, such as when to switch to a generic drug, since employees get to keep tax-free for tomorrow whatever they save today.

■ When a defined contribution plan is used to fund premiums on HSA-qualified individual/family policies, HSAs give employees permanent health insurance because they don't lose their health insurance when they lose or leave their job, and they are never forced to pay the high cost of COBRA health insurance.

■ HSAs cover preventive and wellness care like obesity and smoking cessation—these can be paid for from the HSA itself, but are also fully covered by some HSA-qualified health insurance plans.

■ HSAs provide employees a healthcare safety net between jobs, because contributions may be withdrawn without penalty to pay health insurance premiums if unemployed.

The more you learn about HSAs, the more you will want all your employees to have an HSA with as large a balance as possible.

Three HSA Contribution Options Every Employer Should Consider: 0, 50, and 100 Percent

Health Savings Accounts represent the biggest change in health and retirement care since Social Security and can greatly benefit your employees. But unlike Social Security, HSAs immediately save your business money.

Even if you don't yet offer HSAs, or even health benefits, just giving employees the ability to redirect part of their salary into their HSA costs your company nothing and saves your company up to $804 per year per employee in FICA. And it provides a great new employee benefit—up to $1,313 in income tax savings.

Option 1: 0 Percent Employer Contribution Plan

With this plan, employees redirect their salary to their HSAs via the employer.

You can set up a Section 125 salary redirection plan at virtually no cost. Under such a plan, an employee fills out a simple request form stating the amount of salary per pay period, up to $5,250 per year in 2005, to be redirected to an employer contribution to their HSA. Employees could still receive the same $1,313 in income tax savings by making a personal contribution to their HSAs, but that's only if they are disciplined enough to make the up-to-$5,250 annual HSA contribution on their own. Offering your employees this option saves $804 (15.3 percent) combined in FICA and ensures your employees will fully fund their HSA each year.

Money Saved by Allowing Pretax Salary to be Redirected to Employer Contribution to an HSA (Section 125 Salary Redirection Plan)

	Without Section 125 Salary Redirection Plan	With Section 125 Salary Redirection Plan
Employee HSA contribution	$5,250	$5,250
Employer FICA (7.65%)	$ 402	$ 0
Employee FICA (7.65%)	$ 402	$ 0
Employee income taxes (25%)	$1,313	$ 0
Employer tax savings	$ 0	$ 402
Employee tax savings	$ 0	$1,715[a]

[a]$1,313 + $402; see text.

> Aside from the obvious tax savings of a Section 125 salary
> redirection plan, allowing employees to fund their HSA with
> regular contributions every pay period helps them stay disci-
> plined and fully fund their HSA.

Unlike other uses of a Section 125 plan, the federal government does
not consider an HSA contribution Section 125 salary redirection plan to
be an ERISA employee benefit plan—even with employer matching contributions as described next. This exempts your company from the expensive and time-consuming reporting requirements typically associated with
ERISA health plans such as COBRA continuing obligations for ex-
employees.[1]

Option 2: 50 Percent Employer Matching Contribution Plan

With this plan, the employer matches employee HSA contributions up to
a specified amount. It need not be exactly 50 percent, but rather could be
any ratio you can afford.

If your business can afford it, you should strongly consider establishing a
Section 125 HSA matching contribution plan. In this case, your company
would match, dollar for dollar, employee salary redirected HSA contributions up to the maximum $5,250 (in 2005) amount—$2,625 by the
employee and $2,625 by the company. Such a matching program sends the
right message to your employees and rewards those employees who are
committed to helping themselves.

The tax benefits are substantial. The employee gets $5,250, after taxes,
in their HSA, but at a cost of only $2,625 to the employer and $1,567
(after tax) to the employee ($2,625 – 7.65% FICA – 25% income tax).

Although this type of matching contribution is not considered an
employee benefits program subject to ERISA regulations, employers are
required to make "comparable" contributions to all employees who are in
the same employment class or group. (This does not include voluntary
contributions employees make under employer salary redirection plans.)
Employers cannot discriminate in making HSA contributions based on
age, seniority, or length of service, but employers can make different contributions based on, for example, the size of the annual deductible on the
employee's employer-sponsored health insurance. Employers also do not
have to make comparable contributions to part-time versus full-time
employees or single versus married employees.

TIP: Employers typically allow employees to choose their benefits only once a year, during the "open enrollment period,"
and at the occurrence of a "qualifying event," like a birth or

marriage. However, unlike with traditional benefits, there is no limit to how many times an employer should allow employees to change their Section 125 HSA contribution amount. The more flexibility you allow your employees, the more they will contribute to their HSA and the more you will save on FICA.

Option 3: 100 Percent Employer Contribution Plan

You should also consider funding 100 percent of each employee's HSA contribution, up to $5,250 (in 2005) per year, through a Section 125 HSA contribution plan. Before you think you can't afford it, think of which employees in your company will go out and get a Health Savings Account with the highest deductible so they can take full advantage of this benefit—probably your most savvy managers and top producers who receive regular raises based on their performance.

> Your sophisticated employees will view this option as a raise—a raise that would have cost your company $3,141 more without the HSA contribution plan.

It would cost your company $8,391 to give your employees the same $5,250 after-tax benefit they would get with a $5,250 HSA employer contribution—thus saving $3,141 per year in FICA and income taxes.

Cost to Give an Employee a $5,250 After-Tax Benefit

	Without HSA Contribution Plan
Pretax salary	$7,795
Employer FICA (7.65%)	$ 596
Total employer cost	$8,391
Pretax salary	$7,795
Employee FICA (7.65%)	$ 596
Employee income taxes (25%)	$1,949
Net employee after-tax benefit	$5,250

Employer cost with HSA contribution plan = $5,250.
Employer cost without HSA contribution plan = $8,391.

TIP: An LLC or an S corporation cannot make pretax above-the-line contributions to HSAs for owners, shareholders, or partners.

HSA Plans for Employers Who Offer Health Insurance

Health Savings Accounts are a win-win situation for employers.

HSAs for Employers with Defined Contribution Health Insurance Plans

Companies that already have defined contribution plans, as described in Chapter 11, can today have the best health benefits available anywhere. A two-step HSA defined contribution health benefits program works as follows:

Two-Step HSA Defined Contribution Health Benefits Program

> 1. Each employee chooses and pays for his or her own individual/family health insurance policy and receives reimbursement from a company HRA. Employees can keep what they don't spend; some employees will have to pay more than others.
> 2. Employees who choose an HSA-qualified individual/family policy open a Health Savings Account and make monthly salary contributions to their HSA, which are matched by their employer with a Section 125 HSA matching contribution plan (as described in this chapter).

That's it. End of story. Not only does this give your employees the best health benefits with the most tax advantages, it is also the simplest of all programs to administer. It can be managed by a third-party administrator for as little as $5 per month per employee. Employer savings on FICA alone pay for much more than the administration costs of the program.

Employees receive every possible benefit of an HSA explained in Chapter 6 and then some (e.g., employee FICA savings). Employers don't have to design an HSA health insurance program because each employee who wants an HSA chooses his or her own HSA-qualified individual/family policy.

The only remaining decision for the employer is which, if any, wellness and preventive care programs they should offer—like smoking cessation HRAs, weight loss HRAs, and group accident/hospitalization coverage, which are allowed under HSA rules. These are discussed in Chapter 13.

HSA Options for Employers with Defined Benefit (Traditional Employer-Sponsored) Group Health Insurance

Although this section explores ways to create HSA-qualified employer-sponsored group health insurance, the best option is to discontinue your group plan and switch to the defined contribution program described in this chapter and in Chapter 11.

Employers with traditional group employer-sponsored health plans can make their employees eligible for Health Savings Accounts simply by offering an HSA-qualified group health insurance plan. This can be offered as an option in lieu of the traditional low-deductible company plan or as the only choice available. Most large companies are taking the former approach rather than forcing HSAs on their employees.

TIP: While HSA-type plans are typically optional for employees today, many large-company benefits managers expect HSA and other high-deductible plans to be the only choices available in 5 to 10 years. Ask your CEO or board for a mandate to invest in what it takes today to wean your employees off of expensive low-deductible plans as soon as possible.

Employees are very savvy about their health benefits. Employers commonly complain that they wish employees would be as savvy about their work as they are about their benefits. At larger companies, employees often view benefits as "rights" and check their wallets whenever changes are proposed. Some of the early corporate offerings of high-deductible HSA-qualified health insurance in 2004 and 2005 lived up to their suspicions.

In some cases, employers merely raised the annual deductible on an existing group plan family option from $500 to $5,450 and called it an HSA-qualified health insurance option—with no corresponding reduction in employee participation cost or new employer HSA contributions. Few employees chose this option—the tax benefits of an HSA are not enough to justify paying up to $4,950 more in medical expenses. Moreover, employees know that their employers are making thousands of dollars when an employee chooses a high-deductible option, and employees rightfully expect this money to go mostly to them for taking the increased risk.

Here is a four-step solution (only one of many) for designing an HSA-qualified health insurance plan.

1. Raise the family deductible from $500 to $5,450—and compute the amount your company would save if employees chose this option. Let's say that the company would save, on average, $1,337 in medical expenses for each of the roughly 80 percent of employees who are healthy, and $4,950 for each of the roughly 20 percent who are unhealthy.

TIP: When calculating potential savings from a high-deductible plan, include the processing costs for each claim along with the actual amount paid to the medical provider.

---

2. Throw away the figure for the 20 percent group, because few of these unhealthy employees are going to choose the HSA option, and any who mistakenly do choose it are going to switch back as soon as possible.

3. Offer a new family a $5,450 deductible HSA-qualified plan option with the company to match, 50/50, employee HSA contributions up to $2,725 per employee ($5,450 total HSA contribution in 2006). This would cost your company $1,387 ($2,725 − $1,337) for each employee who chooses the HSA-qualified plan option, except that, on average, only about half of the eligible employees will fully fund their HSA and qualify for the matching funds.

4. For each of the healthy 80 percent of employees who choose the HSA option, your company saves $1,337 in medical expenses but, on average, spends $1,387 in HSA contributions.

This example costs the employer nothing and gives employees a competitive HSA-qualified insurance plan that has the potential to double the employee's annual contribution ($1,337 per year) on a pretax basis. On an after-tax basis, this plan potentially triples the employee's money, since a $2,725 after-tax benefit is equivalent to about $4,000 pretax (after income tax and FICA).

The End of Health Insurance Risk
for Large Employers

If you are following this example and you work for a company that is self-insured for health benefits (as most large companies are), you are probably already seeing the pot of gold that lies at the end of the rainbow for HSA plans. From the standpoint of financial risk, your company can now get out of the health insurance business. Here's how.

Virtually all employers that self-insure their health benefits purchase *re-insurance*—typically a stop-loss policy that covers employee healthcare when an employee spends more than $50,000 or $100,000 in medical expenses. These stop-loss, or re-insurance, policies are now available at levels of $10,000 or $20,000. If your company purchased re-insurance at a $5,000 level and converted all your employees to $5,000-deductible HSA-qualified plans, from a risk standpoint you would be out of the healthcare business.

Since the 2005 collapse of GM's stock price partially due to health benefit obligations, analysts on Wall Street are asking questions about the biggest risk many companies face today—the cost of their health benefits. Announcing that your company is out of the health benefits business altogether could be the best news you could report at the next meeting of your shareholders.

How to Make Sure Your HSA Plan Is Enthusiastically Adopted by Your Employees

To hasten the day when you are out of the health benefits business, you need to give incentives to your employees to open Health Savings Accounts and high-deductible health insurance. Here are some things to do today to accelerate adoption of HSAs by your employees.

- Price your HSA-qualified health insurance plan options so they make financial sense to your most savvy employees. HSAs can only lower your total healthcare costs if your employees choose them. It may be worth it to your company to lose a few dollars on HSA contributions today in order to lower your total healthcare costs tomorrow.

- Add a group insurance rider to your HSA-plan covering all expenses resulting from an accident or requiring hospitalization up to a maximum of $5,000 per year. These accident/hospitalization policies typically cost about $10 per month per employee because of their very low annual maximum ($5,000). They alleviate most employees' main fear about switching to high-deductible health insurance—having an accident or something requiring hospitalization, and they do not violate the regulations for HSA-qualified health insurance.

- Offer your employees an unlimited choice of banks and investment options for their Health Savings Accounts by making sure your third-party administrator (TPA) will make HSA contributions to any bona fide HSA.

- Consider covering the following list of medical items with no deductible for employees who choose HSA-qualified health insurance. These are all allowed for first-dollar coverage under HSA rules, and covering these items sends the right message to your employees regarding HSAs being the best option for the long term:

Annual physical exams

Screening services (e.g., mammograms)

Routine prenatal and well-child care

Child and adult immunizations

Tobacco cessation programs

Obesity weight-loss programs

Specific disease insurance (optional)

Long-term-care insurance options (optional)

Vision care (annual allowance)

In the next chapter, we discuss HRAs and other new cutting-edge tools for employers to offer better health benefits to their employees at less cost, and you learn how all of these new tools integrate with your company Health Savings Account program.

CHAPTER 13

HRAs for Employers: How to Use HRAs to Save $2,000 to $6,000 per Employee Each Year While Getting Your Employees Better Health Insurance

This chapter is intended for employers as a supplement to Chapter 5 (which discusses HRAs and FSAs for employees) and as a continuation of Chapters 11 and 12.

H RAs are the future of employer-sponsored health insurance—they are the only employee-benefits vehicle allowed to pay for premiums on individual/family health insurance, and are therefore a critical part of any defined contribution health plan (see Chapter 11).

Whether your company has a traditional employer-sponsored (defined benefit) group health plan or a defined contribution health plan, HRA programs can save your company and your employees thousands each year—from the day they are first hired until years after they are retired. The new-employee HRA program alone (described in this chapter) can save employers with a group health plan $1,950 per single and $6,528 per family on every new person they hire.

How Health Reimbursement Arrangements (HRAs) Work

The IRS recently began allowing employers to establish Health Reimbursement Arrangements (HRAs) to reimburse employees tax-free for certain medical expenses, including premiums paid for individual health insurance—similar to the way employers routinely reimburse employees for travel, meals, and other qualified business expenses. Employees incur medical expenses and then submit receipts for reimbursement in accordance with the rules of the specific HRA.

HRAs today are about twice as popular as Health Savings Accounts— approximately 4 million U.S. households are covered by employer HRA programs versus 2 million for HSAs. These numbers are expected to double by the beginning of 2007, and then double again to approximately 16 million HRAs and 8 million HSAs in 2009. HRAs are sometimes called Section 105 plans after the IRS Code section that governs them.

HRAs represent the future of employer-sponsored health benefits because they are so flexible and allow employers to reimburse employees for premiums on individual/family and short-term health insurance. The IRS is continually expanding the benefits allowed to be covered by HRAs, so check with your benefits administrator or benefits consultant for the latest information, as well as the web site for this book (www.TNHIS.com).

Basic Rules and Uses for HRAs Today

■ HRAs must be 100 percent funded by employers and cannot be funded by employees through salary reduction.

■ HRAs can be either "use it or lose it" or "use it or keep it"— whichever the employer chooses to offer for each HRA.

■ HRAs can be used to cover generally everything an FSA or HSA can cover (i.e., virtually all medical and pharmacy expenses) plus:

Individual/family health insurance premiums

Medicare and long-term-care insurance premiums

Preventive care such as weight loss and smoking cessation

A wider list of medical expenses like over-the-counter medicines

---

The main reason employers use HRAs today is to get employees to accept changes to the group health plans (i.e., higher deductibles or exclusions for certain items) that result in significant reductions in the premium paid for employer-sponsored group health insurance.

TIP: HRAs are very powerful tools to get your employees to convert to, or purchase, high-deductible coverage while ensuring that employees will not skip important items that they might otherwise have to pay for themselves. Set up an HRA to reimburse 100 percent for HSA-permitted items like annual checkups, mammograms, weight loss, and smoking cessation programs—keeping your employees healthy and fit gives you more productive employees today and saves you money tomorrow.

The main reason employers will use HRAs tomorrow is to get employees to reject employer-sponsored group health insurance entirely and instead receive tax-free reimbursement for the premiums on individual/family policies that employees purchase on their own.

When it comes to funding employee medical expenses tax-free, HRAs offer the most flexibility in plan design, except that HRAs cannot be employee-funded in any manner. HRAs should be combined with employee-funded vehicles like FSAs, HSAs, or Section 125 plans.

Comparison of Features: FSAs, HRAs, HSAs, and Section 125 Cafeteria Plans

	Health FSA	HRA	HSA	Section 125 Cafeteria
Funding of contributions	Employee-funded through pretax salary contributions	Employer-funded only	Employer- and employee-funded	Employer- and employee-funded
Limitations on contributions	None	None	$5,450 family, $2,700 single (2006)	None
Eligible medical expenses	Unreimbursed medical expenses only—no health or long-term-care (LTC) insurance premiums	Unreimbursed medical expenses + health and LTC insurance premiums + preventive care + OTC medicines	Unreimbursed medical expenses + preventive care + OTC medicines but no health insurance premiums except LTC and health while unemployed	Medical, pharmacy, dental and vision expenses, long-term disability (LTD), and deposits to FSA

(continued)

Comparison of Features: FSAs, HRAs, HSAs, and Section 125 Cafeteria Plans *(continued)*

	Health FSA	HRA	HSA	Section 125 Cafeteria
Administration	Claimant must submit documentation for each expense	Claimant must submit documentation for each expense	Self-administered by claimant	Company administered or via TPA
Flexibility	Limited	Virtually unlimited	Insurance and savings must comply with strict rules	Limited
"Use it or lose it" during employment	Yes	No	No	Yes
Kept by employee after employment	No	No, typically, but unspent balance can be offered as retiree benefit	Yes	No
COBRA requirements	Yes	Yes	No (COBRA applies only to high-deductible health plan)	Yes

Your company can have an unlimited number of HRAs, or one HRA for all HRA-type benefits. There is no legal entity to set up—to establish an HRA you write a Plan Document and a Summary of Plan Description (SPD) that clearly states what employees are entitled to under the HRA.

 TIP: You don't need to spend thousands or more for a lawyer to write these documents. Your third-party administrator (TPA) should be able to provide you with the documents you need for a one-time fee of $1,000 or less.

Unlike with an HSA, the IRS requires employees to submit written documentation for all eligible medical expenses before they are reimbursed from the HRA. However, because of HIPAA and other privacy concerns, virtually all companies use a third-party administrator (TPA) to handle verification of medical expenses and reimbursement to employees. TPAs typically charge about $5 per month per employee to administer an HRA.

A Simple, Money-Saving Health Insurance Solution for Most Employers Today

In general, the most simple health benefits solution today for most employers consists of the following three-step program:

1. A defined contribution HRA program (see Chapter 11) to fund employer contributions to individual/family health insurance premiums and other medical expenses.
2. A Section 125 HSA matching contribution program (see Chapter 5) matching, dollar for dollar, employee salary redirected HSA contributions, which encourages employees to purchase HSA-qualified individual/family health insurance.
3. An HRA to fund wellness and preventive care.

Here's how such a three-step program would work.

Three-Step HRA/HSA Defined Contribution Health Benefits Program

1. Each employee chooses and pays for his or her own individual/family health insurance policy and receives reimbursement for all or part of the premium from a defined contribution HRA.
2. Those employees that choose an HSA-qualified individual/family policy open a Health Savings Account and make monthly salary-redirected contributions to their HSA, which are matched by their employer with a Section 125 HSA matching contribution plan.
3. Employees are encouraged to seek wellness and preventive care because these items are paid 100 percent by their employer, tax-free. Such care includes routine medical exams, health screening, smoking cessation, weight loss, maternity, and many other items that will improve the health and performance of your employees.

Optional: Additional HRAs may be included, as described in this chapter, to cover medical items (maternity, etc.) either not covered by individual/family health plans or desired by employees and deemed cost-effective for the employer.

The list of ways employers can use HRAs to improve benefits and lower health plan costs grows every day. In the rest of this chapter we examine five uses of HRAs and then summarize how HRAs work, so you can design the best customized HRA programs for your employees.

1. *New-employee HRA.* Provides health insurance coverage from first day of hire until employees become eligible for regular health benefits.

2. *Former-employee and early-retiree HRA.* Provides a safer, extended, and much less expensive alternative to temporary, expensive COBRA health insurance, and can help older employees with early retirement.

3. *High-deductible HRA.* Encourages employees to choose high-deductible health insurance and incentivizes smart shopping (i.e., buying generics, medical shopping).

4. *Supplemental HRA.* Fills the gaps that some group and individual/family plans do not cover (e.g., accidents, maternity).

5. *Wellness HRA.* Provides programs to improve employee health and productivity (e.g., weight loss, smoking cessation).

New-Employee HRAs——Short-Term Health Insurance Coverage for New Hires ("Waiting Period Coverage")

New employees historically became eligible for health benefits from their first day on the job. However, due to the high cost of employer-sponsored health insurance and to protect the health benefits of their existing employees, many companies have been forced to add "waiting periods" before new hires become eligible for health benefits.

This is because today some employees choose jobs more for health benefits than for wages—especially in lower-paying industries like retail and hospitality. You really can't blame them:

■ What would you do if you had a child who needed a $30,000 operation?

■ What would you do if your spouse had a condition requiring $500 or more in medication per month?

■ What would you do if you just found out that you had cancer and you didn't have health insurance?

To protect their employer-sponsored group health benefit plans, many employers offering good health benefits have added waiting periods of 30 to 270 days before new hires become eligible for health benefits.

TIP: If your company doesn't have a waiting period, start one, or consider lengthening your existing waiting period. Your employer-sponsored group health plan is a sitting duck for people with health issues in their family who want your health benefits more than they want to work for your company. The cost of such people joining your plan is borne by both the company and your existing employees.

Waiting periods have created a difficult situation for personnel departments—many managers claim that to effectively recruit the best employees their company must offer health insurance coverage immediately from date of hire.

TIP: Under HIPAA, waiting period time is excluded when determining whether a new hire with a health issue has had the "continuous coverage" required in order for their new employer to cover their preexisting condition (i.e., they have not had a gap in coverage greater than 63 days, see Chapter 3)—so starting or increasing a waiting period will not prevent new employees with preexisting health conditions from getting the protection they are entitled to under federal law.

Short-Term Health Insurance Policies (Waiting Period Coverage)

The solution to be able to protect your company's group plan while still being able to recruit the best employees with coverage from day of hire is to extend your waiting period and offer *waiting period coverage*—a short-term health insurance policy funded by your company with a new-employee HRA.

Short-term health insurance policies are virtually the same as high-deductible HSA-qualified individual/family policies, except that they are:

- *Instantly underwritten.* Applications are approved or rejected over the telephone or online and are much easier to qualify for than ordinary individual/family policies. Nationally, about 90 percent of applicants for short-term policies are accepted versus about 80 percent for permanent individual/family policies.

- *Of limited duration.* Most short-term policies offer coverage for only 6 months, although some go up to 12 months—they are not guaranteed renewable.

■ *Much less expensive.* They are much cheaper than comparable permanent coverage because they accept only healthy people, take the risk (of them remaining healthy) for only a very short period of time, and typically don't cover pharmacy and other out-of-pocket medical expenses.

Following are typical premiums for quality short-term policies from major carriers in 10 states—note that they cost about 50 percent less than an equivalent high-deductible HSA policy offering permanent coverage. For the actual cost of short-term policies for your employees, visit www.ehealthinsurance.com, www.zaneben.com, the web site for this book (www.TNHIS.com) or contact the department of insurance in your state (see Appendix A).

Short-Term versus Permanent High-Deductible HSA Policies (2006)

Single Applicants   **Monthly Premium, 10 States**

	HSA Policy[a]	Short-Term Policy[b]
Missouri	$ 76	$55
Texas	$ 77	$42
Maryland	$ 66	$44
California	$ 97	$46
Connecticut	$ 94	$54
Kentucky	$ 55	$44
Illinois	$ 85	$32
South Carolina	$ 91	$60
Pennsylvania	$ 69	$43
Georgia	$104	$62
Average	$ 81	$50

Family Applicants

	HSA-Policy[c]	Short-Term Policy[d]
Missouri	$272	$119
Texas	$188	$123
Maryland	$180	$117
California	$294	$129
Connecticut	$259	$115

	HSA-Policy[c]	Short-Term Policy[d]
Kentucky	$262	$152
Illinois	$308	$ 95
South Carolina	$292	$133
Pennsylvania	$181	$115
Georgia	$404	$138
Average	$264	$124

[a]See Appendix A.
[b]Applicant: Male, 35, healthy, from state capitals. Policies are from the following providers' plans: Fortis Temporary Medical Insurance (Missouri, California, Connecticut, South Carolina, Georgia); Unicare Plan 2000 (Texas, Illinois); Golden Rule Short Term Medical 1500 (Maryland, Pennsylvania); Fairmont Specialty Group Select STM Plan 2500 (Kentucky).
[c]See Appendix A.
[d]Applicant: Male, 35, spouse (F/35), and children (F/8, M/5) from state capitals. Policies are from the following providers' plans: Fortis Temporary Medical Insurance (Missouri, California, Connecticut, South Carolina, Georgia); Unicare Plan 2000 (Texas, Illinois); Golden Rule Short Term Medical 1500 (Maryland, Pennsylvania).

> Short-term policies are about 50 percent of the price of equivalent permanent HSA-qualified policies, but they are only 11 percent of the cost of a typical employer-sponsored group plan.

Comparison of Short-Term Policies Monthly Premium Cost (2006)

	Single	Family
Employer-sponsored (2006)[a]	$375	$1,167
Individual/family traditional[a]	$173	$ 541
Individual/family HSA-policy[a]	$ 92	$ 272
Short-term high deductible[b]	$ 50	$ 124

[a]See Chapter 2 and Appendix A for details, male age 35 or family of four.
[b]Average of 10 states in following chart.

Short-term policy coverage is ordinarily not comparable to employer-sponsored group coverage primarily because it is (1) temporary, typically offering six months of nonrenewable coverage, and (2) high deductible, with no co-pays for doctor visits or prescriptions. However, short-term policy coverage during a waiting period in this case is comparable to employer-sponsored group coverage for two reasons:

1. The temporary coverage of a short-term policy is unimportant since these employees are guaranteed acceptance into their employer's group plan at the end of their waiting period.

2. Companies that need to offer full company benefits from date of hire can inexpensively supplement the benefits of a short-term policy with a new-employee HRA (explained momentarily).

If you are following this closely, and you should be if your company hires new employees every year, you probably already see how your company plan can save up to $325 per month ($1,950 for six months) for every new single employee, and $1,043 per month ($6,528 for six months) for every employee with a family.

Savings by Offering/Extending 180-Day Waiting Period (2006)

	Monthly Unless Noted	
	Single	Family
Employer-sponsored (2006)	$ 375	$1,167
Short-term high deductible	$ 50	$ 124
Savings (per month)	$ 325	$1,043
Savings (6 months)	$1,950	$6,528

These enormous savings on health benefits for each new employee are shared by your company and your existing employees depending on the level to which your existing employees contribute to your group plan.

Note that these figures assume your company is able to competitively recruit and hire, with new employees receiving a lower level of health benefits during their first six months. If your personnel recruiters and/or managers insist on all new employees getting full benefits from date of hire, your company can inexpensively add step 3 (see following chart) to your new-employee HRA program.

Three-Step New-Employee HRA Program for Waiting Period Coverage

1. Your company institutes (or extends) a 180-day waiting period for all new employees and offers waiting period coverage reimbursement for short-term health insurance—about $50/month single and $124/month family.[a] This 180-day delay in joining your company plan saves $1,950/single and $6,528/family for each new employee hired (see chart).

2. Ninety percent of your new employees choose and qualify for short-term health insurance—the remaining 10 percent receive the same

monthly monetary allowance to cover other qualified medical expenses during their waiting period (in lieu of actual coverage).[b] Note that your company may be less competitive in hiring some of the approximately 10 percent of new employees who have major health issues in their family and cannot qualify for short-term coverage.

3. *Optional:* Your new-employee HRA also provides reimbursement for out-of-pocket medical expenses incurred by employees during the "waiting period" up to what they would have paid had their waiting period ended (e.g., if your company plan has a $20 doctor co-pay, and your new employee incurs a $75 doctor visit, the HRA would reimburse that person $55).

[a]Or whatever the actual average premium costs in your state for your typical employee.
[b]Giving all employees the same allowance for qualified medical expenses makes your HRA compliant with HIPAA non-discrimination rules.

TIP: Step 3 offers limited exposure (probably $100 to $300 per month), because a major illness during the waiting period would be covered by the short-term policy versus the company-provided HRA—but it would be wise to set the maximum HRA reimbursement for out-of-pocket medical expenses to $1,800, or to the amount of the OOP max of the short-term insurance policy (typically $4,000 per year).

TIP: Make sure you offer your employees short-term policies from a wide selection of carriers—if you make their options look like a limited "cafeteria plan," you run the risk of your HRA being considered a "group health plan" under ERISA and thus subject to costly regulations and restrictions on benefits. Always consult with a benefits administrator and/or benefits counsel when setting up an HRA (see following).

If you are in the retail (100 percent annual turnover) or hospitality business (200 percent annual turnover), a 180-day waiting period program can save you 50 percent or more of your total group plan cost—because 50 percent or more of your employees at any given time would be covered with inexpensive short-term policies versus your group plan.

TIP: A major component of all health insurance premiums, both for group and individual/family plans, is the long-term risk taken by the carrier that a healthy insured could become ill—something you are paying for today but don't need for most of your employees if the average tenure with your company is 12 months or less.

If you already have a defined contribution plan (see Chapter 11) with HRA program(s) that reimburse employees for the cost of a traditional individual/family policy ($173 per month single and $541 per month family), you can similarly set up a waiting period new-employee HRA program that offers a much lower level of reimbursement to new hires for their first 180 days ($50 per month single and $124 per month family).

TIP: Adding such a waiting period to a defined contribution plan is riskier for your employees than with an employer-sponsored guaranteed-acceptance group defined benefit plan—short-term policies are *not* "guaranteed renewable," and each employee risks not getting accepted for an affordable permanent individual/family policy at the end of their waiting period. If you choose a lower level of reimbursement during a waiting period, you should encourage employees to still purchase a permanent individual/family policy versus short-term coverage.

Former-Employee HRAs—COBRA Alternatives (CAP) and Early Retiree Programs

HRAs can also help your ex-employees and early retirees get much better coverage at far less cost.

COBRA Alternative Program

When employees are terminated, or a covered spouse becomes divorced from an employee, they must be offered the right to participate in the company's group health plan for 18 to 36 months. Refer to Chapter 3 for a detailed explanation of COBRA eligibility and its cost.

The only ones who dislike COBRA more than employees and their families are employers. In addition to bearing the costs of administration, former employees and ex-spouses can be hostile participants in your group health plan. While former employees must be offered COBRA for 18 months, an ex-spouse of a current or former employee must be offered COBRA for 36 months.

To ease the burden on their ex-employees, especially during times of layoffs or furloughs, many large companies pay the cost of COBRA for the first one to three months. Automatically paying for COBRA is wasteful for the employer and dangerous for the employee—since it encourages employees to delay seeking permanent coverage until they have to start paying for COBRA themselves.

Temporary COBRA coverage typically costs $408 per month for a single or $1,428 per month for a family (see Chapter 3)—about 200 to 300 percent the cost of a permanent individual/family policy with similar benefits.

To encourage employees to get permanent, affordable individual/family coverage the day they become qualified for COBRA, your company should have a COBRA Alternative Program (CAP) offering individual/family coverage, and a former-employee HRA reimbursing them for the average cost of either a short-term policy or for individual/family health insurance.

The majority of people on COBRA have no idea that affordable individual/family policies exist—many employees blindly accept COBRA and don't start looking for alternatives until the end of their 18 to 36 months of coverage, after they have needlessly wasted $10,000 or more on COBRA premiums.

A typical former-employee HRA might offer three to nine months of reimbursement for the premiums of an individual/family policy as an option to one to three months of COBRA coverage—this costs your company the same amount and gets your former employees or ex-spouses of employees the permanent coverage they need.

 TIP: Offering a former-employer HRA program does not eliminate your obligation to offer COBRA—it just reduces the number of people who accept COBRA, and thus mitigates your risk by 80 to 90 percent.

TIP: Even if your company doesn't currently pay for any part of COBRA, you should have a former-employer HRA covering at least one month of individual/family or short-term premium reimbursement to encourage COBRA-eligible individuals to reject COBRA and get permanent coverage.

Three-Step Former-Employee HRA Program (COBRA Alternative)

1. Your company offers all individuals eligible for **COBRA** a **COBRA Alternative Program (CAP)** funded by a former-employee HRA—offering (ex-employees only) reimbursement for one to nine months of the premium for individual/family or short-term health insurance. You may also limit eligibility for your former-employee HRA to the length of service or class of employee.

2. The **CAP** option should be described in the same **COBRA** Qualifying Event Letter you must send employees regarding their eligibility for **COBRA** (see Chapter 3). Most employees who would have elected **COBRA** will choose permanent coverage for much less money if it is initially paid for by the company.

3. *Optional:* If your company doesn't pay any amount of **COBRA** and does not want to contribute anything toward a **CAP**, your **COBRA** Qualifying Event Letter should nonetheless explain (unfunded) **CAP** as a less expensive, safer, and better alternative to expensive, temporary **COBRA**.

Early Retiree HRA

Some employees age 55 and older no longer want to work and can afford to retire, but remain working just to participate in your company's defined benefit group health plan. Offering these employees a defined contribution health benefit plan, whereby you pay the first one to three years of premiums on an individual/family policy, combined with an early-retiree HRA, can improve your company's workplace and save thousands on your health benefits cost—employees age 55 to 65 consume, on average, three times as much in health benefits as do employees age 35. Here's how a good HRA-retiree medical plan design might work.

Employers should be giving employees over age 40 financial incentives to opt out of the employer-sponsored group plan and purchase their own individual/family health insurance—with the employer reimbursing each employee's premium through an HRA. The amount of reimbursement should be the same as the amount the company was paying for the group plan premium, typically about $350 a month per employee. Most employees age 50 or younger can purchase an individual/family policy with even greater benefits for this much money. Employees can keep their individual/family policy permanently (even if they lose their job or change jobs) until age 65. Unlike the typical employer-sponsored group health insurance plan, the cost of any catastrophically expensive employee medical expenses will no longer be passed on to the employer in the form of astronomical premium increases. This risk will now be borne by an insurance carrier or by the state.

For employees who retire before age 65, the HRA might still reimburse for the entire premium in year 1, and then a declining percentage of the premium, say two-thirds and one-third, in years 2 and 3—weaning the long-term employee off employer-provided health insurance.

An early-retiree HRA can be incorporated into your former-employee HRA offering to pay COBRA premiums or COBRA alternative benefits to ex-employees. Your early retirees deserve the same additional health insurance benefits that an employee gets after being furloughed or fired.

TIP: In 2005, the IRS issued a ruling that employers may make tax-free contributions to a retirement HRA up to the value of the retiree's accumulated vacation and sick leave—which means the employee will not have to pay income taxes on their accumulated vacation and sick leave. The retirement HRA can cover only qualified medical expenses during retirement, including premiums for individual/family or short-term health policies. An early-retiree HRA offering this benefit sends the right message and delivers the right reward—that employees will be compensated, tax-free, for working extra hours and for staying healthy even after their tenure with the company.

High-Deductible HRAs—A Way to Encourage Your Employees to Adopt High-Deductible Insurance

As illustrated throughout this book, high-deductible health insurance is:

- Better for your company, because it saves thousands per employee on the premium for your group health plan
- Better for your employees, because they get to choose their medical providers and their type of treatment
- Less expensive for most of your employees, since the cost is typically less than their out-of-pocket, below-deductible medical expenses
- Much better for U.S. healthcare, since employees with high-deductible coverage are smart healthcare shoppers

Why Don't All Employees Choose High-Deductible Plans?

Many employees have received low- or no-deductible health coverage from their employer for their entire life. It will take time before some of these employees accept high-deductible health insurance, despite the fact that they can save money immediately by switching to a high-deductible policy.

When it comes to healthcare, many healthy employees do not worry about developing an illness—they worry about themselves or a child having an accident costing thousands of dollars in medical expenses. This is one of the biggest reasons that people don't choose high-deductible health insurance, even when it would clearly save them money.

Another reason people don't choose money-saving high-deductible health insurance is the fear of a specific disease, like cancer, that may have plagued one of their parents. Of course, cancer and every other specific disease are covered by high-deductible plans, but employees sometimes feel less secure with high-deductible plans, for purely emotional reasons.

Another reason that some people reject high-deductible coverage that would save them money is dental benefits—they simply don't want to pay out-of-pocket dental expenses regardless of how much more it costs them in premium.

This same is true for vision benefits and many other specific medical items.

The solution is a high-deductible HRA that offers first-dollar coverage of $1,000 a year or more for all of these items. Employees incur these expenses and send their receipts to your third-party administrator (TPA) for reimbursement. Any unspent amounts each year are carried forward to be used in future years, but forfeited if the employee leaves the company.

How High-Deductible HRAs Save Employers Money

Let's assume the current annual deductible on your group plan is $1,000 and you want to raise this deductible to $5,450 (in 2006) so your employees can qualify for HSAs and make the maximum HSA contributions. Your insurance carrier would probably lower your group premium by about $1,500 per employee for this large an increase in your deductible.

To make this change acceptable to your employees, you offer each employee a $1,000 per year high-deductible HRA in combination with the new high-deductible health plan. The high-deductible HRA pays 100 percent of all medical expenses up to $1,000 a year, with unspent amounts carried forward for future years.

Roughly 80 percent of your employees consume less than $1,000 a year in healthcare—these employees would immediately get up to $1,000 a year improvement in their health benefits, and your company would save $500 in health premiums plus any unspent HRA amounts. Among the remaining 20 percent of employees who consume more than $1,000 a year on healthcare, those who consume $1,000 to $2,000 would also benefit, while those who consume $2,000 to $5,450 in healthcare would have out-of-pocket expenses up to a maximum of $3,450.

Offering a high-deductible HRA combined with an increase in the deductible on your health plan can immediately save your company $500 or more in premiums while substantially improving health benefits for 80 percent of your employees.

Coordinating High-Deductible (and Other) HRAs with Health Savings Accounts

But what about Health Savings Accounts? Won't an HRA that covers the first $1,000 of health expenses disqualify your employees from having a Health Savings Account? The answer is no if you limit the medical items allowed for reimbursement to only those allowed for first-dollar coverage on HSA-qualified health plans.

All of the preceding items are allowed under HSA rules for HSA-qualified health insurance. As detailed in Chapter 6, with an HSA you can have a high-deductible HRA (or health insurance) offering unlimited first-dollar coverage for the following items:

Accidents

Hospitalizations

Specific diseases (e.g., cancer, heart disease)

Dental care

Vision care

Wellness and preventive care (see following)

In addition, your employees can leverage their HRA money by purchasing guaranteed-issue insurance policies that cover accidents, hospitalizations, and specific diseases for as little as $10 to $20 per month. Such policies are typically very inexpensive because they often have $5,000 to $10,000 annual limits on benefits—which is all they need because that is typically more than the deductible and/or OOP maximum on their high-deductible insurance coverage.

TIP: Even if you don't have a high-deductible HRA, you should offer your employees accident, hospitalization, and specific disease insurance to encourage adoption of high-deductible insurance plans. These can be purchased by employees individually or by the company on a group basis for all employees.

Most employees like feeling that their employer covers "all" of their medical expenses. Having a $1,000 high-deductible HRA will give this feeling to 80 percent of your employees and costs you less than $1,000 per employee, because not everyone will use their HRA allowance each year. (Except in cases of early retirement, employees typically forfeit balances carried forward in HRAs upon termination of employment.)

Moreover, if your employees have read Chapter 6, they know not to spend the money in their HSA until retirement—so a high-deductible HSA-qualifying HRA gives them additional tax-free money to spend on medical care without touching their HSA balance.

Supplemental HRAs for Dental, Vision, and Other Items—Filling the Gaps in Group and Individual/Family Health Insurance

In addition to having a high-deductible HRA, you can have an unlimited number of similar HRAs to cover almost whatever you wish. These are typically used to keep a benefit for your employees that is being removed from your group health plan or being lost by switching from defined benefit group health insurance to defined contribution individual/family policies.

For example, you might be facing a 20 percent or greater increase in your group health insurance plan premium and want to switch carriers—but the more affordable carrier you select may not offer a specific benefit, like dental coverage, that is popular with your employees. The solution is to accept the lower-cost carrier and offer a supplemental HRA to cover this benefit.

 TIP: The health insurance market is often irrational. If a carrier has had a bad loss experience on a specific disease or issue, it may overreact and charge irrational surcharges or premium increases to cover it. You can save money on your premium by deleting this disease or issue from your group plan and providing your own coverage for employees who want it with a supplemental HRA that has limited exposure.

Another popular use for a supplemental HRA would be to smooth the transition from a defined benefit to a defined contribution plan by covering items not covered by individual/family policies. As noted in Chapter 11, maternity is typically offered in individual/family health insurance plans, but with a $5,000 deductible—adding a $5,000 maximum benefit maternity supplemental HRA program can make an individual/family plan virtually identical in benefits to the best group health insurance plan.

> **TIP:** By changing maternity coverage from a group health policy to an HRA combined with an individual/family policy, you can also set your own eligibility requirements—such as requiring that an employee must have worked for your company for at least two years to get maternity benefits.

Wellness HRAs—Programs to Improve Health and Productivity

As explained in Chapter 10 and in my previous book, *The Wellness Revolution*, there is a new emerging "wellness industry" offering products and services to keep your employees healthy, to slow the effects of aging, and to prevent diseases from developing in the first place. These include programs for weight loss and smoking cessation.

As an employer, you might think that getting your employees involved in wellness is not part of your business. Wrong. The health of your employees affects your profit in three ways: (1) Healthy employees are the most productive employees. (2) Unhealthy and obese employees who smoke are the least productive. (3) The cost of health benefits for sickness care now exceeds profits for most large businesses. Moreover, busy employees typically look to their employer for their health benefits, and they expect any treatments to keep them healthy to be offered and paid for by their employer.

The federal government now allows employers to provide tax-free wellness care (e.g., weight loss and smoking cessation programs) to their employees through HRAs. In addition to saving your company money in the long run on sickness expenses, employees who successfully take advantage of wellness programs will be more loyal and will thank you for the rest of their lives, as will their coworkers and family members.

Moreover, the new rules for Health Savings Accounts allow a wellness HRA to offer unlimited first-dollar coverage for wellness and preventive care (see Chapter 6), including:

Periodic health evaluations (e.g., annual physicals)

Screening services (e.g., mammograms)

Routine prenatal and well-child care

Child and adult immunizations

Tobacco cessation programs

Obesity weight loss programs

Preventive care

Every employer encouraging employees to choose high-deductible and/or HSA-qualified health plans should have a wellness HRA offering first-dollar coverage for wellness items ranging from annual physicals to obesity treatment programs—doing so will encourage your employees to stay healthy, keep them from skipping important screening items like mammograms, and save you and them thousands on future major medical expenses.

HRAs are the newest tool to improve the health of your employees and save employers and employees money on health benefits. They are deliberately designed to be easy to use and flexible enough to allow innovation in healthcare.

Epilogue: The Future of Affordable Health Insurance in America—Who Wins and Who Loses?

The New Health Insurance Solution is not about what should or could be done to change health insurance—the legislation and regulations allowing the changes described in this book have already been passed, and the changes are taking place right now. The sooner you or your company take advantage of these changes, the safer you will be, and the more money you (or your employees) will have for your future health expenses in your Health Savings Account(s).

As illustrated throughout this book, there is a great paradigm shift under way: As a country, we are moving from employer-sponsored group health insurance plans to individual/family health insurance policies and from wasteful, low-deductible "other-people's-money" health plans to efficient, high-deductible "keep-what-you-don't-spend" HSA/HRA health plans.

Employer-Sponsored Group Health Insurance—The Old Way

■ In 2004, 5 million fewer U.S. jobs provided health benefits than in 2001 (see Chapter 1)—and health benefits will be eliminated from millions more jobs in 2007 and the years to come (see Chapter 5).

- Among those jobs still providing health benefits, from 2001 to 2004 the average employee's contribution (per family) increased 49 percent, from $149 per month to $222 per month,[1] and the average employee's annual deductible increased 35 percent (see Chapter 5).

- In 2004, 50 percent fewer large employers offered retiree health benefits than in 1993 (21 percent in 2004 versus 40 percent in 1993, see Chapter 8)—and soon no employers will offer retiree health benefits except those that are obligated to under expiring union contracts.

- The cost of health benefits now exceeds profits for most large employers and is rising much faster than GDP—the average $14,000 per year ($1,166 per month) family premium in 2006 for employer-sponsored health insurance was more than the annual wages earned by some employees.

- U.S. healthcare costs have risen from one-twentieth of GDP in 1960 to almost one-sixth of GDP in 2006, and, unless something is done, healthcare costs threaten to bankrupt the U.S. economy by 2020 (see Chapter 1). A primary reason for rising costs is that most doctors and patients are still spending "other people's money" when it comes to healthcare—see Chapters 9 and 10 for examples of how much you could save if you wanted to on your medical expenses.

While about 50 percent of Americans today receive health insurance from an employer, this number is rapidly declining due to employers either dropping health coverage entirely or increasing the amount contributed by employees and their families for health insurance.

Individual/Family Health Insurance— The New Way

Fortunately, there is a much better alternative now available— individual/family health insurance.

- Close to 4 percent of Americans, or about 13 million people, now have individual or family health insurance policies that they have purchased themselves—the premium on these policies cannot be substantially increased, nor can the policy be canceled or benefits reduced because of illness.

- High-quality, affordable individual/family policies are now available in all 50 states (plus Washington, D.C.) at an average monthly premium of $173 per single and $541 per family in 2006 (see Appendix

A). This is less than half the monthly price for similar coverage from employer-sponsored group plans ($375 per single and $1,166 per family).

- Individual/family policies theoretically cost about half the price of employer-sponsored plans *for similar coverage,* but in practice cost as little as one quarter the price because many people don't choose "similar coverage" when spending their own money—they choose to purchase less expensive, higher-deductible policies excluding benefits (like maternity and pharmacy) they don't think they need. High-deductible HSA-qualified individual/family plans were available nationwide at an average monthly premium of $92 per single individual and $272 per family in 2006—about one-fourth the price of employer-sponsored low-deductible plans.

- In 2006, instead of an employer-sponsored group plan, some employers began offering defined contribution health benefit plans, whereby the employer simply reimburses the employee, tax-free, for the cost of their individual/family policy. This effectively lowers the cost of an individual/family policy up to 50 percent, since the employer receives a tax deduction and the employee is not taxed on the reimbursed amount. Most people today with individual/family policies are paying their premiums themselves without an employer—which effectively costs them up to twice as much on an after-tax basis.

- Since only about 80 percent of applicants medically qualify at the lowest rates for these affordable individual/family policies, every state now has state-guaranteed coverage for people with preexisting health conditions—coverage is typically the same as for healthy individuals except that the state pays the insurance carrier for any losses. Consumers pay about twice the normal (healthy) price for state-guaranteed coverage, but only for the one family member with the health issue, so the blended price is not that much more for an entire family (see Appendix A for examples in your state).

- Health Savings Accounts and other new health benefit financial tools like "use it or keep it" HRAs will convert U.S. healthcare from a bureaucratic, wasteful industry into an efficient sector of our economy, similar to restaurants or communications, and will offer consumers an unlimited choice of providers, better quality, and more service for less money each year due to technological advances.

The change from expensive employer-sponsored group plans to affordable individual/family policies is already under way, and will accelerate as more employers adopt new plans to pay employee premiums on individual/family policies with pretax

dollars—effectively lowering the after-tax price of such policies by up to 50 percent.

The change is also under way from wasteful low- or no-
deductible health plans to efficient HSA and HRA-type high-
deductible plans—in which consumers make their own
medical purchases and receive the savings and rewards for a
healthy lifestyle as tax-free deposits to their HSA or HRA.

The Complete Reform of U.S. Healthcare

High-deductible health insurance and other consumer-directed health
benefits tools will do much more than just save money on paperwork—
they will cause nothing short of a revolution in how and where medical
care is delivered.

Once consumers are choosing their own medical providers and using
their own money for healthcare, they will demand and receive better service for lower prices—just as they do now in every other sector of our
economy except healthcare and public education. Healthcare "category
busters," like Office Depot, PETsMART, and Home Depot in their areas
of the economy, will supply the widest selection of medical products and
services at the lowest possible prices. Specialty medical providers will
open faster than fast-food restaurants.

High-quality discount healthcare is already here: Costco has
begun offering individual health insurance, and Target is
opening "Minute Clinics" in selected department stores.
Customers (i.e., patients) are served on a first-come, first-
served basis and are given a pager so they can shop around
the store while they wait.[2] Customer satisfaction is much
higher than with traditional doctor's office visits.

Since every treatment has a cost paid by the patient, patients will
become more knowledgeable about their ailments when they speak to
their physicians, and they will consider the costs and benefits of each sug-
gested treatment. New medical providers will offer money-back guarantees or charge prices based on delivering what they promise—such as
lowering blood pressure, lowering cholesterol, or helping patients lose
weight. The emphasis in medical-related R&D will shift from products
that can be sold to health insurers to those that give consumers real bene-

fits—consumers spending their own money are more savvy customers than executives working at health insurance companies.

When LASIK eye surgery first came out in the 1990s it cost $3,000 or more per eye and was performed mostly in hospitals. Because LASIK was not covered by health insurance, it was one of the few major medical procedures subject to free market forces. After only 10 years, in response to popular demand from consumers spending their own money, the quality greatly increased, the price dropped to $500 or less per eye, and the treatment is now mostly performed at convenient retail locations. This is what will eventually happen to most of the U.S. healthcare system.

As the LASIK example shows, most operations in hospitals are extremely inefficient, which is why they currently consume 45 percent of medical spending. This will change once hospitals are subject to genuine competition, especially from hospitals outside the United States. For example, some of the best private hospitals in the world today are located outside the United States in countries like Thailand and India. These hospitals cater to an international clientele seeking the best service, not necessarily the lowest price, and yet they cost only a small fraction of what hospitals cost in the United States. They often have U.S.-trained physicians, deliver safer and better services in a comfortable, resort-type atmosphere, and some have full-time local facilities inside the United States for patient recruitment and follow-up treatment. As illustrated on a recent *60 Minutes* television segment,[3] a typical patient facing a $100,000 quintuple bypass operation is able to get much better service at one of these hospitals for $12,000, and similar savings exist for patients electing voluntary procedures like cosmetic plastic surgery.

Of course, most people will not want or be able to fly overseas for hospital care, but this competition will force U.S. hospitals to retool their operations to provide better care at a lower cost—just as competition similarly forces the U.S. auto and computer businesses to constantly offer more for less.

Many people reading this book can remember when making a long-distance phone call or flying across the United States was a significant expense. U.S. business history is rampant with what happens when the free market, driven by intelligent consumers, is allowed to work its magic—to the betterment of all. We are about to find out how good quality can get, and how low prices can fall, with *The New Health Insurance Solution.*

Who Wins and Who Loses with *The New Health Insurance Solution?*

Eventually, everyone wins with *The New Health Insurance Solution.* When medical care finally joins the free market, consumers will learn what medical services actually cost. Then they will drive down prices and increase quality—just as competition has done in every other sector of our economy.

However, as with any change, over the short term somebody loses and somebody gains until the free market increases the total size of the health-care pie for everyone.

Unhealthy People Lose $ and Healthy People Gain $ with HSAs

If you are unhealthy, whether you participate in an employer-sponsored group plan or have your own individual/family policy, you are probably going to see an increase in the cost of your health benefits.

For example, suppose today your employer plan has a $500 annual deductible and your employer unilaterally (1) raises the annual deductible to $5,000 and (2) contributes $2,000 a year to each employee's HSA. The 80 percent of healthy employees who spend less than $500 a year effectively receive a $2,000 tax-free raise and tax-free investment growth of this amount for future medical expenses. Unhealthy employees are now out of pocket up to $2,500 a year—they pay up to $4,500 more for their medical expenses (because of the increase in their deductible) less the $2,000 employer contribution to their HSA.

Similarly, if you have an individual/family policy, let's say you increase your annual deductible from $500 to $5,000 for a $2,000 reduction in your annual premium. If you are healthy, you save $2,000 that you can deposit tax-free into your HSA. If you become unhealthy, you are also out of pocket up to $2,500 a year—you pay up to $4,500 more for your medical expenses less the $2,000 you save on your annual premium. Separately, if you are overweight or a smoker, the cost of your monthly premium is likely to increase 25 to 50 percent with an individual/family policy.

Increasing the annual deductible to $5,000 coupled with a $2,000 employer HSA contribution (or reduction in premium) gives healthy people the equivalent of a $2,000 raise and costs unhealthy people up to $2,500 a year for each year they remain unhealthy.

However, this $2,500 per year or more additional burden may turn into a blessing for some people whose unhealthiness is caused by their lifestyle.

The increased expense could cause them to change their diet and exercise routine to become healthier. Today, for many people, being unhealthy is a lifestyle choice rather than a random event.

The majority of healthcare expenses today are spent on the two-thirds of Americans who are overweight and the one-fourth who smoke. Increasing the amount they pay for health insurance while offering them wellness programs like weight loss and smoking cessation could provide the impetus some of them need to change their lifestyle.

Healthy and Especially Unhealthy Individuals Gain Peace of Mind

The biggest financial worry most unhealthy people have is not the extra money it costs to be unhealthy—their biggest worry is losing their health insurance if they are no longer able to work. Between cutting expenses, working at home, and support from family and friends, they know they will get by if they lose their job—but they will be in real trouble if they lose their health insurance.

Three-fourths of the millions of families who have filed medical bankruptcy had health insurance when they became ill but lost their health insurance when they could no longer work. Individual/family health insurance solves this problem because you don't lose your insurance when you lose your job.

This fear of losing your health insurance applies equally to healthy individuals—anyone can develop a major illness or be involved in an accident.

When you obtain your own individual or family health insurance policy, either a normal policy from a private carrier (because you are healthy) or roughly the same coverage guaranteed by your state (because you are unhealthy), you get a priceless benefit—the peace of mind that comes with guaranteeing your family affordable health insurance regardless of what happens to your job or to their health.

One of the biggest benefits of *The New Health Insurance Solution* is the peace of mind you get from knowing you have your own individual/family health insurance policy regardless of what happens to your health or your employment—a policy on which the premium cannot be raised nor the policy canceled because of your future health problems.

Some State Governments Lose Short Term, but All Win Long Term

Some state governments may initially lose money as employers switch from defined benefit group plans to defined contribution individual/family plans—because more unhealthy employees and members of their families will require state-guaranteed, state-subsidized coverage.

However, this cost will be offset by millions of currently uninsured people who will be purchasing for themselves, or through their employer, affordable high-deductible individual/family policies—saving state and local governments money they currently spend providing care to the uninsured through publicly funded hospitals. As shown in Appendices A and B, high-deductible HSA-qualified health insurance policies cost less than $90 per month per adult ($272 per month per family) in most states and only one-fourth the price of traditional employer-sponsored group coverage.

The cost of more unhealthy individuals receiving state-guaranteed coverage will be offset by millions of people no longer relying on public hospitals because they (or their employer) can now afford individual/family high-deductible health insurance—which typically costs one-fourth the price of employer-sponsored group plans.

If everyone purchased at least a high-deductible HSA-qualified policy when they turned 18, almost no one would require state-guaranteed coverage, since a future illness would be covered by a private insurance carrier. Some states are considering mandating that employers withhold wages and/or contribute to defined contribution plans to fund catastrophic health insurance as a condition of employment—just as all states today require drivers to have automobile liability insurance. This is far superior to mandating, as does Hawaii, that employers pay for employer-sponsored group defined benefit plans—such a mandate would bankrupt many small businesses and drive jobs overseas.

Some states may soon require employees to submit "proof of health insurance" to employers as a condition of employment, just as drivers today are required to have automobile liability insurance.

The states that take the lead in promoting a competitive individual/family and HSA health insurance marketplace, plus take care of their uninsurables through state-guaranteed coverage, will benefit the most—they will yield increased taxes, employment, and revenues from businesses seeking to locate or expand within their borders.

The availability of affordable individual/family health insurance policies for employees, plus state-guaranteed coverage for unhealthy individuals, will become an important factor for employers when choosing states in which to locate or to expand.

The U.S. Economy and U.S. Consumers Benefit the Most

U.S. healthcare currently costs almost one-sixth of total GDP—about one out of every six employees works in the healthcare industry. But millions of these people don't do anything to help anyone's health.

Medical providers spend a significant amount of their time and personnel fighting a paper war with employers and insurance companies to get paid—a war fought by millions of people who could otherwise be serving patients or more positively adding to our GDP. "At a rough guess, between 2 million and 3 million Americans are employed by insurers and healthcare providers not to deliver healthcare, but to pass the buck for that care to someone else."[4]

Amazingly, about 31 percent ($620 billion) of the roughly $2 trillion each year we currently spend on healthcare goes toward administration costs[5]—that's twice the $325 billion annual cost of Medicare, and 1.5 times the $400 billion we spend on defense.

The most immediate gain from the switch to high-deductible health insurance is saving billions on paperwork, since most medical transactions will now be paid for at time of service by consumers themselves.

Over the long term, the biggest winners are the U.S. economy and U.S. consumers.

Employers will be relieved of a crushing moral and financial obligation that they should never have taken on in the first place. The obligation to provide health insurance will be rightfully returned to individuals, with government providing only for those too poor, too old, or too ill to take care of themselves—just as it is today with higher education, life insurance, retirement, and every other aspect of our lives except defense.

Hundreds of billions of dollars now wasted on bureaucratic "sickness care" will be given back to consumers as cash savings and as contributions to their health savings accounts—they will spend this money to improve their lives on preventive care, education, retirement, and new products and services.

Businesses will flourish as billions in new profits (from cost savings) are multiplied sevenfold in our economy—creating tens of millions of new jobs producing real products and services that consumers want, jobs that will be first available to the millions of displaced paper pushers from the healthcare industry.

What Should Be Done Now to Improve Health Insurance?

Major pieces of legislation have already been passed to allow (1) tax-deductible employer-reimbursed individual/family health insurance and (2) high-deductible health insurance with Health Savings Accounts. However, there are six important governmental changes left to complete to ensure better health insurance for every American at less cost. You should contact your congressman, senator, and appropriate state officials on each of the following six issues.

Allow Health Insurance to Be Sold Across State Lines

The largest determinant of the monthly premium for individual/family health insurance is not your age or health but the state in which you live. In 2006, a single individual living in New Hampshire was able to get a low-deductible individual/family policy for $163 per month, but paid three times the price, $503 per month ($4,080 more each year), if he or she lived just across the border in Massachusetts. A family of four paid $342 per month for similar coverage in Philadelphia, but paid almost four times the price, $1,244 per month ($10,824 more each year), if they lived just across the border in Cherry Hill, New Jersey (see Appendix A).

Amazingly, because of an outdated federal law passed in 1945, it is currently illegal for a carrier to sell health insurance to an out-of-state individual—unless the out-of-state insurer goes through an expensive filing process and meets the unique health insurance requirements of the individual's state of residence. If this law were repealed, anyone could purchase a health insurance policy from any carrier in any state—take a look at Appendix A to see how much you could save. A resident of Maine paying $278 per month for an HSA-qualified single policy could have purchased similar coverage from Humana in Michigan for one-fifth the price, $54 a month—saving $2,688 per year. A family of four living in West Virginia and paying $453 per month for an HSA-qualified family policy could have purchased similar coverage from United Healthcare in Ohio for one-third the price, $151 per month—saving $3,624 per year.

In Michigan in 1908, when Henry Ford produced the Model T costing $825, there were thousands of small auto manufacturers in the United States making cars costing $10,000 or more. To protect their own manufacturers, neighboring states passed laws claiming that the Model T was dangerous and thus not allowed to drive on their roads. Eventually, the federal government stepped in and regulated the automobile industry—mandating that any automobile meeting certain minimum standards could be freely driven in every state.

As of this writing, there is a simple 14-page bill in Congress designed to do exactly the same for health insurance, The Health Care Choice Act (HR 2355).[6] Opposing this bill are the hundred or so small regional health insurance companies that are terrified of competition and a few overpaid bureaucrats in state insurance departments who would rather see their citizens go uninsured than be able to purchase quality, affordable health insurance regulated by someone else.

Allowing consumers to purchase health insurance from carriers in any state will not just increase competition 50-fold and drive down prices; the massive increase in competition will also allow millions more individuals with preexisting conditions to get private health insurance without having to rely on more expensive state-guaranteed coverage.

Make All Health Insurance Premiums Tax Deductible

Also at the time of this writing, a different bill in Congress would make all health insurance premiums tax deductible for individuals, The Health Care Freedom of Choice Act (HR 66).[7]

This extremely simple bill would take away the main reason employers are involved in health insurance and finally level the playing field for all Americans, whether they are employed, self-employed, or unemployed. Overnight, this bill could reduce the after-tax price of individual/family health insurance for consumers 25 to 50 percent. This change will not substantially affect the federal budget deficit since most U.S. citizens effectively already have tax-deductible health insurance through their employer-sponsored plan.

Making all health insurance premiums tax deductible for all consumers is long overdue—this simple change in our tax code

will correct a terrible inequity and eventually return responsibility for health insurance to where it belongs—individuals and government instead of employers.

Make All Healthcare Providers Disclose Prices

As illustrated in Chapter 4, almost all healthcare providers, from major hospitals to individual doctor's offices, charge wildly varying prices for the exact same service depending on the network (PPO) in which the patient is a participant. The same doctor visit might cost a cash-paying immigrant $110, while a person whose employer bargained down the price pays only $42. Hospitals such as the Cleveland Clinic routinely charge one patient $14,367 and another $3,010 for the exact same service.

While there is nothing wrong with large customers bargaining for better prices, today there is no longer any true "retail" price in medical care. Providers have artificially inflated their retail prices two to five times just to meet ridiculous contracts forcing them to give 50 to 80 percent discounts to large purchasers. The terrible side effect is that the working poor and other people without health insurance are charged two to five times the price paid by most people for healthcare—and often are driven to bankruptcy when they cannot pay these exorbitant prices.

In 1934 the Securities Exchange Act created the SEC and mandated that U.S. public companies disclose accurate financial information. This act did not tell businesspeople how to run their business—it merely told them that they must disclose pertinent facts to investors or be subject to criminal prosecution. A similar act is now needed for all U.S. healthcare providers who receive direct or indirect federal subsidies (through tax benefits) for their services.

Healthcare providers and especially pharmaceutical companies should be required to disclose their prices and all discounts given off these prices. Open disclosure will drive consumerism and lower prices for all—plus help stop the terrible way medical providers overcharge their poorest customers 200 to 500 percent. A consumer paying a $14,367 hospital bill has a right to know that another person is being charged only $3,010 for the exact same service. People standing in line at a pharmacy have a right to know when they are being charged two to three times the price of the person next to them for the exact same drug.

Armed with this information, consumers will be able to seek out the best networks and be able to negotiate fairly with medical providers. Moreover, once their prices are out in the open, some employees of medical providers will refuse to work for organizations that price-gouge the poorest of families when they are most vulnerable.

Allow International Competition for Pharmaceuticals

The peace and prosperity of the United States and the free world is based mostly on free trade with other nations. It is simply ludicrous that the federal government currently does not openly allow, and force the FDA to regulate, the importation of less-expensive, identical brand-name prescription drugs from other countries—some of which have better consumer protection standards than those the FDA provides for Americans.

As illustrated in Chapter 9, prescription drugs from pharmacies in countries like Canada cost about half the price of the identical name-brand drugs in the United States.

Protect Bankrupt Families from 200 to 500 Percent Medical Bills

When the United States was founded in 1776, one of the founding principles was that a person in economic trouble should be able to file bankruptcy and start over—bankruptcy protection was incorporated by our founding fathers into the original U.S. Constitution. On April 20, 2005, a new bankruptcy code was signed into law that, sadly, prevents millions of American families from being able to discharge their debts and start over. People who earn above the median income in their state are now required to pay off certain medical expenses and credit card balances even after filing for bankruptcy.

Two very important exemptions were left out of this new bankruptcy code—you should contact your congressmen and senators to amend their legislation as follows:

- *Medical expenses.* When families are forced to pay medical expenses after filing bankruptcy, the amount they pay should be reduced to the "usual and customary" amount of medical services actually consumed, not the two to five times inflated amount that the hospital never really expects most people to pay (e.g., the $3,010 figure in the Cleveland Clinic example versus the exorbitant $14,367 fake "retail" price).

- *Credit card balances.* By the time a family files for bankruptcy, $4,000 worth of actual purchases has often turned into a $10,000 credit card balance, including 24 percent interest, penalties, and late fees. Similar to passing through medical expenses, the now-bankrupt family should be held responsible only for the actual $4,000 amount they spent, not the $6,000 in bank-added interest and fees. If this law is not amended, banks will be issuing credit to millions more people not capable of handling credit—gambling that one day the bank will get its $6,000 in interest and fees even if the cardholder files for bankruptcy.

No one wins, especially children, when a family is forced to seek federal bankruptcy protection to maintain basic food, clothing, and shelter. Forcing these families to then pay off 200–500 percent inflated medical bills is cruel and unusual punishment for some of our nation's least fortunate citizens.

End Federal Lifetime Health Benefits for Congressmen, Senators, and Government Officials

The primary reason that we need the first five changes is because, when it comes to health insurance, we have created an elite class of a certain type of animal straight out of George Orwell's *Animal Farm*. This elite class consists of our elected federal and state officials who have voted themselves and their associates unlimited lifetime health benefits paid for by taxpayers (see Chapter 8).[8] In doing so, they have removed themselves from being participants in solving the terrible health insurance crisis that affects the rest of American citizens. They do not directly feel the pain of America's health insurance problems.

Make the following pledge now if you would like to ensure that all Americans, and not just those savvy enough to read this book, can one day get affordable health insurance:

I pledge not to vote for any politician unless he or she refuses to accept government-provided health insurance. Instead, all elected and appointed government employees should receive a defined contribution allowance and be forced to purchase health insurance on their own from an insurance carrier in their home state.

Regardless of whether these six suggestions are enacted, the revolution from employer-sponsored health insurance toward individual opportunity and responsibility is well under way. Decades from now we will look back at the period from 1945 to 2005 as the Dark Ages for U.S. health insurance, and 2006 as the beginning of the New Health Insurance Revolution.

In the 1980s, when I was a lecturer at Moscow University in the former USSR, I was embarrassed when questions were asked of me about U.S.

health insurance—this embarrassment led me to testify before Congress about the problems with employer-sponsored healthcare. Today I am no longer embarrassed—I am gushing with American patriotic pride in our free enterprise system.

In writing this book, I sat down each week to write about a different problem with U.S. health insurance—from buying long-term-disability insurance to getting affordable coverage for a sick child. And each week I found that some enterprising entrepreneur, corporate health benefits executive, or dedicated government official had already focused on the problem I was writing about and had created a solution. The main problem is that because the solutions are so new, most people don't yet know about them. My goal with this book is to let America know about these new solutions. I hope this book and its web site (www.TNHIS.com) help you find health insurance solutions that will save money for your future medical expenses and better protect your family.

State-by-State Guide to Individual/Family Health Insurance Costs

This appendix shows the monthly cost, in each state, of representative individual/family health insurance policies for a healthy single person (male, age 35), a healthy family of four (parents, age 35, and children, ages 5 and 8), and a person (male, age 35) with a preexisting medical condition who does not medically qualify for private health insurance. See each state for policy details.

The following two pages contain a summary of representative or typical health insurance costs in all states. While the policies for each state were chosen to be as similar as possible, they are not directly comparable—benefits vary between states and between carriers.

Please refer to the index for explanations of terms not listed here (e.g., *prescription co-pay*).

Definition of Key Terms in Appendix A

PP   Per person.

Average cost of individual policy sold in 2004   This figure is based on 82,000 policies sold to single individuals online by ehealthinsurance .com in 44 states during a six-month period in 2004 (see Chapter 2).

Guaranteed issue   A legal requirement in some states that health insurance carriers accept all applicants regardless of health status, age, etc. New York, New Jersey, Massachusetts, Maine, and Vermont are guaranteed-issue states.

Community rated   A legal requirement in some states that all applicants (both high- and low-risk) are charged the same health insurance premium for the same coverage regardless of health status, age, etc. New York, New Jersey, Massachusetts, Maine, and Vermont are community-rated states.

HIPAA-eligible (federally eligible) individual   Person whose health insurance has been terminated and who has elected and exhausted COBRA (if offered). Federal law requires that each state offer its HIPAA-eligible residents individual health insurance without exclusions for preexisting conditions (see Chapter 3).

State-guaranteed coverage   All states have a state risk pool or its equivalent to provide state-subsidized coverage to individuals who cannot medically qualify for private health insurance—in 10 states you must be HIPAA-eligible to get this state-guaranteed coverage (see Chapter 7).

Applicants Who Cannot Afford Health Insurance

All states have programs (e.g., Medicaid) for residents receiving public assistance or who cannot afford health insurance—these programs vary greatly and are not included in this appendix. See Chapter 7 and contact your department of health insurance to learn about programs for low-income residents in your state.

Monthly Cost in All States of a Typical Individual Health Insurance Policy (Male, Age 35, 2006)

State	Traditional (Low-Deductible) Policy	HSA Policy (High-Deductible)	State	Traditional (Low-Deductible) Policy	HSA Policy (High-Deductible)
AL	$210	$118	MT	$257	$131
AK	$192	$104	NE	$109	$ 79
AZ	$120	$ 83	NV	$121	$ 89
AR	$123	$ 58	NH	$163	$133
CA	$204	$ 97	NJ[a]	$411	—
CO	$148	$ 90	NM	$131	$ 90
CT	$132	$ 94	NY[a]	$302	—
DE	$143	$ 88	NC	$125	$102
DC	$146	$109	ND	$169	$ 88
FL	$168	$ 73	OH	$100	$ 55
GA	$154	$104	OK	$183	$ 88
HI	$162	$ 82	OR	$157	$116
ID	$146	$ 70	PA	$119	$ 69
IL	$ 98	$ 85	RI[a]	$203	—
IN	$126	$ 81	SC	$148	$ 91
IA	$116	$ 55	SD	$163	$113
KS	$167	$ 98	TN	$137	$ 74
KY	$ 79	$ 55	TX	$117	$ 77
LA	$188	$102	UT	$115	$ 99
ME	$445	$278	VT[a]	$374	—
MD	$134	$ 66	VA	$138	$ 63
MA[a]	$503	—	WA	$167	$ 98
MI	$103	$ 54	WV	$191	$125
MN	$142	$100	WI	$118	$ 68
MS	$161	$ 77	WY	$162	$101
MO	$124	$ 76	Avg	$173	$ 92

Note: See individual state pages for details on each policy.
[a]A few states have either not yet modified their regulations to allow HSAs or carriers are not yet offering individual/family HSA-qualified policies.

Nationally, the average monthly premium is $173 per month for a traditional policy and $92 per month for a high-deductible HSA-qualified policy. The average annual deductible is $1,001 per year traditional and $2,596 per year HSA.

Cost of Health Insurance for a Single Applicant—National Average (2006)

	Traditional (Low-Deductible) Policy	HSA-Qualified Policy (High-Deductible)
Average premium	$173/month	$92/month
Average deductible	$1,001/year	$2,596/year

Monthly Cost in all 50 States of a Typical Family Health Insurance Policy (Two Parents, Age 35; Children, Ages 5 and 8, 2006)

State	Traditional (Low-Deductible) Policy	HSA Policy (High-Deductible)	State	Traditional (Low-Deductible) Policy	HSA Policy (High-Deductible)
AL	$ 622	$317	MT	$ 637	$295
AK	$ 695	$370	NE	$ 422	$291
AZ	$ 394	$267	NV	$ 388	$264
AR	$ 430	$169	NH	$ 503	$469
CA	$ 617	$294	NJ[a]	$1,244	—
CO	$ 460	$267	NM	$ 418	$287
CT	$ 465	$259	NY[a]	$ 734	—
DE	$ 480	$237	NC	$ 482	$271
DC	$ 396	$296	ND	$ 425	$201
FL	$ 586	$204	OH	$ 402	$151
GA	$ 595	$404	OK	$ 637	$251
HI	$ 485	$328	OR	$ 399	$325
ID	$ 539	$253	PA	$ 341	$181
IL	$ 348	$308	RI[a]	$ 625	—
IN	$ 506	$299	SC	$ 556	$292
IA	$ 398	$151	SD	$ 592	$371
KS	$ 581	$323	TN	$ 491	$202
KY	$ 413	$262	TX	$ 403	$188
LA	$ 566	$282	UT	$ 351	$302
ME	$1,123	$430	VT[a]	$1,010	—
MD	$ 462	$180	VA	$ 502	$172
MA[a]	$ 906	—	WA	$ 525	$255
MI	$ 358	$180	WV	$ 743	$453
MN	$ 501	$294	WI	$ 428	$184
MS	$ 551	$209	WY	$ 472	$267
MO	$ 382	$272	Avg	$ 541	$272

Note: See individual state pages for details on each policy.
[a]A few states have either not yet modified their regulations to allow HSAs, or carriers are not yet offering individual/family HSA-qualified policies.

Nationally, the average monthly premium is $541 per month for a traditional policy and $272 per month for a high-deductible HSA-qualified policy. The average annual deductible is $2,428 per year traditional and $5,171 per year HSA.

Cost of Family Health Insurance—National Average (2006)

	Traditional (Low-Deductible) Policy	HSA-Qualified Policy (High-Deductible)
Average premium	$541/month	$272/month
Average deductible	$2,428/year	$5,171/year

Alabama Department of Insurance
(334) 269-3550
www.aldoi.org
Guaranteed Issue ☐
Community Rated ☐

Montgomery
★

Average Cost of Individual Policy Sold in 2004: $173/month[a]
(single, average age 28, healthy)

Typical Healthy Individual/Family Coverage (2006)

	Traditional Co-Pay Policy[b]		High-Deductible Policy[c]	
	Single	Family	Single	Family
Monthly premium	$210	$622	$97	$294
Annual deductible	$1,000	$3,000	$2,400	$4,800
Annual out-of-pocket max	$2,500	$5,000	$3,200	$5,800
Doctor visit co-pay	$25/2 visits then 50% after ded	$25/2 visits then 50% after ded	—	—
Prescription co-pay	$10–25+ 20% after $500 ded	$10–25+ 20% after $500 ded	—	—
Lifetime maximum	$7 million	$6 million	$6 million	$6 million

State-Guaranteed Coverage for People with Preexisting Conditions

Alabama Health Insurance Plan for HIPAA-Eligible Applicants (AHIP)[d]

Monthly Premium	Annual Deductible	Annual OOP Max	Doctor Visit Co-Pay	Prescription Co-Pay	Lifetime Maximum
$309	$1,000	$1,500 + hospital ded	$25	20% + $500 ded	$1 million

HIPAA-eligible individuals: Applicants are guaranteed acceptance into AHIP with no exclusions for preexisting conditions.

Alabama guarantees coverage only to residents with health issues who are HIPAA-eligible or low-income individuals.

For More Information: See www.TNHIS.com/AL

---

[a]From 82,000 policies sold nationally online in 2004, see first page of Appendix A.
[b]Fortis PPO X-tra; single applicant (M/35); family applicant (M/35), spouse (F/35), children (F/8, M/5) from Montgomery, AL 36104; quoted 5.2.05.
[c]Fortis One Deductible; single applicant (M/35); family applicant (M/35), spouse (F/35), children (F/8, M/5) from Montgomery, AL 36104; quoted 5.2.05.
[d]AHIP Traditional Indemnity Plan C; single applicant (M/35); quoted 5.5.05 from www.seib.state.al.us.

Alaska Division of Insurance
(907) 465-2515
www.commerce.state.ak.us/insurance/
Guaranteed Issue ☐
Community Rated ☐

Average Cost for an Individual Policy: $157/month[a]
(single, age 36, healthy, sold in 2004)

Typical Healthy Individual/Family Coverage

	Traditional Co-Pay Policy[b]		High-Deductible Policy[c]	
	Single	Family	Single	Family
Monthly premium	$192	$695	$104	$370
Annual deductible	$1,000	$3,000	$2,600	$5,150
Annual out-of-pocket max	$2,000	$6,000	$2,600	$5,150
Doctor visit co-pay	20% after ded	20% after ded	—	—
Prescription co-pay	80–85% (discount card)	80–85% (discount card)	—	—
Lifetime maximum	$5 million	$5 million	$5 million	$5 million

State-Guaranteed Coverage for People with Preexisting Conditions

Alaska Comprehensive Health Insurance Association (ACHIA)[d]

Monthly Premium	Annual Deductible	Annual OOP Max	Doctor Visit Co-Pay	Prescription Co-Pay	Lifetime Maximum
$486	$1,000	$2,500	20%	20%	$1 million

Eligibility: (1) Alaska resident for 12 months, (2) ineligible for coverage under any other health insurance plan, and (3) rejected from health insurer within the past six months, accepted with restrictive riders substantially reducing coverage or accepted with qualifying condition, or (4) federally eligible.

HIPAA-eligible individuals: Applicants are guaranteed health insurance coverage through ACHIA with no exclusions for preexisting conditions and without a 12-month residency requirement.

For More Information: See www.TNHIS.com/AK

---

[a]From 82,000 policies sold nationally online in 2004, see first page of Appendix A.
[b]Celtic Managed Indemnity 80/20 Plan; single applicant (M/35); family applicant (M/35), spouse (F/35), children (F/8, M/5) from Juneau, AK 99801; quoted 5.2.05.
[c]CelticSaver HSA PPO; single applicant (M/35); family applicant (M/35), spouse (F/35), two children from Anchorage, AK 99501 (HSA for this company not available in Juneau); quoted 5.13.05 from www.celtic-net.com.
[d]ACHIA PPO Plan; single applicant (M/35); quoted 5.5.05 from www.achia.com.

Arizona Department of Insurance
(602) 912-8444
www.id.state.az.us/
Guaranteed Issue ☐
Community Rated ☐

AZ

Phoenix
★

Average Cost of Individual Policy Sold in 2004: $153/month[a]
(single, average age 34, healthy)

Typical Healthy Individual/Family Coverage (2006)

	Traditional Co-Pay Policy[b]		High-Deductible Policy[c]	
	Single	Family	Single	Family
Monthly premium	$120	$394	$83	$267
Annual deductible	$1,500	$3,000	$2,750	$5,500
Annual out-of-pocket max	$3,000	$6,000	$5,000	$10,000
Doctor visit co-pay	$20–35	$20–35	—	—
Prescription co-pay	$15–40 + $250 ded	$15–40 + $250 ded	—	—
Lifetime maximum	$5 million	$5 million	$5 million	$5 million

State-Guaranteed Coverage for People with Preexisting Conditions (2006)

Individual Portability Coverage for HIPAA-Eligible Applicant[d]

Monthly Premium	Annual Deductible	Annual OOP Max	Doctor Visit Co-Pay	Prescription Co-Pay	Lifetime Maximum
$493	$1,000	$2,000	$25–40	$15–120	$3 million

HIPAA-eligible individuals: Arizona requires that all private insurance companies offer HIPAA-eligible applicants an individual policy without exclusions for preexisting conditions.

Arizona guarantees coverage only to residents with health issues who are HIPAA-eligible or low-income individuals.

For More Information: See www.TNHIS.com/AZ

---

[a]From 82,000 policies sold nationally online in 2004, see first page of Appendix A.
[b]Aetna PPO 1500; single applicant (M/35); family applicant (M/35), spouse (F/35), children (F/8, M/5) from Phoenix, AZ 85003; quoted 4.29.05.
[c]Aetna High Deductible PPO 1 (HSA Compatible); single applicant (M/35); family applicant (M/35), spouse (F/35), children (F/8, M/5) from Phoenix, AZ 85003; quoted 4.29.05.
[d]AZ Blue Cross Blue Shield BluePreferred $1,000 deductible; single applicant (M/35) from Phoenix, AZ 85003; quoted 5.11.05 www.bcbsaz.com.

Arkansas Insurance Department
(501) 371-2600
www.state.ar.us/insurance
Guaranteed Issue ☐
Community Rated ☐

AR

Little Rock
★

Average Cost of Individual Policy Sold in 2004: $209/month[a]
(single, average age 37, healthy)

Typical Healthy Individual/Family Coverage (2006)

	Traditional Co-Pay Policy[b]		High-Deductible Policy[c]	
	Single	Family	Single	Family
Monthly premium	$123	$430	$58	$169
Annual deductible	$750	$1,500	$2,650	$5,250
Annual out-of-pocket max	$3,000	$6,000	$2,650	$5,250
Doctor visit co-pay	$35	$35	—	—
Prescription co-pay	$20–50 + $250 ded	$20–50 + $250 ded	—	—
Lifetime maximum	$3 million	$3 million pp	$3 million	$3 million pp

State-Guaranteed Coverage for People with Preexisting Conditions (2006)

Arkansas Comprehensive Health Insurance Pool (CHIP)[d]

Monthly Premium	Annual Deductible	Annual OOP Max	Doctor Visit Co-Pay	Prescription Co-Pay	Lifetime Maximum
$193	$1,000	$2,000	20%	20%	$1 million

Eligibility: (1) Arkansas resident for 90 days, (2) ineligible for coverage through a group health plan, Medicare, or Medicaid, (3) not enrolled in any other health insurance policy, (4) not previously terminated from CHIP coverage, and (5) CHIP premium cannot be paid by government sponsored program, or (6) federally eligible.

HIPAA-eligible individuals: Applicants are guaranteed acceptance into the CHIP with no exclusions for preexisting conditions.

For More Information: See www.TNHIS.com/AR

---

[a]From 82,000 policies sold nationally online in 2004, see first page of Appendix A.
[b]Golden Rule Copay 35; single applicant (M/35); family applicant (M/35), spouse (F/35), children (F/8, M/5) from Little Rock, AR 72201; quoted 5.2.05.
[c]Golden Rule Single HSA Saver; single applicant (M/35); family applicant (M/35), spouse (F/35), children (F/8, M/5) from Little Rock, AR 72201; quoted 5.2.05.
[d]AR Comprehensive Health Insurance Plan; single applicant (M/35); quoted 5.7.05 from http://chiparkansas.org/.

California Department of Insurance
Consumer Communications Bureau
(213) 897-8921
www.insurance.ca.gov/
Guaranteed Issue ☐
Community Rated ☐

CA

 Sacramento

Average Cost of Individual Policy Sold in 2004: $140/month[a]
(single, average age 32, healthy)

Typical Healthy Individual/Family Coverage (2006)

	Traditional Co-Pay Policy[b]		High-Deductible Policy[c]	
	Single	Family	Single	Family
Monthly premium	$204	$617	$97	$294
Annual deductible	$1,500	$3,000	$2,400	$4,800
Annual out-of-pocket max	$4,500	$9,000	$3,200	$5,800
Doctor visit co-pay	$40	$40	—	—
Prescription co-pay	$7–60 + $250 brandname ded	$7–60 + $250 brandname ded	—	—
Lifetime maximum	$5 million	$5 million	$5 million	$5 million

State-Guaranteed Coverage for People with Preexisting Conditions (2006)

California Major Risk Medical Insurance Program (MRMIP)[d]

Monthly Premium	Annual Deductible	Annual OOP Max	Doctor Visit Co-Pay	Prescription Co-Pay	Lifetime Maximum
$356	$0	$2,500	$25	20%	$1.5 million

Eligibility: (1) California resident, (2) ineligible for COBRA/CalCOBRA, and (3) denied coverage within the past 12 months with rejection letter from insurance carrier, involuntarily terminated from coverage for reasons other than fraud, or offered coverage with premium higher than MRMIP, or (4) federally eligible.

HIPAA-eligible individuals: State requires mandatory acceptance by all individual insurance carriers without exclusions for preexisting conditions. Each company independently determines the monthly premium.

For More Information: See www.TNHIS.com/CA

[a]From 82,000 policies sold nationally online in 2004, see first page of Appendix A.
[b]Blue Shield of CA Shield Spectrum PPO Plan 1500; single applicant (M/35); family applicant (M/35), spouse (F/35), children (F/8, M/5) from Sacramento, CA 95814; quoted 4.25.05.
[c]Blue Shield of CA Shield Spectrum PPO Savings Plan 2400 (single) 4800 (family); single applicant (M/35); family applicant (M/35), spouse (F/35), children (F/8, M/5); quoted 4.29.05.
[d]The Blue Cross Plan for MRMIP; applicant (M/35) from Sacramento, California, based on quote from Leslie at Major Risk Enrollment Unit at 800.289.6574.

Colorado Division of Insurance
(303) 894-7499
www.dora.state.co.us/insurance/
Guaranteed Issue   ☐
Community Rated   ☐

Average Cost of Individual Policy Sold in 2004: $120/month[a]
(single, average age 33, healthy)

Typical Healthy Individual/Family Coverage (2006)

| | Traditional Co-Pay Policy[b] | | High-Deductible Policy[c] | |
	Single	Family	Single	Family
Monthly premium	$148	$460	$90	$267
Annual deductible	$1,000	$4,000	$2,500	$5,500
Annual out-of-pocket max	$5,000	$8,000	$5,000	$10,000
Doctor visit co-pay	$25	$25	—	—
Prescription co-pay	$15–60	$15–60	—	—
Lifetime maximum	$2 million	$2 million pp	$2 million	$2 million pp

State-Guaranteed Coverage for
People with Preexisting Conditions (2006)

CoverColorado (CC)[d]

Monthly Premium	Annual Deductible	Annual OOP Max	Doctor Visit Co-Pay	Prescription Co-Pay	Lifetime Maximum
$493	$1,000	$2,000	20% after ded	20–60% after ded	$1 million

Eligibility: (1) Colorado resident for six months, (2) ineligible for Medicare and Medicaid, and (3) denied coverage, proof of inability to get coverage, diagnosed with qualifying condition, or acceptance with preexisting condition limitation or higher premium than CC, or (4) federally eligible.

HIPAA-eligible individuals: Applicants are guaranteed acceptance into CC with no exclusions for preexisting conditions.

For More Information: See www.TNHIS.com/CO

---

[a]From 82,000 policies sold nationally online in 2004, see first page of Appendix A.
[b]Anthem Blue Preferred $10K Coinsurance; single applicant (M/35); family applicant (M/35), spouse (F/35), children (F/8, M/5) from Denver, CO 80012; quoted 5.2.05.
[c]Anthem Blue 2500D/5000-80% Individual/Family Plan; single applicant (M/35); family applicant (M/35), spouse (F/35), children (F/8, M/5) from Denver, CO 80012; quoted 5.2.05.
[d]CoverColorado PPO Plan; single applicant (M/35) from Denver, CO 80012; quoted 5.7.05 from www.covercolorado.org.

Connecticut Insurance Dept.
(860) 297-3800
www.ct.gov/cid/
Guaranteed Issue ☐
Community Rated ☐

CT

★
Hartford

Average Cost of Individual Policy Sold in 2004: $174/month[a]
(single, average age 35, healthy)

Typical Healthy Individual/Family Coverage (2006)

	Traditional Co-Pay Policy[b]		High-Deductible Policy[c]	
	Single	Family	Single	Family
Monthly premium	$132	$465	$94	$259
Annual deductible	$1,500	$3,000	$2,600	$5,150
Annual out-of-pocket max	$3,000	$6,000	None	None
Doctor visit co-pay	$0 after ded	$0 after ded	—	—
Prescription co-pay	$10–40	$10–40	—	—
Lifetime maximum	$5 million	$5 million	$3 million	$3 million pp

State-Guaranteed Coverage for People with Preexisting Conditions (2006)

Health Reinsurance Association (HRA)[d]

Monthly Premium	Annual Deductible	Annual OOP Max	Doctor Visit Co-Pay	Prescription Co-Pay	Lifetime Maximum
$290	$1,500	$7,500	20%	20%	$1 million

Eligibility: (1) Connecticut resident age 19 to 64 and (2) rejected from an individual provider due to a preexisting health condition or (3) federally eligible.

HIPAA-eligible individuals: Applicants are guaranteed acceptance into HRA with no exclusions for preexisting conditions.

For More Information: See www.TNHIS.com/CT

---

[a]From 82,000 policies sold nationally online in 2004, see first page of Appendix A.
[b]Anthem Century Preferred Direct; single applicant (M/35); family applicant (M/35), spouse (F/35), children (F/8, M/5) from Hartford, CT 95814; quoted 5.2.05.
[c]Golden Rule Single/Family HSA 100 Plan; single applicant (M/35); family applicant (M/35), spouse (F/35), children (F/8, M/5) from Hartford, CT 95814; quoted 5.2.05.
[d]United Health Care PPO Plan; single applicant (M/35) from Hartford, CT 95814; quoted 5.4.05 from www.hract.org.

Delaware Insurance Commissioner
(302) 739-6775
www.state.de.us/inscom/default.shtml
Guaranteed Issue ☐
Community Rated ☐

Dover

Average Cost of Individual Policy Sold in 2004: $131/month[a]
(single, age 34, healthy)

Typical Healthy Individual/Family Coverage (2006)

	Traditional Co-Pay Policy[b]		High-Deductible Policy[c]	
	Single	Family	Single	Family
Monthly premium	$143	$480	$88	$237
Annual deductible	$750	$750	$2,600	$5,150
Annual out-of-pocket max	$10,000	$10,000	None	None
Doctor visit co-pay	$35	$35	—	—
Prescription co-pay	$20–50 + $250 ded	$20–50 + $250 ded	—	—
Lifetime maximum	$3 million	$3 million pp	$3 million	$3 million pp

State-Guaranteed Coverage for People with Preexisting Conditions (2006)

Individual HIPAA-Eligible Applicant Policy[d]

Monthly Premium	Annual Deductible	Annual OOP Max	Doctor Visit Co-Pay	Prescription Co-Pay	Lifetime Maximum
$709	$250	$3,000	0% for first $150 then 30%	Not Covered	$3 million

HIPAA-eligible individuals: Delaware requires Delaware-licensed insurance companies to offer a minimum of two policies without medical underwriting to HIPAA-eligible individuals.

Delaware only guarantees coverage to residents with health issues who are HIPAA-eligible or low-income individuals.

For More Information: See www.TNHIS.com/DE

---

[a]From 82,000 policies sold nationally online in 2004, see first page of Appendix A.
[b]Golden Rule Copay 35; single applicant (M/35); family applicant (M/35), spouse (F/35), children (F/8, M/5) from Dover, DE 19901; quoted 5.2.05.
[c]Golden Rule Single/Family HSA 100 Plan; single applicant (M/35); family applicant (M/35), spouse (F/35), children (F/8, M/5) from Dover, DE 19901; quoted 5.2.05.
[d]Blue Classic Basic HIPAA—Delaware; single applicant (M/35) quoted 5.11.05 from www.carefirst.com.

DC Dept. of Insurance, Sec., & Bnkng
(202) 727-8000
dc.gov/agencies/detail.asp?id=1011
Guaranteed Issue ☐
Community Rated ☐

District of ★
Columbia

Average Cost of Individual Policy Sold in 2004: $193/month[a]
(single, average age 32, healthy)

Typical Healthy Individual/Family Coverage (2006)

	Traditional Co-Pay Policy[b]		High-Deductible Policy[c]	
	Single	Family	Single	Family
Monthly premium	$146	$396	$109	$296
Annual deductible	$750	$1,500	$2,600	$5,200
Annual out-of-pocket max	$3,500	$7,000	$4,600	$9,200
Doctor visit co-pay	$25	$25	—	—
Prescription co-pay	$10–45 + $100 ded	$10–45 + $100 ded	—	—
Lifetime maximum	Unlimited	Unlimited	$8 million	$8 million

State-Guaranteed Coverage for People with Preexisting Conditions (2006)

PPO HIPAA Plan Coverage Blue Preferred Low Option[d]

Monthly Premium	Annual Deductible	Annual OOP Max	Doctor Visit Co-Pay	Prescription Co-Pay	Lifetime Maximum
$506	$300	$2,500	$25	$10–45 + $100 ded	Unlimited

HIPAA-eligible individuals: Applicants must be offered a choice of at least two policies on a guaranteed issue basis without exclusions for preexisting conditions.

Applicants who are not HIPAA-eligible have access to an individual health policy on a guaranteed issue basis through CareFirst BCBS if they are (1) living in the covered DC area, (2) at least 18 years of age, and (3) not currently enrolled in another insurance plan. Premium is based on health status.

For More Information: See www.TNHIS.com/DC

---

[a]From 82,000 policies sold nationally online in 2004, see first page of Appendix A.
[b]CareFirst Blue Cross Blue Shield Blue Preferred; single applicant (M/35); family applicant (M/35), spouse (F/35), children (F/8, M/5) from Washington, DC 20374; quoted 5.2.05.
[c]Fortis One Deductible; single applicant (M/35); family applicant (M/35), spouse (F/35), children (F/8, M/5) from Washington, DC 20374; quoted 5.2.05.
[d]Blue Cross Blue Shield Blue Preferred HIPAA PPO Plan; single applicant (M/35) quoted 5.12.05 from Dorothy at 800.544.8703.

Florida Dept of Financial Services
(800) 413-3100 (customer helpline)
www.fldfs.com
Guaranteed Issue ☐
Community Rated ☐

Average Cost for an Individual Policy: $148/month[a]
(single, age 34, healthy, sold in 2004)

Typical Healthy Individual/Family Coverage

	Traditional Co-Pay Policy[b]		High-Deductible Policy[c]	
	Single	Family	Single	Family
Monthly premium	$168	$586	$73	$204
Annual deductible	$750	$1,500	$3,500	$7,500
Annual out-of-pocket max	$3,000	$6,000	$3,500	$7,500
Doctor visit co-pay	$35	$35	—	—
Prescription co-pay	$20–50 + $250 ded	$20–50 + $250 ded	—	—
Lifetime maximum	$3 million	$3 million	$3 million	$3 million pp

State-Guaranteed Coverage for People with Preexisting Conditions (2006)

Approximation for an Individual Policy for HIPAA-Eligible Applicant[d]

Monthly Premium	Annual Deductible	Annual OOP Max	Doctor Visit Co-Pay	Prescription Co-Pay	Lifetime Maximum
$244	$1,000	$4,000	$20	20–40%	$2 million

HIPAA-eligible individuals: Every insurance company is required to provide applicants with a policy with no exclusions for preexisting conditions.

Florida guarantees coverage only to residents with health issues who are HIPAA-eligible or low-income individuals. Businesses with 1 to 50 employees have access to open enrollment guaranteed-issue plans if they can provide proof of business income in at least one of the two preceding calendar years.

Florida's state risk pool is not accepting new enrollees pending state funding.

For More Information: See www.TNHIS.com/FL

---

[a]From 82,000 policies sold nationally online in 2004, see first page of Appendix A.
[b]Golden Rule Copay 35; single applicant (M/35); family applicant (M/35), spouse (F/35), children (F/8, M/5) from Tallahassee, FL 32301.
[c]Golden Rule Single/Family HSA Saver; single applicant (M/35); family applicant (M/35), spouse (F/35), children (F/8, M/5) from Tallahassee, FL 32301.
[d]Blue Cross Blue Shield of Florida PPO Blue Choice Plan 1; single applicant (M/35); quoted 5.12.05 from www.bcbsfl.com and phone call with Keith at 800.766.3737. Without specific health condition disclosures, BCBS cannot provide a HIPAA-eligible quote. Blue Choice benefits are available for HIPAA-eligible plans, and that premium is about two times the normal premium. For specific quotes, please call BCBS directly at 800.766.3737.

Georgia Insurance Commissioner
(404) 656-2085
www.inscomm.state.ga.us/
Guaranteed Issue ☐
Community Rated ☐

GA

Atlanta ★

Average Cost of Individual Policy Sold in 2004: $159/month[a]
(single, average age 31, healthy)

Typical Healthy Individual/Family Coverage (2006)

	Traditional Co-Pay Policy[b]		High-Deductible Policy[c]	
	Single	Family	Single	Family
Monthly premium	$154	$595	$104	$404
Annual deductible	$1,000	$3,000	$2,600	$5,150
Annual out-of-pocket max	$2,000	$6,000	$5,000	$10,000
Doctor visit co-pay	$30	$30	—	—
Prescription co-pay	$15–45 + $200 ded	$15–45 + $200 ded	—	—
Lifetime maximum	$5 million	$5 million	$5 million	$5 million

State-Guaranteed Coverage for People with Preexisting Conditions (2006)

Georgia Assignment Plan Policy for HIPAA-Eligible Applicant[d]

Monthly Premium	Annual Deductible	Annual OOP Max	Doctor Visit Co-Pay	Prescription Co-Pay	Lifetime Maximum
$172	$2,000	$5,000	30%	30%	None

HIPAA-eligible individuals: Applicants must elect and exhaust available COBRA coverage. If the applicant is coming off a self-insured plan, the state assigns a private insurer to provide individual health insurance. If the applicant is coming off an employer plan provided by an insurance company, the insurer is required to convert coverage to an individual policy.

Georgia guarantees coverage only to residents with health issues who are HIPAA-eligible or low-income individuals.

For More Information: See www.TNHIS.com/GA

---

[a]From 82,000 policies sold nationally online in 2004, see first page of Appendix A.
[b]Blue Cross Blue Shield of GA Blue Value Select PPO; single applicant (M/35); family applicant (M/35), spouse (F/35), children (F/8, M/5) from Atlanta, GA 30303; quoted 5.2.05.
[c]Blue Cross Blue Shield of GA High Deductible H.S.A.; single applicant (M/35); family applicant (M/35), spouse (F/35), children (F/8, M/5) from Atlanta, GA 30303; quoted 5.2.05.
[d]GA Assignment Program (from a pool of providers); single applicant (M/35) quoted 5.12.05 by Tanya at 404.656.2070.

Dept. of Commerce & Consumer Affairs
Insurance Division
(808) 586-2790
www.hawaii.gov/dcca/areas/ins
Guaranteed Issue ☐
Community Rated ☐

Average Cost of Individual Policy Sold in 2004: NA[a]

Typical Healthy Individual/Family Coverage (2006)

	Traditional Co-Pay Policy[b]		High-Deductible Policy[c]	
	Single	Family	Single	Family
Monthly premium	$162	$485	$82	$328
Annual deductible	$2,000	$4,000	$2,550	$5,100
Annual out-of-pocket max	$3,000	$6,000	$2,550	$5,100
Doctor visit co-pay	$20	$20	—	—
Prescription co-pay	$0–15 for diabetic; others not included	$0–15 for diabetic; others not included	—	—
Lifetime maximum	$5 million	$5 million	$7 million	$7 million

State-Guaranteed Coverage for People with Preexisting Conditions (2006)

Individual Conversion Policy for HIPAA-Eligible Applicant[d]

Monthly Premium	Annual Deductible	Annual OOP Max	Doctor Visit Co-Pay	Prescription Co-Pay	Lifetime Maximum
$102[e]	$1,000	$5,000	Not covered	Not covered	$5 million

HIPAA-eligible individuals: Every private insurance company must provide HIPAA-eligible applicants with a policy on a guaranteed-issue basis without a limit on the premium.

Hawaii guarantees coverage only to residents with health issues who are HIPAA-eligible or low-income individuals. Hawaii requires that any employee working more than 20 hours per week be provided with health insurance from their employer in a group plan with no preexisting condition limitations.

For More Information: See www.TNHIS.com/HI

[a]From 82,000 policies sold nationally online in 2004, see first page of Appendix A.
[b]HMSA Blue Cross Blue Shield PPO Conversion Plan; single applicant (M/35); family applicant (M/35), spouse (F/35), children (F/8, M/5) from Honolulu, HI 96813; quoted 5.2.05.
[c]American National PPO HSA Complete Series ANL-2004-P; single applicant (M/35); family applicant (M/35), spouse (F/35), children (F/8, M/5) from Honolulu, HI 96813; quoted 5.2.05.
[d]American Champion Plus Select; single applicant (M/35) quoted 5.11.05.
[e]This is the basic policy—it has not yet been medically underwritten for applicant. Monthly premium will increase according to the health status of applicant.

Idaho Department of Insurance
(208) 334-4250
www.doi.state.id.us/
Guaranteed Issue ☐
Community Rated ☐

★ Boise

Average Cost of Individual Policy Sold in 2004: $162/month[a]
(single, average age 36, healthy)

Typical Healthy Individual/Family Coverage (2006)

	Traditional Co-Pay Policy[b]		High-Deductible Policy[c]	
	Single	Family	Single	Family
Monthly premium	$146	$539	$70	$253
Annual deductible	$1,000	$2,000	$3,000	$6,000
Annual out-of-pocket max	$3,000	$12,000	$5,000	$10,000
Doctor visit co-pay	$25	$25	—	—
Prescription co-pay	50%	50%	—	—
Lifetime maximum	$1 million	$1 million pp	$1 million	$1 million

State-Guaranteed Coverage for People with Preexisting Conditions (2006)

High Risk Reinsurance Pool (HRP)[d]

Monthly Premium	Annual Deductible	Annual OOP Max	Doctor Visit Co-Pay	Prescription Co-Pay	Lifetime Maximum
$493	$1,000	$10,000	30%	50% after $250 ded	$1 million

Eligibility: (1) Idaho resident, (2) under 65, (3) ineligible for Medicare and Medicaid, (4) without health insurance coverage, (5) applied for and denied coverage because of health status or accepted with a higher premium, and (6) unable to obtain substantially similar health insurance coverage, or (7) federally eligible.

HIPAA-eligible individuals: Applicants are guaranteed acceptance into the HRP with no exclusions for preexisting conditions.

For More Information: See www.TNHIS.com/ID

---

[a]From 82,000 policies sold nationally online in 2004, see first page of Appendix A.
[b]Blue Cross of ID BlueCare PPO 1000; single applicant (M/35); family applicant (M/35), spouse (F/35), children (F/8, M/5) from Boise, ID 83702; quoted 5.2.05.
[c]Blue Cross of ID HSA Blue PPO Single 3K90/Family 6K90; single applicant (M/35); family applicant (M/35), spouse (F/35), children (F/8, M/5) from Boise, ID 83702; quoted 5.2.05.
[d]HRP Standard Plan; single applicant (M/35); quoted 5.9.05 from www.doi.state.id.us/health/quarterlya4.pdf.

Illinois Dept. of Financial and Prof. Reg.
Division of Insurance
(217) 782-4515
www.idfpr.com
Guaranteed Issue ☐
Community Rated ☐

Springfield ★

Average Cost of Individual Policy Sold in 2004: $140/month[a]
(single, average age 33, healthy)

Typical Healthy Individual/Family Coverage (2006)

	Traditional Co-Pay Policy[b]		High-Deductible Policy[c]	
	Single	Family	Single	Family
Monthly premium	$98	$348	$85	$308
Annual deductible	$1,000	$1,000	$2,250	$4,500
Annual out-of-pocket max	$3,000	$9,000	$2,200	$4,500
Doctor visit co-pay	$30	$30	—	—
Prescription co-pay	20% after ded	20% after ded	—	—
Lifetime maximum	$5 million	$5 million	$5 million	$5 million

State-Guaranteed Coverage for People with Preexisting Conditions (2006)

Illinois Comprehensive Health Insurance Plan (CHIP)[d]

Monthly Premium	Annual Deductible	Annual OOP Max	Doctor Visit Co-Pay	Prescription Co-Pay	Lifetime Maximum
$257	$1,000	$7,000	20%	20% from $5–200	$1 million

Eligibility: (1) U.S. citizen, (2) Illinois resident for more than 179 days, and (3) with written proof of inability to purchase insurance coverage because of a preexisting condition or evidence of qualifying medical condition with confirming physician letter, or (4) federally eligible.

HIPAA-eligible individuals: Applicants are guaranteed a CHIP plan with no exclusions for preexisting conditions.

For More Information: See www.TNHIS.com/IL

---

[a]From 82,000 policies sold nationally online in 2004, see first page of Appendix A.
[b]Blue Cross Blue Shield of IL Select Blue Advantage $1,000/80%; single applicant (M/35); family applicant (M/35), spouse (F/35), children (F/8, M/5) from Springfield, IL 62701; quoted 5.2.05.
[c]Blue Cross Blue Shield of IL High Deductible Health Plan $2,250 (Single) $4,500 (Family)/100%; single applicant (M/35); family applicant (M/35), spouse (F/35), children (F/8, M/5) from Springfield, IL 62701; quoted 5.2.05.
[d]IL CHIP Plan 3; single applicant (M/35) from Springfield, IL 62701; quoted 5.4.05 from www.chip.state.il.us.

Indiana Department of Insurance
(317) 232-2385
www.in.gov/idoi
Guaranteed Issue ☐
Community Rated ☐

IN

Indianapolis

Average Cost of Individual Policy Sold in 2004: $125/month[a]
(single, average age 34, healthy)

Typical Healthy Individual/Family Coverage (2006)

	Traditional Co-Pay Policy[b]		High-Deductible Policy[c]	
	Single	Family	Single	Family
Monthly premium	$126	$506	$81	$299
Annual deductible	$1,000	$2,000	$2,400	$4,800
Annual out-of-pocket max	$3,000	$6,000	$3,025	$6,050
Doctor visit co-pay	$25	$25	—	—
Prescription co-pay	$15–90	$15–90	—	—
Lifetime maximum	$5 million	$5 million	$5 million	$5 million

State-Guaranteed Coverage for People with Preexisting Conditions (2006)

Indiana Comprehensive Health Insurance Association (ICHIA)[d]

Monthly Premium	Annual Deductible	Annual OOP Max	Doctor Visit Co-Pay	Prescription Co-Pay	Lifetime Maximum
$952	$1,000	$3,000	20%	20% + $300 deductible	Unlimited

Eligibility: (1) Resident of Indiana for 12 months, (2) ineligible for Medicaid, and (3) ineligible for insurance plan that equals or exceeds minimum requirements for ICHIA policies, or (4) federally eligible.

HIPAA-eligible individuals: Applicants are guaranteed acceptance into risk pool with no exclusions for preexisting conditions.

For More Information: See www.TNHIS.com/IN

---

[a]From 82,000 policies sold nationally online in 2004, see first page of Appendix A.
[b]Anthem Individual Blue Access—Plan 2; single applicant (M/35); family applicant (M/35), spouse (F/35), children (F/8, M/5) from Indianapolis, IN 46201; quoted 5.2.05.
[c]Anthem Individual Blue Access Saver—Plan 2; single applicant (M/35); family applicant (M/35), spouse (F/35), children (F/8, M/5) from Indianapolis, IN 46201; quoted 5.2.05.
[d]IN ICHIA Plan 3A; single applicant (M/35) from Indianapolis, IN 46201; quoted 5.9.05 from www.onlinehealthplan.com.

Iowa Insurance Division
(515) 281-5705
www.iid.state.ia.us/
Guaranteed Issue ☐
Community Rated ☐

Des Moines
★

Average Cost of Individual Policy Sold in 2004: $103/month[a]
(single, average age 35, healthy)

Typical Healthy Individual/Family Coverage (2006)

	Traditional Co-Pay Policy[b]		High-Deductible Policy[c]	
	Single	Family	Single	Family
Monthly premium	$116	$398	$55	$151
Annual deductible	$750	$1,500	$2,650	$5,250
Annual out-of-pocket max	$3,000	$6,000	$2,650	$5,250
Doctor visit co-pay	$35	$35	—	—
Prescription co-pay	$20–50 + $250 namebrand ded	$20–50 + $250 namebrand ded	—	—
Lifetime maximum	$3 million	$3 million pp	$3 million	$3 million pp

State-Guaranteed Coverage for People with Preexisting Conditions (2006)

Iowa Comprehensive Health Association (HIPIOWA)[d]

Monthly Premium	Annual Deductible	Annual OOP Max	Doctor Visit Co-Pay	Prescription Co-Pay	Lifetime Maximum
$493	$1,000	$2,000	$25–40	$15–120	$3 million

Eligibility: (1) Iowa resident for 60 days and (2) with notice of rejection for health insurance coverage within past nine months, benefit reduction, qualifying medical condition or increase in premium over HIPIOWA plan or (3) federally eligible.

HIPAA-eligible individuals: Applicants are guaranteed acceptance into HIPIOWA with no exclusions for preexisting conditions.

For More Information: See www.TNHIS.com/IA

---

[a]From 82,000 policies sold nationally online in 2004, see first page of Appendix A.
[b]Golden Rule Copay 35; single applicant (M/35); family applicant (M/35), spouse (F/35), children (F/8, M/5) from Des Moines, IA 50307; quoted 5.2.05.
[c]Golden Rule Single/Family HSA Saver—Plan 2; single applicant (M/35); family applicant (M/35), spouse (F/35), children (F/8, M/5) from Des Moines, IA 50307; quoted 5.2.05.
[d]HIPIOWA Plan B $1,000 Deductible; single applicant (M/35); quoted 5.9.05 from www.hipiowa.com.

Kansas Insurance Department
(785) 296-3071
www.ksinsurance.org
Guaranteed Issue ☐
Community Rated ☐

Average Cost of Individual Policy Sold in 2004: $128/month[a]
(single, average age 30, healthy)

Typical Healthy Individual/Family Coverage (2006)

	Traditional Co-Pay Policy[b]		High-Deductible Policy[c]	
	Single	Family	Single	Family
Monthly premium	$167	$581	$98	$323
Annual deductible	$1,000	$3,000	$2,600	$5,150
Annual out-of-pocket max	$2,000	$8,000	$4,600	$9,150
Doctor visit co-pay	$25–40/ 4 visits then 20%	$25–40/ 4 visits then 20%	—	—
Prescription co-pay	$10–50	$10–50	—	—
Lifetime maximum	$5 million	$5 million pp	$5 million	$5 million pp

State-Guaranteed Coverage for People with Preexisting Conditions (2006)

Kansas Health Insurance Association (KHIA)[d]

Monthly Premium	Annual Deductible	Annual OOP Max	Doctor Visit Co-Pay	Prescription Co-Pay	Lifetime Maximum
$441	$1,000	None	30% after ded	50% after ded	$1 million

Eligibility: (1) Kansas resident for six months, (2) ineligible for insurance coverage, and (3) rejected by two carriers due to health condition, quoted rate higher than KHIA rate, or accepted with preexisting condition exclusions, or (4) federally eligible.

HIPAA-eligible individuals: Applicants are guaranteed acceptance into KHIA with no exclusions for preexisting conditions.

For More Information: See www.TNHIS.com/KS

---

[a]From 82,000 policies sold nationally online in 2004, see first page of Appendix A.
[b]HumanaOnePlan with Office Visit Copay, $0 Rx Deductible; single applicant (M/35); family applicant (M/35), spouse (F/35), children (F/8, M/5) from Topeka, KS 66603; quoted 5.2.05.
[c]HumanaOne HSA Plan 49, Option 201; single applicant (M/35); family applicant (M/35), spouse (F/35), children (F/8, M/5) from Topeka, KS 66603; quoted 5.13.05 from Carla at 800.833.6917.
[d]KHIA Individual Plan B $1,000 Plan; single applicant (M/35); quoted 5.9.05 from www.benefitmanagementks.com.

Kentucky Office of Insurance
(800) 595-6053
doi.ppr.ky.gov/kentucky
Guaranteed Issue ☐
Community Rated ☐

Frankfort

Average Cost of Individual Policy Sold in 2004: $125/month[a]
(single, average age 33, healthy)

Typical Healthy Individual/Family Coverage (2006)

	Traditional Co-Pay Policy[b]		High-Deductible Policy[c]	
	Single	Family	Single	Family
Monthly premium	$79	$413	$55	$262
Annual deductible	$1,000	$2,000	$2,400	$4,800
Annual out-of-pocket max	$3,000	$6,000	$3,025	$6,500
Doctor visit co-pay	$25	$25	—	—
Prescription co-pay	$15–90	$15–90	—	—
Lifetime maximum	$5 million	$5 million	$5 million	$5 million

State-Guaranteed Coverage for
People with Preexisting Conditions (2006)

Kentucky Access (KA)[d]

Monthly Premium	Annual Deductible	Annual OOP Max	Doctor Visit Co-Pay	Prescription Co-Pay	Lifetime Maximum
$249	$750	$3,750	$20	20% after $500 ded	$1 million

Eligibility: (1) Kentucky resident for one year and (2) rejected by private insurer or offered higher premium than Kentucky Access premiums, with qualifying medical condition, or qualified for state's Guaranteed Acceptance Program or (3) federally eligible.

HIPAA-eligible individuals: Applicants are guaranteed acceptance into KA with no exclusions for preexisting conditions.

For More Information: See www.TNHIS.com/KY

---

[a]From 82,000 policies sold nationally online in 2004, see first page of Appendix A.
[b]Anthem Individual Blue Access—Plan 2; single applicant (M/35); family applicant (M/35), spouse (F/35), children (F/8, M/5) from Frankfort, KY 40601; quoted 5.2.05.
[c]Anthem Individual Blue Access Saver—Plan 2; single applicant (M/35); family applicant (M/35), spouse (F/35), children (F/8, M/5) from Frankfort, KY 40601; quoted 5.2.05.
[d]KY Preferred Access $750 Deductible Plan; single applicant (M/35); quoted 5.4.05 from www.kentuckyaccess.com.

Louisiana Department of Insurance
(225) 342-5900
www.ldi.la.gov/
Guaranteed Issue   ☐
Community Rated   ☐

Baton Rouge

Average Cost of Individual Policy Sold in 2004: $135/month[a]
(single, average age 30, healthy)

Typical Healthy Individual/Family Coverage (2006)

	Traditional Co-Pay Policy[b]		High-Deductible Policy[c]	
	Single	Family	Single	Family
Monthly premium	$188	$566	$102	$282
Annual deductible	$1,000	$3,000	$2,600	$5,200
Annual out-of-pocket max	$3,500	$8,000	$4,600	$9,200
Doctor visit co-pay	$25/2 visits then 50%	$25/2 visits then 50%	—	—
Prescription co-pay	$10–25 + 20% + $500 ded	$15–40 + 20% + $500 ded	—	—
Lifetime maximum	$7 million	$7 million	$8 million	$8 million

State-Guaranteed Coverage for
People with Preexisting Conditions (2006)

Louisiana Health Plan[d]

Monthly Premium	Annual Deductible	Annual OOP Max	Doctor Visit Co-Pay	Prescription Co-Pay	Lifetime Maximum
$407	$1,000	$3,500	25%	20–30%	$500,000

Eligibility: (1) Louisiana resident for six months, (2) not covered by or eligible for other health insurance coverage, and (3) with a minimum of two written denials of coverage within one year of date of application for pool, or (4) federally eligible.

HIPAA-eligible individuals: Applicants are guaranteed acceptance into the Louisiana Health Plan with no exclusions for preexisting conditions.

For More Information: See www.TNHIS.com/LA

---

[a]From 82,000 policies sold nationally online in 2004, see first page of Appendix A.
[b]Fortis PPO X-tra; single applicant (M/35); family applicant (M/35), spouse (F/35), children (F/8, M/5) from Baton Rouge, LA 70801; quoted 5.2.05.
[c]Fortis One Deductible; single applicant (M/35); family applicant (M/35), spouse (F/35), children (F/8, M/5) from Baton Rouge, LA 70801; quoted 5.2.05.
[d]LA Health Plan A without non-tobacco-user discount; single applicant (M/35) from Baton Rouge, LA 70801; quoted 5.9.05 from www.lahealthplan.org.

Maine Bureau of Insurance
(207) 624-8475
www.state.me.us/pfr/ins/ins_index.htm
Guaranteed Issue □
Community Rated □

Average Cost of Individual Policy Sold in 2004: NA[a]

Typical Healthy Individual/Family Coverage (2006)

	Traditional Co-Pay Policy[b]		High-Deductible Policy[c]	
	Single	Family	Single	Family
Monthly premium	$445	$1,123	$278	$430
Annual deductible	$1,000	$1,500	$2,250	$5,000
Annual out-of-pocket max	$2,000	$2,500	$2,250	$5,000
Doctor visit co-pay	40% after ded	40% after ded	—	—
Prescription co-pay	$20–30	$20–30	—	—
Lifetime maximum	$1 million	$1 million	$3 million	$3 million

State-Guaranteed Coverage for People with Preexisting Conditions (2006)

Representative Policy[d]

Monthly Premium	Annual Deductible	Annual OOP Max	Doctor Visit Co-Pay	Prescription Co-Pay	Lifetime Maximum
$493	$1,000	$2,000	$25–40	$15–120	$3 million

Maine does not have a state risk pool—every policy sold in Maine is effectively a state risk pool policy because all citizens must be accepted ("guaranteed issue") at the same premium ("community rated") regardless of their health. Both HIPAA-eligible applicants and applicants who are not HIPAA-eligible are guaranteed a policy at the same community rate.

For More Information: See www.TNHIS.com/ME

---

[a]From 82,000 policies sold nationally online in 2004, see first page of Appendix A.
[b]Anthem Health Choice Basic; single applicant (M/35); family applicant (M/35), spouse (F/35), children (F/8, M/5) from Augusta, ME 04330; quoted 5.2.05.
[c]Anthem Health Choice; single applicant (M/35); family applicant (M/35), spouse (F/35), children (F/8, M/5) from Augusta, ME 04330; quoted 5.2.05.
[d]Anthem Health Choice Basic; single applicant (M/35); family applicant (M/35), spouse (F/35), children (F/8, M/5) from Augusta, ME 04330; quoted 5.2.05.

Maryland Insurance Administration
(410) 468-2000
www.mdinsurance.state.md.us/
Guaranteed Issue ☐
Community Rated ☐

Average Cost of Individual Policy Sold in 2004: $166/month[a]
(single, average age 32, healthy)

Typical Healthy Individual/Family Coverage (2006)

	Traditional Co-Pay Policy[b]		High-Deductible Policy[c]	
	Single	Family	Single	Family
Monthly premium	$134	$462	$66	$180
Annual deductible	$750	$1,500	$2,650	$5,250
Annual out-of-pocket max	$3,000	$6,000	$2,650	$5,250
Doctor visit co-pay	$35	$35	—	—
Prescription co-pay	$20–50 + $250 namebrand ded	$20–50 + $250 namebrand ded	—	—
Lifetime maximum	$3 million	$3 million pp	$3 million	$3 million pp

State-Guaranteed Coverage for People with Preexisting Conditions (2006)

Maryland Health Insurance Plan (MHIP)[d]

Monthly Premium	Annual Deductible	Annual OOP Max	Doctor Visit Co-Pay	Prescription Co-Pay	Lifetime Maximum
$194	$1,000	$4,500	$20–20%	$15–35 + $250 ded	$2 million

Eligibility: (1) Maryland resident and (2) denied or offered restricted health coverage within past six months for health reasons, with qualifying medical condition, or at a premium higher than MHIP or (3) federally eligible.

HIPAA-eligible individuals: Applicants are guaranteed acceptance into MHIP with no exclusions for preexisting conditions.

For More Information: See www.TNHIS.com/MD

---

[a]From 82,000 policies sold nationally online in 2004, see first page of Appendix A.
[b]Golden Rule Copay 35; single applicant (M/35); family applicant (M/35), spouse (F/35), children (F/8, M/5) from Annapolis, MD 21401; quoted 5.2.05.
[c]Golden Rule Single/Family HSA Saver; single applicant (M/35); family applicant (M/35), spouse (F/35), children (F/8, M/5) from Annapolis, MD 21401; quoted 5.2.05.
[d]MHIP $1,000 PPO Plan; single applicant (M/35); quoted 5.9.05 from www.marylandhealthinsuranceplan.state.md.us.

Massachusetts Division of Insurance
(617) 521-7794
www.mass.gov/doi/home.html
Guaranteed Issue ☐
Community Rated ☐

Average Cost of Individual Policy Sold in 2004: NA[a]

Typical Healthy Individual/Family Coverage (2006)

	Traditional Co-Pay Policy[b]		High-Deductible Policy	
	Single	Family	Single	Family
Monthly premium	$503	$906	NA	NA
Annual deductible	$250	$500	NA	NA
Annual out-of-pocket max	$2,250	$4,500	NA	NA
Doctor visit co-pay	10%	10%	—	—
Prescription co-pay	$20–25 $250 ded	$20–25 $250 ded	—	—
Lifetime maximum	$1 million	$1 million pp	NA	NA

State-Guaranteed Coverage for People with Preexisting Conditions (2006)

Representative Policy[c]

Monthly Premium	Annual Deductible	Annual OOP Max	Doctor Visit Co-Pay	Prescription Co-Pay	Lifetime Maximum
$503	$250	$2,250	10%	$20–25	$1 million

Massachusetts does not have a state risk pool—every policy sold in Massachusetts is effectively a state risk pool policy because all citizens must be accepted ("guaranteed issue") at the same premium ("community rated") regardless of their health. Both HIPAA-eligible applicants and applicants who are not HIPAA-eligible are guaranteed a policy at the same community rate.

For More Information: See www.TNHIS.com/MA

---

[a]From 82,000 policies sold nationally online in 2004, see first page of Appendix A.
[b]Blue Cross Blue Shield of MA PPO Blue Direct; single applicant (M/35); family applicant (M/35), spouse (F/35), children (F/8, M/5) from Boston, MA 02108; quoted 5.2.05.
[c]Blue Cross Blue Shield of MA PPO Blue Direct; single applicant (M/35); family applicant (M/35), spouse (F/35), children (F/8, M/5) from Boston, MA 02108; quoted 5.2.05.

Michigan Office of Finan. and Ins. Svcs.
(517) 373-0220
www.michigan.gov/cis
Guaranteed Issue ☐
Community Rated ☐

Lansing ★

Average Cost of Individual Policy Sold in 2004: $112/month[a]
(single, average age 33, healthy)

Typical Healthy Individual/Family Coverage (2006)

	Traditional Co-Pay Policy[b]		High-Deductible Policy[c]	
	Single	Family	Single	Family
Monthly premium	$103	$358	$54	$180
Annual deductible	$1,000	$3,000	$2,600	$5,150
Annual out-of-pocket max	$3,000	$8,000	$4,600	$9,150
Doctor visit co-pay	$25–40/ 2 visits then 20%	$25–40/ 2 visits then 20%	—	—
Prescription co-pay	$10–50	$10–50	—	—
Lifetime maximum	$5 million	$5 million pp	$5 million	$5 million pp

State-Guaranteed Coverage for People with Preexisting Conditions (2006)

Guaranteed Issue PPO[d]

Monthly Premium	Annual Deductible	Annual OOP Max	Doctor Visit Co-Pay	Prescription Co-Pay	Lifetime Maximum
$493	$1,000	$2,000	$25–40	$15–120	$3 million

Eligibility: (1) Michigan resident for six months out of the year and (2) ineligible for other group coverage or (3) federally eligible.

HIPAA-eligible individuals: Applicants are guaranteed an individual health insurance policy issued by Blue Cross Blue Shield.

Michigan requires Blue Cross Blue Shield Michigan to sell individual health insurance to any resident ("guaranteed issue"). BCBS Michigan cannot charge higher premiums because of applicant's health status.

For More Information: See www.TNHIS.com/MI

---

[a]From 82,000 policies sold nationally online in 2004, see first page of Appendix A.
[b]HumanaOne Plan with Office Visit Copay, $0 Rx Deductible; single applicant (M/35); family applicant (M/35), spouse (F/35), children (F/8, M/5) from Lansing, MI 48908; quoted 5.2.05.
[c]HumanaOne HSA; single applicant (M/35); family applicant (M/35), spouse (F/35), children (F/8, M/5) from Lansing, MI 48908; quoted 5.2.05.
[d]Blue Cross Blue Shield ValueBluePPO; single applicant (M/35) quoted 5.12.05 from Tara 800.848.5101.

Minnesota Department of Commerce
(303) 894-7499
www.state.mn.us/
Guaranteed Issue ☐
Community Rated ☐

MN

St. Paul
★

Average Cost of Individual Policy Sold in 2004: $143/month[a]
(single, average age 33, healthy)

Typical Healthy Individual/Family Coverage (2006)

	Traditional Co-Pay Policy[b]		High-Deductible Policy[c]	
	Single	Family	Single	Family
Monthly premium	$142	$501	$100	$294
Annual deductible	$1,000	$3,000	$2,600	$5,150
Annual out-of-pocket max	$1,800	$5,400	$5,000	$10,000
Doctor visit co-pay	20% after ded	20% after ded	—	—
Prescription co-pay	20% after ded	20% after ded	—	—
Lifetime maximum	$3 million	$3 million	$3 million	$3 million

State-Guaranteed Coverage for People with Preexisting Conditions (2006)

Minnesota Comprehensive Health Association (MCHA)[d]

Monthly Premium	Annual Deductible	Annual OOP Max	Doctor Visit Co-Pay	Prescription Co-Pay	Lifetime Maximum
$197	$1,000	$3,000	20% after ded	20%	$2.8 million

Eligibility: (1) Minnesota resident for six months and (2) rejected for individual health coverage within past six months, 65 and ineligible for Medicare, or with qualifying condition or (3) federally eligible.

HIPAA-eligible individuals: Applicants are guaranteed acceptance into MCHA with no exclusions for preexisting conditions.

For More Information: See www.TNHIS.com/MN

---

[a]From 82,000 policies sold nationally online in 2004, see first page of Appendix A.
[b]Blue Cross Blue Shield of MN Aware Care Plan; single applicant (M/35); family applicant (M/35), spouse (F/35), children (F/8, M/5) from St. Paul, MN 55101; quoted 5.2.05.
[c]Blue Cross Blue Shield of MN Options Blue; single applicant (M/35); family applicant (M/35), spouse (F/35), children (F/8, M/5) from St. Paul, MN 55101; quoted 5.2.05.
[d]MCHA $1,000 Deductible Plan; single applicant (M/35); quoted 5.9.05 from www.mchamn.com.

Mississippi Department of Insurance
(601) 359-3569
www.doi.state.ms.us/
Guaranteed Issue ☐
Community Rated ☐

MS

Jackson ★

Average Cost of Individual Policy Sold in 2004: $131/month[a]
(single, average age 34, healthy)

Typical Healthy Individual/Family Coverage (2006)

	Traditional Co-Pay Policy[b]		High-Deductible Policy[c]	
	Single	Family	Single	Family
Monthly premium	$161	$551	$77	$209
Annual deductible	$750	$1,500	$2,650	$5,250
Annual out-of-pocket max	$3,000	$6,000	$2,650	$5,250
Doctor visit co-pay	$35	$35	—	—
Prescription co-pay	$20–50 + $250 namebrand ded	$20–50 + $250 namebrand ded	—	—
Lifetime maximum	$3 million	$3 million pp	$3 million	$3 million pp

State-Guaranteed Coverage for People with Preexisting Conditions (2006)

MS Comprehensive Health Insurance Risk Pool Assoc. (MCHIRPA)[d]

Monthly Premium	Annual Deductible	Annual OOP Max	Doctor Visit Co-Pay	Prescription Co-Pay	Lifetime Maximum
$295	$1,000	None	20%	0–50% + $250 ded	$500,000

Eligibility: (1) Mississippi resident for 6 months, (2) with qualified health condition or rejection for individual health coverage within past 12 months, (3) ineligible for Medicare, Medicaid, or other government program, and (4) without coverage under another policy, or (5) federally eligible.

HIPAA-eligible individuals: Applicants are guaranteed acceptance into MCHIRPA without exclusions for preexisting conditions.

For More Information: See www.TNHIS.com/MS

---

[a]From 82,000 policies sold nationally online in 2004, see first page of Appendix A.
[b]Golden Rule Copay 35; single applicant (M/35); family applicant (M/35), spouse (F/35), children (F/8, M/5) from Jackson, MS 39201; quoted 5.2.05.
[c]Golden Rule Single/Family HSA Saver; single applicant (M/35); family applicant (M/35), spouse (F/35), children (F/8, M/5) from Jackson, MS 39201; quoted 5.2.05.
[d]MCHIRPA $1000 Deductible/$250 Pharmacy Plan; single applicant (M/35); quoted 5.9.05 from www.doi.state.ms.us.

Missouri Health Insurance
(573) 751-4363
www.insurance.state.mo.us/
Guaranteed Issue   ☐
Community Rated   ☐

MO

Jefferson City

Average Cost of Individual Policy Sold in 2004: $139/month[a]
(single, average age 32, healthy)

Typical Healthy Individual/Family Coverage (2006)

	Traditional Co-Pay Policy[b]		High-Deductible Policy[c]	
	Single	Family	Single	Family
Monthly premium	$124	$382	$76	$272
Annual deductible	$1,000	$3,000	$3,000	$6,000
Annual out-of-pocket max	$3,000	$6,000	$5,000	$10,000
Doctor visit co-pay	$30	$30	—	—
Prescription co-pay	10–50% + $2000 namebrand ded	10–50% + $2000 namebrand ded	—	—
Lifetime maximum	Unlimited	Unlimited	Unlimited	Unlimited

State-Guaranteed Coverage for People with Preexisting Conditions (2006)

Missouri Health Insurance Pool (MHIP)[d]

Monthly Premium	Annual Deductible	Annual OOP Max	Doctor Visit Co-Pay	Prescription Co-Pay	Lifetime Maximum
$270	$1,000	$5,000	20%	30% after $100 ded	$1 million

Eligibility: (1) Missouri resident and (2) rejected for individual health insurance within past six months, offered coverage with premium exceeding 300% of standard rate, or elected and exhausted COBRA coverage or (3) federally eligible.

HIPAA-eligible individual: Applicants are guaranteed acceptance into MHIP with no exclusions for preexisting conditions.

For More Information: See www.TNHIS.com/MO

---

[a]From 82,000 policies sold nationally online in 2004, see first page of Appendix A.
[b]Blue Cross Blue Shield Alliance Rate Saver; single applicant (M/35); family applicant (M/35), spouse (F/35), children (F/8, M/5) from Jefferson City, MO 65101; quoted 5.2.05.
[c]Blue Cross Blue Shield Alliance HSA Plan Single/Family; single applicant (M/35); family applicant (M/35), spouse (F/35), children (F/8, M/5) from Jefferson City, MO 65101; quoted 5.2.05.
[d]MHIP $1,000 Deductible Plan; single applicant (M/35); quoted 5.9.05 www.mhip.org/benefits.pdf.

Montana Insurance Division
(406) 444-3246
www.state.mt.us/sao/
Guaranteed Issue ☐
Community Rated ☐

MT

★ Helena

Average Cost of Individual Policy Sold in 2004: $145/month[a]
(single, average age 31, healthy)

Typical Healthy Individual/Family Coverage (2006)

	Traditional Co-Pay Policy[b]		High-Deductible Policy[c]	
	Single	Family	Single	Family
Monthly premium	$257	$637	$131	$295
Annual deductible	$1,000	$3,000	$2,600	$5,200
Annual out-of-pocket max	$3,500	$8,000	$4,600	$9,200
Doctor visit co-pay	$25/2 visits then 50%	$25/2 visits then 50%	—	—
Prescription co-pay	$10–25 + 20% + $500 ded	$10–25 + 20% + $500 ded	—	—
Lifetime maximum	$7 million	$7 million	$8 million	$8 million

State-Guaranteed Coverage for People with Preexisting Conditions (2006)

Montana Comprehensive Health Association (MCHA)[d]

Monthly Premium	Annual Deductible	Annual OOP Max	Doctor Visit Co-Pay	Prescription Co-Pay	Lifetime Maximum
$385	$1,000	$5,000	20%	$10–50 +30%	$1 million

Eligibility: (1) Montana resident and (2) rejected or offered a restrictive rider by two insurers within the past six months, with qualifying condition and ineligible for other health insurance coverage, or paying higher than 150% of the average premium rate or (3) federally eligible.

HIPAA-eligible individuals: Applicants are guaranteed acceptance into MCHA without exclusions for preexisting conditions.

For More Information: See www.TNHIS.com/MT

---

[a]From 82,000 policies sold nationally online in 2004, see first page of Appendix A.
[b]Fortis PPO X-tra; single applicant (M/35); family applicant (M/35), spouse (F/35), children (F/8, M/5) from Helena, MT 59601; quoted 5.2.05.
[c]Fortis One Deductible; single applicant (M/35); family applicant (M/35), spouse (F/35), children (F/8, M/5) from Helena, MT 59601; quoted 5.2.05.
[d]MCHA Traditional Plan Option A $1,000 Deductible; single Applicant (35); quoted 5.9.05 from www.mthealth.org.

Nebraska Department of Insurance
(402) 471-2201
www.doi.ne.gov
Guaranteed Issue ☐
Community Rated ☐

Average Cost of Individual Policy Sold in 2004: $129/month[a]
(single, average age 32, healthy)

Typical Healthy Individual/Family Coverage (2006)

	Traditional Co-Pay Policy[b]		High-Deductible Policy[c]	
	Single	Family	Single	Family
Monthly premium	$109	$422	$79	$291
Annual deductible	$1,000	$1,000	$2,600	$5,200
Annual out-of-pocket max	$3,000	$3,000	$4,600	$9,200
Doctor visit co-pay	$30	$20–35	—	—
Prescription co-pay	$10–45	$10–45	—	—
Lifetime maximum	$10 million	$10 million pp	$10 million	$10 million pp

State-Guaranteed Coverage for People with Preexisting Conditions (2006)

Nebraska Comprehensive Health Insurance Pool (CHIP)[d]

Monthly Premium	Annual Deductible	Annual OOP Max	Doctor Visit Co-Pay	Prescription Co-Pay	Lifetime Maximum
$316	$1,000	$2,500	$10	$10–20	$1 million

Eligibility: (1) Nebraska resident for six months and (2) rejected or offered a restrictive rider by an insurer within the past six months, accepted with qualifying condition, or refused health coverage or offered coverage with a higher premium or (3) federally eligible.

HIPAA-eligible individuals: Applicants are guaranteed acceptance into CHIP with no exclusions for preexisting conditions.

For More Information: See www.TNHIS.com/NE

---

[a]From 82,000 policies sold nationally online in 2004, see first page of Appendix A.
[b]Blue Cross Blue Shield BluePreferred Value Plan 1000; single applicant (M/35); family applicant (M/35), spouse (F/35), children (F/8, M/5) from Lincoln, NE 68502; quoted 5.2.05.
[c]Blue Cross Blue Shield BluePreferred Single/Family Value Plan HSA Eligible Plan; single applicant (M/35); family applicant (M/35), spouse (F/35), children (F/8, M/5) from Lincoln, NE 68502; quoted 5.2.05.
[d]CHIP Option 3; single applicant (35); quoted 5.9.05 from www.bcbsne.com.

Nevada Division of Insurance
(775) 687-4270
www.doi.state.nv.us/
Guaranteed Issue ☐
Community Rated ☐

Carson City
★

Average Cost of Individual Policy Sold in 2004: $155/month[a]
(single, average age 33, healthy)

Typical Healthy Individual/Family Coverage (2006)

	Traditional Co-Pay Policy[b]		High-Deductible Policy[c]	
	Single	Family	Single	Family
Monthly premium	$121	$388	$89	$264
Annual deductible	$1,000	$3,000	$2,000	$4,000
Annual out-of-pocket max	$4,000	$9,000	$5,000	$10,000
Doctor visit co-pay	$35–70	$35–70	—	—
Prescription co-pay	$15–60	$15–60	—	—
Lifetime maximum	$2 million	$2 million pp	$2 million	$2 million pp

State-Guaranteed Coverage for People with Preexisting Conditions (2006)

Nevada HIPAA-Eligible Applicant Plan[d]

Monthly Premium	Annual Deductible	Annual OOP Max	Doctor Visit Co-Pay	Prescription Co-Pay	Lifetime Maximum
$328	$1,500	$3,500	30%	30%	$1 million

HIPAA-eligible individuals: Applicants are guaranteed the right to purchase individual insurance coverage from any company that provides individual health plans in Nevada. Nevada also has a special program with a discounted premium for healthy HIPAA-eligible individuals.

Nevada guarantees coverage only to residents with health issues who are HIPAA-eligible or low-income individuals.

For More Information: See www.TNHIS.com/NV

---

[a]From 82,000 policies sold nationally online in 2004, see first page of Appendix A.
[b]Anthem BluePreferred Plan 1000-35-80/50; single applicant (M/35); family applicant (M/35), spouse (F/35), children (F/8, M/5) from Carson City, NV 89701; quoted 5.2.05.
[c]Anthem NV HSA-Qualified High Deductible Health Plan; single applicant (M/35); family applicant (M/35), spouse (F/35), children (F/8, M/5) from Carson City, NV 89701; quoted 5.13.05.
[d]Anthem NV HIPAA Basic with Health Conditions; single applicant (M/35) quoted 5.12.05 from Shania at 800.873.2261.

New Hampshire Insurance Department
(603) 271-2261
www.nh.gov/insurance/
Guaranteed Issue ☐
Community Rated ☐

Concord
★

Average Cost of Individual Policy Sold in 2004: NA[a]

Typical Healthy Individual/Family Coverage (2006)

	Traditional Co-Pay Policy[b]		High-Deductible Policy[c]	
	Single	Family	Single	Family
Monthly premium	$163	$503	$133	$469
Annual deductible	$1,000	$2,000	$2,500	$4,000
Annual out-of-pocket max	None	$10,000	$2,500	$8,000
Doctor visit co-pay	$20	$40	—	—
Prescription co-pay	$10	$10	—	—
Lifetime maximum	$2 million	$2 million	$2 million	$2 million

State-Guaranteed Coverage for People with Preexisting Conditions (2006)

New Hampshire Health Plan (NHHP)[d]

Monthly Premium	Annual Deductible	Annual OOP Max	Doctor Visit Co-Pay	Prescription Co-Pay	Lifetime Maximum
$235	$1,000	$3,500	20%	$10–45 + 20% with $500 ded	$2 million

Eligibility: (1) New Hampshire resident and (2) applied and rejected for individual coverage, offered a higher premium than NHHP, with qualifying medical condition, or offered insurance with a rider excluding coverage for a condition or (3) federally eligible.

HIPAA-eligible individuals: Applicants are guaranteed acceptance into NHHP with no exclusions for preexisting conditions.

For More Information: See www.TNHIS.com/NH

---

[a]From 82,000 policies sold nationally online in 2004, see first page of Appendix A.
[b]Anthem Blue Direct $1,000/$2,000; single applicant (M/35); family applicant (M/35), spouse (F/35), children (F/8, M/5) from Concord, NH 03301; quoted 5.2.05.
[c]Anthem Blue Direct HSA; single applicant (M/35); family applicant (M/35), spouse (F/35), children (F/8, M/5) from Concord, NH 03301; quoted 5.2.05.
[d]NHHP Managed Care Plan Option A; single applicant (M/35); quoted 5.9.05 from www.nhhealthplan.org.

NJ Dept. of Banking and Insurance
(609) 292-5427
www.nj.gov/dobi/life.htm
Guaranteed Issue ☐
Community Rated ☐

Average Cost of Individual Policy Sold in 2004: $340/month[a]
(single, average age 38, healthy)

Typical Healthy Individual/Family Coverage (2006)

	Traditional Co-Pay Policy[b]		High-Deductible Policy	
	Single	Family	Single	Family
Monthly premium	$411	$394	NA	NA
Annual deductible	$0	$3,000	NA	NA
Annual out-of-pocket max	None	$6,000	NA	NA
Doctor visit co-pay	$30	$20–35	—	—
Prescription co-pay	Discount card	Discount card	—	—
Lifetime maximum	Unlimited	Unlimited	NA	NA

State-Guaranteed Coverage for People with Preexisting Conditions (2006)

Representative Policy[c]

Monthly Premium	Annual Deductible	Annual OOP Max	Doctor Visit Co-Pay	Prescription Co-Pay	Lifetime Maximum
$411	$0	None	$30	About 50%	Unlimited

New Jersey does not have a state risk pool—every policy sold in New Jersey is effectively a state risk pool policy because all citizens must be accepted ("guaranteed issue") at the same premium ("community rated") regardless of their health. Both HIPAA-eligible applicants and applicants who are not HIPAA-eligible are guaranteed a policy at the same community rate.

For More Information: See www.TNHIS.com/NJ

---

[a]From 82,000 policies sold nationally online in 2004, see first page of Appendix A.
[b]Horizon Blue Cross Blue Shield of NJ Horizon HMO; single applicant (M/35); family applicant (M/35), spouse (F/35), children (F/8, M/5) from Trenton, NJ 08608; quoted 5.2.05.
[c]Horizon Blue Cross Blue Shield of NJ Horizon HMO; single applicant (M/35); family applicant (M/35), spouse (F/35), children (F/8, M/5) from Trenton, NJ 08608; quoted 5.2.05.

New Mexico Insurance Division
(505) 827-4601
www.nmprc.state.nm.us/
Guaranteed Issue ☐
Community Rated ☐

NM

Santa Fe

Average Cost of Individual Policy Sold in 2004: $121/month[a]
(single, average age 32, healthy)

Typical Healthy Individual/Family Coverage (2006)

	Traditional Co-Pay Policy[b]		High-Deductible Policy[c]	
	Single	Family	Single	Family
Monthly premium	$131	$418	$90	$287
Annual deductible	$1,000	$3,000	$2,600	$5,150
Annual out-of-pocket max	$2,000	$5,000	$5,000	$10,000
Doctor visit co-pay	$20	$20	—	—
Prescription co-pay	$15–40	$15–40	—	—
Lifetime maximum	Unlimited	Unlimited	Unlimited	Unlimited

State-Guaranteed Coverage for People with Preexisting Conditions (2006)

Individual Portability Coverage for HIPAA-Eligible Applicant[d]

Monthly Premium	Annual Deductible	Annual OOP Max	Doctor Visit Co-Pay	Prescription Co-Pay	Lifetime Maximum
$315	$1,000	$3,500	20%	30%	Unlimited

Eligibility: (1) New Mexico resident, (2) ineligible for Medicaid or Medicare, and (3) rejected from a health insurer, accepted with rate higher than NMMIP, accepted with restrictive rider, with coverage involuntarily terminated because carrier stopped providing insurance in NM, or with physician letter confirming qualifying medical condition, or (4) federally eligible.

HIPAA-eligible individuals: Applicants are guaranteed acceptance into NMMIP with no exclusions for preexisting conditions.

For More Information: See www.TNHIS.com/NM

---

[a]From 82,000 policies sold nationally online in 2004, see first page of Appendix A.
[b]Blue Cross Blue Shield of NM BlueChoice; single applicant (M/35); famly applicant (M/35), spouse (F/35), children (F/8, M/5) from Santa Fe, NM 87501; quoted 5.2.05.
[c]Blue Cross Blue Shield of NM BlueEdge Individual HSA; single applicant (M/35); family applicant (M/35), spouse (F/35), children (F/8, M/5) from Santa Fe, NM 87501; quoted 5.13.05 from www.bcbsnm.com.
[d]NMMIP 80 Percent Plan with $1,000 deductible; single applicant (M/35); quoted 5.9.05 from www.nmmip.com.

New York Insurance Department
(212) 480-6400
www.ins.state.ny.us
Guaranteed Issue   ☐
Community Rated   ☐

> Average Cost of Individual Policy Sold in 2004: $295/month[a]
> (single, average age 40, healthy)

Typical Healthy Individual/Family Coverage (2006)

	Traditional Co-Pay Policy[b]		High-Deductible Policy	
	Single	Family	Single	Family
Monthly premium	$302	$734	NA	NA
Annual deductible	$250	$500	NA	NA
Annual out-of-pocket max	$10,000	$10,000	NA	NA
Doctor visit co-pay	Not covered	Not covered	—	—
Prescription co-pay	$10 + $50 ded	$10 + $50 ded	—	—
Lifetime maximum	$1 million	$1 million	NA	NA

State-Guaranteed Coverage for People with Preexisting Conditions (2006)

Representative Policy[c]

Monthly Premium	Annual Deductible	Annual OOP Max	Doctor Visit Co-Pay	Prescription Co-Pay	Lifetime Maximum
$302	$250	$10,000	Not covered	$10 with $50 ded	$1 million

New York does not have a state risk pool—every policy sold in New York is effectively a state risk pool policy because all citizens must be accepted ("guaranteed issue") at the same premium ("community rated") regardless of their health. Both HIPAA-eligible applicants and applicants who are not HIPAA-eligible are guaranteed a policy at the same community rate.

For More Information: See www.TNHIS.com/NY

---

[a]From 82,000 policies sold nationally online in 2004, see first page of Appendix A.
[b]GHI Alliance Value Plan; single applicant (M/35); family applicant (M/35), spouse (F/35), children (F/8, M/5) from Albany, NY 12202; quoted 5.2.05.
[c]GHI Alliance Value Plan; Single Applicant (M/35); family applicant (M/35), spouse (F/35), children (F/8, M/5) from Albany, NY 12202; quoted 5.2.05.

North Carolina Dept. of Insurance
(919) 733-2032
www.ncdoi.com
Guaranteed Issue ☐
Community Rated ☐

NC

Raleigh

Average Cost of Individual Policy Sold in 2004: $130/month[a]
(single, average age 32, healthy)

Typical Healthy Individual/Family Coverage (2006)

	Traditional Co-Pay Policy[b]		High-Deductible Policy[c]	
	Single	Family	Single	Family
Monthly premium	$125	$482	$102	$271
Annual deductible	$1,000	$3,000	$2,600	$5,200
Annual out-of-pocket max	$3,000	$6,000	$4,600	$9,200
Doctor visit co-pay	$20–50	$25–50	—	—
Prescription co-pay	$10–50 + $200 ded	$10–50 + $200 ded	—	—
Lifetime maximum	$5 million	$5 million	$8 million	$8 million

State-Guaranteed Coverage for People with Preexisting Conditions (2006)

Guaranteed-Issue Policy without Medical Underwriting[d]

Monthly Premium	Annual Deductible	Annual OOP Max	Doctor Visit Co-Pay	Prescription Co-Pay	Lifetime Maximum
$1,389	$1,200	$2,500	20%	20%	$500,000

HIPAA-eligible individuals: Applicants are guaranteed the right to purchase an insurance policy from any company that provides individual coverage without exclusions for pre-existing conditions.

For applicants who are not HIPAA-eligible, Blue Cross Blue Shield in North Carolina will sell at least one individual health insurance policy to any resident on a guaranteed-issue basis if the applicant (1) resides within the North Carolina coverage area and (2) is under age 65. Premium is based on health status.

For More Information: See www.TNHIS.com/NC

---

[a]From 82,000 policies sold nationally online in 2004, see first page of Appendix A.
[b]Blue Cross Blue Shield of NC Blue Advantage—Plan B, $1,000 Deductible; single applicant (M/35); family applicant (M/35), spouse (F/35), children (F/8, M/5) from Raleigh, NC 27601; quoted 5.2.05.
[c]Fortis One Deductible; single applicant (M/35); family applicant (M/35), spouse (F/35), children (F/8, M/5) from Raleigh, NC 27601; quoted 5.2.05.
[d]Blue Cross Blue Shield of NC Blue Assurance for HIPAA-eligibles; single applicant (M/35) quoted 5.11.05 from Jenea at 800.863.1213.

North Dakota Insurance Department
(701) 328-2440
www.state.nd.us/ndins/
Guaranteed Issue ☐
Community Rated ☐

Bismarck
★

Average Cost of Individual Policy Sold in 2004: NA[a]

Typical Healthy Individual/Family Coverage (2006)

	Traditional Co-Pay Policy[b]		High-Deductible Policy[c]	
	Single	Family	Single	Family
Monthly premium	$169	$425	$88	$201
Annual deductible	$1,000	$3,000	$2,600	$5,200
Annual out-of-pocket max	$3,500	$8,000	$4,600	$9,200
Doctor visit co-pay	$25/2 visits; 50% after ded	$25/2 visits; 50% after ded	—	—
Prescription co-pay	$15–40 + $250 ded	$15–40 + $250 ded	—	—
Lifetime maximum	$7 million	$7 million	$8 million	$8 million

State-Guaranteed Coverage for People with Preexisting Conditions (2006)

Comp. Health Association of North Dakota (CHAND)[d]

Monthly Premium	Annual Deductible	Annual OOP Max	Doctor Visit Co-Pay	Prescription Co-Pay	Lifetime Maximum
$493	$1,000	$2,000	$25–40	$15–120	$3 million

Eligibility: (1) North Dakota resident for 183 days, (2) denied health coverage, offered restricted coverage, offered premium above CHAND rate, or with written evidence of qualifying medical condition, and (3) ineligible for North Dakota's medical assistance program, or (4) federally eligible.

HIPAA-eligible individuals: Applicants are guaranteed acceptance into CHAND without exclusions for preexisting conditions.

For More Information: See www.TNHIS.com/ND

---

[a]From 82,000 policies sold nationally online in 2004, see first page of Appendix A.
[b]Fortis PPO X-tra; single applicant (M/35); family applicant (M/35), spouse (F/35), children (F/8, M/5) from Bismarck, ND 58501; quoted 5.2.05.
[c]Fortis One Deductible; single applicant (M/35); family applicant (M/35), spouse (F/35), children (F/8, M/5) from Bismark, ND 58501; quoted 5.2.05.
[d]CHAND Major Medical Without Optional Chiropractic Option 1; single applicant (35); quoted 5.9.05 from www.chand.org/rates.html.

Ohio Department of Insurance
(614) 644-2658 (customer helpline)
www.ohioinsurance.gov
Guaranteed Issue   ☐
Community Rated   ☐

OH

Columbus
★

Average Cost for an Individual Policy: $132/month[a]
(single, age 34, healthy, sold in 2004)

Typical Healthy Individual/Family Coverage

	Traditional Co-Pay Policy[b]		High-Deductible Policy[c]	
	Single	Family	Single	Family
Monthly premium	$100	$399	$55	$151
Annual deductible	$1,000	$2,000	$2,650	$5,250
Annual out-of-pocket max	$3,000	$6,000	$2,650	$5,250
Doctor visit co-pay	$25	$25	—	—
Prescription co-pay	$15–90	$15–90	—	—
Lifetime maximum	$5 million	$5 million	$3 million	$3 million pp

State-Guaranteed Coverage for People with Preexisting Conditions

HIPAA-Eligible Applicant Individual Policy[d]

Monthly Premium	Annual Deductible	Annual OOP Max	Doctor Visit Co-Pay	Prescription Co-Pay	Lifetime Maximum
$351	$1,000	$5,000	50%	0% up to $2,500 then 100%	None

HIPAA-eligible individuals: Applicants are guaranteed the right to purchase insurance from individual health insurance providers at any time during the year.

Individuals who are not HIPAA-eligible must be accepted by any carrier that offers individual plans during an open enrollment period (30 days) where a limited number of applicants are accepted without health screening in the order in which they applied.

For More Information: See www.TNHIS.com/OH

---

[a]From 82,000 policies sold nationally online in 2004, see first page of Appendix A.
[b]Anthem Individual Blue Access—Plan 2; single applicant (M/35); family applicant (M/35), spouse (F/35), children (F/8, M/5) from Columbus, OH 43083; quoted 4.25.05.
[c]United Healthcare Single/Family HSA Saver; single applicant (M/35); family applicant (M/35), spouse (F/35), children (F/8, M/5); quoted 4.25.05.
[d]Blue Cross Blue Shield Basic CMM Plan; applicant (M/35) quoted 5.12.05 from phone call with Mary Jo at 800.467.8065.

Oklahoma Insurance Department
(405) 521-2828
www.oid.state.ok.us/
Guaranteed Issue   ☐
Community Rated   ☐

Oklahoma City ★

Average Cost of Individual Policy Sold in 2004: $134/month[a]
(single, average age 35, healthy)

Typical Healthy Individual/Family Coverage (2006)

	Traditional Co-Pay Policy[b]		High-Deductible Policy[c]	
	Single	Family	Single	Family
Monthly premium	$183	$637	$88	$251
Annual deductible	$750	$1,500	$2,650	$5,250
Annual out-of-pocket max	$3,000	$6,000	$2,650	$5,250
Doctor visit co-pay	$35	$35	—	—
Prescription co-pay	$20–50 + $250 namebrand ded	$20–50 + $250 namebrand ded	—	—
Lifetime maximum	$3 million	$3 million pp	$3 million	$3 million pp

State-Guaranteed Coverage for People with Preexisting Conditions (2006)

Individual Portability Coverage for HIPAA-Eligible Applicant[d]

Monthly Premium	Annual Deductible	Annual OOP Max	Doctor Visit Co-Pay	Prescription Co-Pay	Lifetime Maximum
$332	$1,000	$3,000	20%	$10–30 or 30%	$500,000

Eligibility: (1) Resident of Oklahoma for one year, (2) rejected or quoted very high premiums for health insurance by two companies, and (3) not institutionalized in penal, drug, or alcohol facility, or (4) federally eligible.

HIPAA-eligible individuals: Applicants are guaranteed acceptance into the Oklahoma High Risk Pool with no exclusions for preexisting conditions.

For More Information: See www.TNHIS.com/OK

---

[a]From 82,000 policies sold nationally online in 2004, see first page of Appendix A.
[b]Golden Rule Copay 35; single applicant (M/35); family applicant (M/35), spouse (F/35), children (F/8, M/5) from Oklahoma City, OK 73102; quoted 5.2.05.
[c]Golden Rule Single/Family HSA Saver; single applicant (M/35); family applicant (M/35), spouse (F/35), children (F/8, M/5) from Oklahoma City, OK 73102; quoted 5.2.05.
[d]OK High Risk Pool Plan (by Epoch Group); single applicant (M/35); quoted 5.10.05 913.362.0040 ext. 4767 from Mike.

Oregon Insurance Division
(503) 947-7980
www.cbs.state.or.us/external/ins
Guaranteed Issue ☐
Community Rated ☐

OR

Salem

Average Cost of Individual Policy Sold in 2004: $145/month[a]
(single, average age 31, healthy)

Typical Healthy Individual/Family Coverage (2006)

	Traditional Co-Pay Policy[b]		High-Deductible Policy[c]	
	Single	Family	Single	Family
Monthly premium	$157	$399	$116	$325
Annual deductible	$1,000	$2,500	$2,500	$5,000
Annual out-of-pocket max	$4,000	$4,000	$5,000	$10,000
Doctor visit co-pay	$20	$20	—	—
Prescription co-pay	50%	50%	—	—
Lifetime maximum	$2 million	$2 million	$2 million	$2 million

State-Guaranteed Coverage for People with Preexisting Conditions (2006)

Oregon Medical Insurance Pool (OMIP)[d]

Monthly Premium	Annual Deductible	Annual OOP Max	Doctor Visit Co-Pay	Prescription Co-Pay	Lifetime Maximum
$235	$1,000	$4,000	20%	$20–20%	$1 million

Eligibility: (1) Oregon resident and (2) rejected for health coverage within the past six months for health reasons, agent refuses to apply to a represented insurer for coverage because of applicant's health issues, health insurance is offered with restrictive waiver or excluded coverage, or choice of plans offered by carrier is limited because of applicant's medical condition or (3) federally eligible.

HIPAA-eligible individuals: Applicants are guaranteed acceptance into OMIP with no exclusions for preexisting conditions.

For More Information: See www.TNHIS.com/OR

---

[a]From 82,000 policies sold nationally online in 2004, see first page of Appendix A.
[b]Regence BCBS Blue Selections Premier; single applicant (M/35); family applicant (M/35), spouse (F/35), children (F/8, M/5) from Salem, OR 97301; quoted 5.2.05.
[c]Regence BCBS Regence HSA Qualified Plan; single applicant (M/35); family applicant (M/35), spouse (F/35), children (F/8, M/5) from Salem, OR 97301; quoted 5.2.05.
[d]OMIP Plan 1000; single applicant (M/35); quoted 5.10.05 www.oregon.gov.

Pennsylvania Insurance Department
(717) 787-2317
www.ins.state.pa.us/
Guaranteed Issue ☐
Community Rated ☐

 PA

 Harrisburg ★

Average Cost of Individual Policy Sold in 2004: $138/month[a]
(single, average age 31, healthy)

Typical Healthy Individual/Family Coverage (2006)

	Traditional Co-Pay Policy[b]		High-Deductible Policy[c]	
	Single	Family	Single	Family
Monthly premium	$119	$341	$69	$181
Annual deductible	$1,000	$3,000	$2,600	$5,200
Annual out-of-pocket max	$3,500	$8,500	$4,600	$9,200
Doctor visit co-pay	$25/2 visits then 50%	$25/2 visits then 50%	—	—
Prescription co-pay	$10–25 + 20% + $500 ded	$15–40 + 20% + $500 ded	—	—
Lifetime maximum	$7 million	$7 million	$8 million	$8 million

State-Guaranteed Coverage for People with Preexisting Conditions (2006)

HIPAA Comprehensive Policy[d]

Monthly Premium	Annual Deductible	Annual OOP Max	Doctor Visit Co-Pay	Prescription Co-Pay	Lifetime Maximum
$325	$1,500	$6,000	20%	50% after $250 ded	$1 million

HIPAA-eligible applicants: Applicants are guaranteed the opportunity to purchase a state-approved policy sold by Blue Cross Blue Shield.

For applicants who are not HIPAA-eligible, BCBS in Pennsylvania will sell at least one individual health insurance policy to any resident on a guaranteed-issue basis if the applicant (1) resides within the coverage area and (2) does not have coverage available elsewhere through a spouse, employer, Medicare, or Medicaid. Premium is based on health status.

For More Information: See www.TNHIS.com/PA

[a]From 82,000 policies sold nationally online in 2004, see first page of Appendix A.
[b]Fortis PPO X-tra; single applicant (M/35); family applicant (M/35), spouse (F/35), children (F/8, M/5) from Harrisburg, PA 17101; quoted 5.2.05.
[c]Fortis One Deductible; single applicant (M/35); family applicant (M/35), spouse (F/35), children (F/8, M/5) from Harrisburg, PA 17101; quoted 5.2.05.
[d]Blue Cross Blue Shield of PA HIPAA Comprehensive1500; single applicant (M/35) quoted 5.11.05.

Rhode Island Division of Insurance
(401) 222-2223
www.dbr.state.ri.us/insurance.html
Guaranteed Issue ☐
Community Rated ☐

Average Cost of Individual Policy Sold in 2004: $116/month[a]
(single, average age 33, healthy)

Typical Healthy Individual/Family Coverage (2006)

	Traditional Co-Pay Policy[b]		High-Deductible Policy	
	Single	Family	Single	Family
Monthly premium	$203	$625	NA	NA
Annual deductible	$300	$600	NA	NA
Annual out-of-pocket max	None	None	NA	NA
Doctor visit co-pay	20%	20%	—	—
Prescription co-pay	20%	20%	—	—
Lifetime maximum	$250,000	$250,000	NA	NA

State-Guaranteed Coverage for People with Preexisting Conditions (2006)

PPO Program for HIPAA-Eligible Applicant[c]

Monthly Premium	Annual Deductible	Annual OOP Max	Doctor Visit Co-Pay	Prescription Co-Pay	Lifetime Maximum
$310	$2,000	$5,000	$15–25	20%	None

HIPAA-eligible applicants: All Rhode Island insurance providers must offer and accept HIPAA-eligible applicants immediately for an individual policy with no exclusions for pre-existing conditions. The state also has a special program with discounted rates for healthy HIPAA-eligible individuals less than 60 years old who pass medical underwriting.

Rhode Island guarantees coverage only to residents with health issues who are HIPAA-eligible or low-income individuals. However, for self-employed individuals working in companies with 1 to 50 employees, guaranteed-issue policies for group plans are available if the individual can prove that he or she is self-employed.

For More Information: See www.TNHIS.com/RI

---

[a]From 82,000 policies sold nationally online in 2004, see first page of Appendix A.
[b]Blue Cross Blue Shield of RI Direct Blue Standard; single applicant (M/35); family applicant (M/35), spouse (F/35), children (F/8, M/5) from Providence, RI 02903; quoted 5.2.05.
[c]Blue Cross Blue Shield Health Mate Coast to Coast PPO Program for HIPAA-Eligibles; single applicant (M/35) quoted 5.12.05 from Anne at 401.459.5000.

South Carolina Department of Insurance
(803) 737-6160
www.doi.state.sc.us/
Guaranteed Issue   ☐
Community Rated   ☐

Average Cost of Individual Policy Sold in 2004: $138/month[a]
(single, average age 35, healthy)

Typical Healthy Individual/Family Coverage (2006)

	Traditional Co-Pay Policy[b]		High-Deductible Policy[c]	
	Single	Family	Single	Family
Monthly premium	$148	$556	$91	$292
Annual deductible	$1,000	$4,000	$2,600	$5,150
Annual out-of-pocket max	$5,000	$5,000	$5,000	$10,000
Doctor visit co-pay	$20	$20	—	—
Prescription co-pay	Discount %	Discount %	—	—
Lifetime maximum	$2 million	$2 million	$2 million	$2 million

State-Guaranteed Coverage for People with Preexisting Conditions (2006)

South Carolina Health Insurance Pool (SCHIP)[d]

Monthly Premium	Annual Deductible	Annual OOP Max	Doctor Visit Co-Pay	Prescription Co-Pay	Lifetime Maximum
$447	$500	$2,000	0% after ded	20%	$1 million

Eligibility: (1) South Carolina resident for six months and (2) with a rejection letter from an insurance carrier and preexisting condition making applicant ineligible for an individual health insurance or qualifying medical condition or (3) federally eligible.

HIPAA-eligible individuals: Applicants are guaranteed acceptance into SCHIP with no exclusions for preexisting conditions.

For More Information: See www.TNHIS.com/SC

---

[a]From 82,000 policies sold nationally online in 2004, see first page of Appendix A.
[b]Blue Cross Blue Shield of SC Plan I 80/60; single applicant (M/35); family applicant (M/35), spouse (F/35), children (F/8, M/5) from Columbia, SC 29201; quoted 5.3.05.
[c]Blue Cross Blue Shield of SC Personal Blue High Deductible Plan 4; single applicant (M/35); family applicant (M/35), spouse (F/35), children (F/8, M/5) from Columbia, SC 29201; quoted 5.3.05.
[d]SCHIP Plan; single applicant (M/35); quoted 5.10.05 from phone call with Darrel 5.10.05.

South Dakota Division of Insurance
(605) 773-3563
www.state.sd.us/drr2/reg/insurance/
Guaranteed Issue ☐
Community Rated ☐

Average Cost of Individual Policy Sold in 2004: $124/month[a]
(single, average age 32, healthy)

Typical Healthy Individual/Family Coverage (2006)

	Traditional Co-Pay Policy[b]		High-Deductible Policy[c]	
	Single	Family	Single	Family
Monthly premium	$163	$592	$113	$371
Annual deductible	$1,000	$3,000	$2,550	$5,100
Annual out-of-pocket max	$2,000	$6,000	$2,550	$5,100
Doctor visit co-pay	20% after ded	20% after ded	—	—
Prescription co-pay	Discount card	Discount card	—	—
Lifetime maximum	$5 million	$5 million	$2 million	$2 million

State-Guaranteed Coverage for People with Preexisting Conditions (2006)

Individual Portability Coverage for HIPAA-Eligible Applicant[d]

Monthly Premium	Annual Deductible	Annual OOP Max	Doctor Visit Co-Pay	Prescription Co-Pay	Lifetime Maximum
$493	$1,000	$2,000	$25–40	$15–120	$3 million

HIPAA-eligible individuals: Applicants are guaranteed coverage by the South Dakota High Risk Pool without exclusions for preexisting conditions.

South Dakota guarantees coverage only to residents with health issues who are HIPAA-eligible or low-income individuals.

For More Information: See www.TNHIS.com/SD

---

[a]From 82,000 policies sold nationally online in 2004, see first page of Appendix A.
[b]Celtic Managed Indemnity 80/20 Plan; single applicant (M/35); family applicant (M/35), spouse (F/35), children (F/8, M/5) from Pierre, SD 57501; quoted 5.3.05.
[c]Wellmark BCBS Blue Priority HSA/Blue Select: Plan B; single applicant (M/35); family applicant (M/35), spouse (F/35), children (F/8, M/5) from Pierre, SD 57501; quoted 5.13.05.
[d]SD High Risk Pool Plan A; single applicant (M/35); quoted 5.10.05 from www.hcmti.com/riskpool/plan_2005.pdf.

Tennessee Dept. of Commerce & Ins.
(615) 741-2241
www.state.tn.us/commerce/contact.html
Guaranteed Issue ☐
Community Rated ☐

TN

Nashville ★

Average Cost of Individual Policy Sold in 2004: $127/month[a]
(single, average age 33, healthy)

Typical Healthy Individual/Family Coverage (2006)

	Traditional Co-Pay Policy[b]		High-Deductible Policy[c]	
	Single	Family	Single	Family
Monthly premium	$137	$491	$74	$202
Annual deductible	$1,000	$3,000	$2,650	$5,250
Annual out-of-pocket max	$2,000	$5,000	$2,650	$5,250
Doctor visit co-pay	$30	$20–35	—	—
Prescription co-pay	$10–50	$10–50	—	—
Lifetime maximum	$5 million	$5 million	$3 million	$3 million pp

State-Guaranteed Coverage for People with Preexisting Conditions (2006)

Individual Portability Coverage for HIPAA-Eligible Applicant[d]

Monthly Premium	Annual Deductible	Annual OOP Max	Doctor Visit Co-Pay	Prescription Co-Pay	Lifetime Maximum
$439	$1,000	$2,000	20%	$10–50	$5 million

HIPAA-eligible individuals: Applicants are guaranteed the right to purchase an insurance policy from any company that provides individual coverage in Tennessee without exclusions for preexisting conditions; premiums are about 300% the cost of the standard healthy rate. For more information, applicants should call individual carriers directly.

As of May 2005, Tennessee guarantees coverage only to residents with health issues who are HIPAA-eligible or low-income individuals pending funding for the state-sponsored TennCare program. For updated information, contact TennCare directly at 866.311.4287.

For More Information: See www.TNHIS.com/TN

---

[a]From 82,000 policies sold nationally online in 2004, see first page of Appendix A.
[b]Blue Cross Blue Shield of TN PPO Plan $30 Copay $1,000 80/60 (H11); single applicant (M/35); family applicant (M/35), spouse (F/35), children (F/8, M/5) from Nashville, TN 37201; quoted 5.3.05.
[c]Golden Rule Single/Family HSA Saver; single applicant (M/35); family applicant (M/35), spouse (F/35), children (F/8, M/5) from Nashville, TN 37201; quoted 5.3.05.
[d]Blue Cross Blue Shield of TN Guaranteed Issue/HIPAA Policy; single applicant (M/35); quoted 5.10.05 at 800.565.9140 by Tanya.

The Texas Dept of Insurance
(512) 463-6169 (customer helpline)
www.tdi.state.tx.us/
Guaranteed Issue ☐
Community Rated ☐

Austin ★

Average Cost of Individual Policy Sold in 2004: $133/month[a]
(single, average age 33, healthy)

Typical Healthy Individual/Family Coverage (2006)

	Traditional Co-Pay Policy[b]		High-Deductible Policy[c]	
	Single	Family	Single	Family
Monthly premium	$117	$403	$77	$188
Annual deductible	$1,500	$4,500	$2,600	$5,200
Annual out-of-pocket max	$3,000	$6,000	$5,000	$10,000
Doctor visit co-pay	$25	$25	—	—
Prescription co-pay	$10–45 + $200 ded	$10–45 + $200 ded	—	—
Lifetime maximum	$5 million	$5 million	$5 million	$5 million

State-Guaranteed Coverage for People with Preexisting Conditions (2006)

Texas Health Insurance Risk Pool[d]

Monthly Premium	Annual Deductible	Annual OOP Max	Doctor Visit Co-Pay	Prescription Co-Pay	Lifetime Maximum
$364	$1,000	$4,000	$30/visit for 2 visits, then 20–40%	$10–40 with $100 ded	$1.5 million

Eligibility: (1) Texas resident for 30 days or permanent resident of the U.S. for three years, (2) less than 65, and (3) with evidence of uninsurability or uprating, or (4) federally eligible.

HIPAA-eligible individuals: Applicants are guaranteed acceptance into the Texas Health Insurance Risk Pool with no exclusions for preexisting conditions.

For More Information: See www.TNHIS.com/TX

---

[a]From 82,000 policies sold nationally online in 2004, see first page of Appendix A.
[b]Blue Cross Blue Shield of TX, PPO Select Choice; single applicant (M/35); family applicant (M/35), spouse (F/35), children (F/8, M/5) from Austin, TX 73301; quoted 4.25.04.
[c]Unicare Life & Health Insurance Company HSA Compatible Plan 2 (Single)/(Family); single applicant (M/35); family applicant (M/35), spouse (F/35), children (F/8, M/5); quoted 4.25.04.
[d]Texas Health Insurance Risk Pool Plan II $1,000 Deductible Area 2; single applicant (M/35) from Austin, Texas 78701; quoted 5.17.05 from www.txhealthpool.org.

Utah Insurance Department
(801) 538-3800
www.insurance.state.ut.us/
Guaranteed Issue ☐
Community Rated ☐

UT

Salt Lake City

Average Cost of Individual Policy Sold in 2004: $114/month[a]
(single, average age 31, healthy)

Typical Healthy Individual/Family Coverage (2006)

	Traditional Co-Pay Policy[b]		High-Deductible Policy[c]	
	Single	Family	Single	Family
Monthly premium	$115	$351	$99	$302
Annual deductible	$1,000	$1,000	$2,500	$5,000
Annual out-of-pocket max	$3,500	$3,500	$5,000	$10,000
Doctor visit co-pay	$20	$20	—	—
Prescription co-pay	$5–50%	$5–50%	—	—
Lifetime maximum	$2 million	$2 million	$1 million	$1 million

State-Guaranteed Coverage for People with Preexisting Conditions (2006)

Utah Comprehensive Health Insurance Pool (HIPUTAH)[d]

Monthly Premium	Annual Deductible	Annual OOP Max	Doctor Visit Co-Pay	Prescription Co-Pay	Lifetime Maximum
$493	$1,000	$2,000	$25–40	$15–120	$3 million

Eligibility: (1) Continuous resident of Utah for 12 months, (2) ineligible for Medicare and Medicaid, (3) unable to get insurance through a group employer plan, (4) ineligible for health insurance coverage in the private market, and (5) meets health underwriting criteria established by the state of Utah, or (6) federally eligible.

HIPAA-eligible individuals: Applicants are guaranteed acceptance into HIPUTAH with no exclusions for preexisting conditions.

For More Information: See www.TNHIS.com/UT

---

[a]From 82,000 policies sold nationally online in 2004, see first page of Appendix A.
[b]Regence Blue Cross Blue Shield BlueAdvantage Copay Plan—Value Care Network; single applicant (M/35); family applicant (M/35), spouse (F/35), children (F/8, M/5) from Salt Lake City, UT 84101; quoted 5.3.05.
[c]Regence Blue Cross Blue Shield HSA $2,500 Single/$5,000 Family—Traditional Network; single applicant (M/35); family applicant (M/35), spouse (F/35), children (F/8, M/5) from Salt Lake City, UT 84101; quoted 5.3.05.
[d]HIPUtah UP2 Plan; single applicant (35); quoted 5.10.05 from www.ut.regence.com.

Vermont Insurance Division
(802) 828-3301
www.bishca.state.vt.us/
Guaranteed Issue ☐
Community Rated ☐

VT

★
Montpelier

Average Cost of Individual Policy Sold in 2004: NAᵃ

Typical Healthy Individual/Family Coverage (2006)

	Traditional Co-Pay Policyᵇ		High-Deductible Policy	
	Single	Family	Single	Family
Monthly premium	$374	$1,010	NA	NA
Annual deductible	$3,500	$7,000	NA	NA
Annual out-of-pocket max	$9,500	$19,000	NA	NA
Doctor visit co-pay	Not covered	Not covered	—	—
Prescription co-pay	Not covered	Not covered	—	—
Lifetime maximum	None	None	NA	NA

State-Guaranteed Coverage for People with Preexisting Conditions (2006)

Representative Policyᶜ

Monthly Premium	Annual Deductible	Annual OOP Max	Doctor Visit Co-Pay	Prescription Co-Pay	Lifetime Maximum
$374	$3,500	$9,500	Not covered	Not covered	None

Vermont does not have a state risk pool—every policy sold in Vermont is effectively a state risk pool policy because all citizens must be accepted ("guaranteed issue") at the same premium ("community rated") regardless of their health. Both HIPAA-eligible applicants and applicants who are not HIPAA-eligible are guaranteed a policy at the same community rate.

For More Information: See www.TNHIS.com/VT

ᵃFrom 82,000 policies sold nationally online in 2004, see first page of Appendix A.
ᵇVT Freedom Plan Nongroup $3,500 Option; single applicant (M/35); family applicant (M/35), spouse (F/35), children (F/8, M/5) from Montpelier, VT 05602; quoted 5.2.05.
ᶜVT Freedom Plan Nongroup $3,500 Option; single applicant (M/35); family applicant (M/35), spouse (F/35), children (F/8, M/5) from Montpelier, VT 05602; quoted 5.2.05.

Virginia Bureau of Insurance
(804) 371-9741
www.scc.virginia.gov/division/boi
Guaranteed Issue ☐
Community Rated ☐

Average Cost of Individual Policy Sold in 2004: $154/month[a]
(single, average age 34, healthy)

Typical Healthy Individual/Family Coverage (2006)

	Traditional Co-Pay Policy[b]		High-Deductible Policy[c]	
	Single	Family	Single	Family
Monthly premium	$138	$502	$63	$172
Annual deductible	$750	$1,500	$2,650	$5,250
Annual out-of-pocket max	$1,500	$3,000	$2,650	$5,250
Doctor visit co-pay	$20–30	$20–30	—	—
Prescription co-pay	Greater of $10 or 40%	Greater of $10 or 40%	—	—
Lifetime maximum	$5 million	$5 million	$3 million	$3 million pp

State-Guaranteed Coverage for People with Preexisting Conditions (2006)

Approximation for a HIPAA-Eligible Applicant Policy[d]

Monthly Premium	Annual Deductible	Annual OOP Max	Doctor Visit Co-Pay	Prescription Co-Pay	Lifetime Maximum
$494	$1,500	$2,500	$30/3 visits then 30%	Generic only: $15–40% + ded	$2 million

HIPAA-eligible individuals: Applicants are guaranteed coverage by any individual health insurance provider with no exclusions for preexisting conditions.

Individuals who are not HIPAA-eligible are guaranteed coverage by Anthem of Virginia if they are (1) residents of Virginia within the coverage area, (2) unable to get insurance from another source, and (3) ineligible for Medicaid and Medicare. Premium is based on health status.

For More Information: See www.TNHIS.com/VA

[a]From 82,000 policies sold nationally online in 2004, see first page of Appendix A.
[b]Anthem Individual KeyCare Preferred; single applicant (M/35); family applicant (M/35), spouse (F/35), children (F/8, M/5) from Richmond, VA 23219; quoted 5.2.05.
[c]Golden Rule Single/Family HSA Saver; single applicant (M/35); family applicant (M/35), spouse (F/35), children (F/8, M/5) from Richmond, VA 23219; quoted 5.2.05.
[d]Anthem Individual Essential KeyCare; single applicant (M/35) quoted 5.12.05 from seca.anthem.com and phone call with Carolyn at 800.334.7676. Without specific health condition disclosures, Anthem is unable to provide a HIPAA-eligible quote. Carolyn said listed benefits are available for HIPAA-eligible plans, and that the premium is about four times the normal premium of a tobacco user. For specific quotes, please call BCBS directly.

Washington Office of the Ins. Comm.
(360) 725-7080
www.insurance.wa.gov/
Guaranteed Issue ☐
Community Rated ☐

★ Olympia

Average Cost of Individual Policy Sold in 2004: $169/month[a]
(single, average age 35, healthy)

Typical Healthy Individual/Family Coverage (2006)

	Traditional Co-Pay Policy[b]		High-Deductible Policy[c]	
	Single	Family	Single	Family
Monthly premium	$167	$525	$98	$255
Annual deductible	$1,000	$4,000	$2,500	$5,000
Annual out-of-pocket max	$2,000	$6,000	$5,000	$10,000
Doctor visit co-pay	$15	$15	—	—
Prescription co-pay	50%	50%	—	—
Lifetime maximum	$1 million	$1 million	$1 million	$1 million

State-Guaranteed Coverage for People with Preexisting Conditions (2006)

Washington State Health Insurance Pool (WSHIP)[d]

Monthly Premium	Annual Deductible	Annual OOP Max	Doctor Visit Co-Pay	Prescription Co-Pay	Lifetime Maximum
$493	$1,000	$2,000	$25–40	$15–120	$3 million

Eligibility: (1) Resident of Washington, (2) rejected from other health coverage within the past 90 days, and (3) not enrolled in a public program that duplicates WSHIP's health benefits or resident of a county where individual health benefit plans aren't marketed to the general public, or (4) federally eligible.

HIPAA-eligible individuals: Applicants are guaranteed acceptance into WSHIP with no exclusions for preexisting conditions.

For More Information: See www.TNHIS.com/WA

---

[a]From 82,000 policies sold nationally online in 2004, see first page of Appendix A.
[b]Regence Blue Shield Selections Comprehensive Plan 1000; single applicant (M/35); family applicant (M/35), spouse (F/35), children (F/8, M/5) from Olympia, WA 98501; quoted 5.3.05.
[c]Regence Blue Shield Preferred Plan 2500/5000 Catastrophic (HSA Qualified); single applicant (M/35); family applicant (M/35), spouse (F/35), children (F/8, M/5) from Olympia, WA 98501; quoted 5.3.05.
[d]WSHIP Plan 3 Network Plan $1,000 Deductible Plan Choice; single applicant (35); quoted 5.10.05 from www.wship.org/summary.asp.

West Virginia Insurance Commission
(304) 558-3386
www.wvinsurance.gov
Guaranteed Issue ☐
Community Rated ☐

★
Charleston

Average Cost of Individual Policy Sold in 2004: NA[a]

Typical Healthy Individual/Family Coverage (2006)

	Traditional Co-Pay Policy[b]		High-Deductible Policy[c]	
	Single	Family	Single	Family
Monthly premium	$191	$743	$125	$453
Annual deductible	$1,000	$2,000	$2,600	$5,150
Annual out-of-pocket max	$2,000	$6,000	$2,600	$5,150
Doctor visit co-pay	20% after ded	20% after ded	—	—
Prescription co-pay	50%	50%	—	—
Lifetime maximum	$1 million	$1 million	$5 million	$5 million pp

State-Guaranteed Coverage for People with Preexisting Conditions (2006)

Guaranteed Issue HIPAA-Eligible Applicant Policy[d]

Monthly Premium	Annual Deductible	Annual OOP Max	Doctor Visit Co-Pay	Prescription Co-Pay	Lifetime Maximum
$724	$1,000	$2,000	20%	50%	$1 million

HIPAA-eligible individuals: Applicants are guaranteed the right to buy an individual health insurance policy from any insurance company that sells policies in West Virginia with no exclusions for preexisting conditions and no limit on the premium.

West Virginia guarantees coverage only to residents with health issues who are HIPAA-eligible or low-income individuals. The state anticipates opening a risk pool on July 1, 2005, that will cover medical uninsurables who are not HIPAA-eligible. Call the Insurance Commission directly for more details.

For More Information: See www.TNHIS.com/WV

---

[a]From 82,000 policies sold nationally online in 2004, see first page of Appendix A.
[b]Blue Cross Blue Shield of WV Super Blue Plus 2000; single applicant (M/35); family applicant (M/35), spouse (F/35), children (F/8, M/5) from Charleston, WV 25301; quoted 5.2.05.
[c]CelticSaver HSA Health Plan; single applicant (M/35); family applicant (M/35), spouse (F/35), children (F/8, M/5) from Charleston, WV 25301; quoted 5.2.05.
[d]One on One Super Blue Plus; single applicant (M/35) quoted 5.12.05 from Laura at 888.644.2583.

Wisconsin Office of the Ins. Comm.
(608) 266-3585
http://oci.wi.gov/
Guaranteed Issue ☐
Community Rated ☐

Madison
★

> Average Cost of Individual Policy Sold in 2004: $126/month[a]
> (single, average age 36, healthy)

Typical Healthy Individual/Family Coverage (2006)

	Traditional Co-Pay Policy[b]		High-Deductible Policy[c]	
	Single	Family	Single	Family
Monthly premium	$118	$428	$68	$267
Annual deductible	$1,000	$3,000	$2,650	$5,500
Annual out-of-pocket max	$500	$1,000	$2,650	$10,000
Doctor visit co-pay	10% after ded	10% after ded	—	—
Prescription co-pay	30% after ded	30% after ded	—	—
Lifetime maximum	$3 million	$3 million	$3 million	$3 million pp

State-Guaranteed Coverage for People with Preexisting Conditions (2006)

Wisconsin Health Insurance Risk Sharing Plan (HIRSP)[d]

Monthly Premium	Annual Deductible	Annual OOP Max	Doctor Visit Co-Pay	Prescription Co-Pay	Lifetime Maximum
$690	$1,000	$2,000	$20%	20% up to $25 per presc	$1 million

Eligibility: (1) Wisconsin resident, (2) ineligible for employer-sponsored group health insurance, (3) ineligible for other government insurance programs, and (4) less than 65 with documentation of insurability because of disability, HIV, or a notice of rejection, cancellation, or significant reduction in coverage over past nine months, or (5) federally eligible.

HIPAA-eligible individuals: Applicants are guaranteed acceptance into the HIRSP with no exclusions for preexisting conditions.

For More Information: See www.TNHIS.com/WI

---

[a]From 82,000 policies sold nationally online in 2004, see first page of Appendix A.
[b]Blue Cross Blue Shield of WI Personal Choice PPO $1,000 Deductible; single applicant (M/35); family applicant (M/35), spouse (F/35), children (F/8, M/5) from Madison, WI 50061; quoted 5.3.05.
[c]Golden Rule Single/Family HSA Saver; single applicant (M/35); family applicant (M/35), spouse (F/35), children (F/8, M/5) from Madison, WI 50061; quoted 5.3.05.
[d]HIRSP Plan I Option A; single applicant (M/35) from Madison, WI 50061; quoted 5.10.05 www.dhfs.state.wi.us.

Wyoming Insurance Department
(307) 777-7401
http://insurance.state.wy.us/
Guaranteed Issue ☐
Community Rated ☐

Cheyenne
★

Average Cost of Individual Policy Sold in 2004: $107/month[a]
(single, average age 28, healthy)

Typical Healthy Individual/Family Coverage (2006)

	Traditional Co-Pay Policy[b]		High-Deductible Policy[c]	
	Single	Family	Single	Family
Monthly premium	$162	$472	$101	$267
Annual deductible	$1,000	$3,000	$2,600	$5,200
Annual out-of-pocket max	$3,500	$8,000	$4,600	$9,200
Doctor visit co-pay	$25/2 visits then 50%	$25/2 visits then 50%	—	—
Prescription co-pay	$10–25 + 20% + $500 ded	$10–25 + 20% + $500 ded	—	—
Lifetime maximum	$7 million	$7 million	$8 million	$8 million

State-Guaranteed Coverage for
People with Preexisting Conditions (2006)

Wyoming Health Insurance Pool (WHIP)[d]

Monthly Premium	Annual Deductible	Annual OOP Max	Doctor Visit Co-Pay	Prescription Co-Pay	Lifetime Maximum
$446	$1,000	$2,000	20%	30%	$600,000

Eligibility: (1) Resident of Wyoming and (2) refused coverage for health reasons by one insurer, provided with coverage more restrictive than pool, or given health insurance coverage at rate exceeding the pool or (3) federally eligible.

HIPAA-eligible individuals: Applicants are guaranteed acceptance into WHIP with no exclusions for preexisting conditions.

For More Information: See www.TNHIS.com/WY

---

[a]From 82,000 policies sold nationally online in 2004, see first page of Appendix A.
[b]Fortis PPO X-tra; single applicant (M/35); family applicant (M/35), spouse (F/35), children (F/8, M/5) from Cheyenne, WY 00050; quoted 5.3.05.
[c]Fortis One Deductible; single applicant (M/35); family applicant (M/35), spouse (F/35), children (F/8, M/5) from Cheyenne, WY 00050; quoted 5.3.05.
[d]WHIP Gold Plan; single applicant (M/35); quoted 5.10.05 from insurance.state.wy.us.

How Americans Get Health Insurance Today . . . and What about the 45 Million Uninsured?

Here's how all 296 million Americans get their health insurance.

How Americans Get Health Insurance[a]

Type of Health Insurance	Millions	% of Population
Employer-sponsored	157	51%
Uninsured	45	15%
Medicare	43	15%
Medicaid/public	38	15%
Individual/family policies	13	4%
Total population	296	100%

[a]*"The Uninsured: A Primer—Key Facts about Americans without Health Insurance,"* 18 December 2003, Kaiser Family Foundation, 7 May 2005, *www.kff.org/uninsured/ 4085.cfm*, November 2004, www.kff.org.

The 45 Million Americans without Health Insurance

The majority of the uninsured are working—8 in 10 have workers in their families. Of these workers, 81 percent work for an employer that does not sponsor health benefits, or they are not eligible for their employer's plan (i.e., they are part-time or independent contractors).[1]

Two reasons that 45 million Americans do not have health
insurance are that their employers do not provide it for them
and that they do not know that affordable individual/family
policies are available.

Few Americans without health insurance are very poor. If
they were, they would qualify for Medicaid and other state-
sponsored programs for low-income families—38 million
Americans qualified for Medicaid and Medicaid-type programs in 2003 (see Chapter 7).

While each state is different, to qualify for Medicaid you must be either
under age 19 in a lower-income family, disabled, or earning an annual
income below 100 to 150 percent of the federal poverty line (FPL)—the
FPL in 2005 was approximately $20,000 per family ($10,000 per single).

The 45 million uninsured can be divided into two categories based on
their 2005 income—the 16 million earning more than $40,000 for a fam-
ily of four ($20,000 per single) and the 29 million earning less than this
amount (but typically not enough less to qualify for Medicaid).

**16 Million (35 Percent) Uninsured Earning More Than $40,000 per Family
($20,000 per Single)**

Category	Millions	%
Adults without children	10	65%
Adult parents	4	21%
Children	2	14%
Total	16	100%

**29 Million (65 Percent) Uninsured Earning Less Than $40,000 per Family
($20,000 per Single)**

Category	Millions	%
Adults without children	15	52%
Adult parents	8	28%
Children	6	20%
Total	29	100%

Of the first category (the 16 million earning more than $40,000 per
family), a primary reason they do not have health insurance is ignorance—they do not know that affordable individual/family policies are
available. As shown in Appendix A, in almost every state, individual HSA-
qualified policies for most of these 10 million adults without children are

available for between $50 and $116 per month—and these quotes are for good policies from top-rated carriers (e.g., Blue Cross Blue Shield plans).

Most of the 10 million uninsured adults without children earning more than $40,000 per year per family could afford individual health insurance policies for a premium of about $92 a month—if only they knew they were available.

In the second category, there are 29 million Americans earning less than $40,000 per family but probably not enough less to qualify for Medicaid (below $20,000 to $30,000 per family).

Many of the 15 million uninsured adults without children earning more than $20,000 to $30,000 but less than $40,000 per year per family could probably afford individual health insurance policies for a premium of about $92 per month—if only they knew they were available.

These 25 million uninsured adults without children comprise 55 percent of the 45 million uninsured. In addition, a significant portion of the 12 million adults with children, and the 2 million children in families earning more than $40,000 per year, could probably qualify for and afford individual/family policies.

Why HSAs Will Lower the Number of Uninsured

HSAs and other high-deductible health insurance policies, now offered by both employers and individual/family policies, should lower the number of uninsured because their premiums are so much more affordable. HSAs are also a particularly good option for the largest group of uninsured—individuals age 19 to 29.

Individuals age 19 to 29 are uninsured at more than twice the rate (33 percent) as the rest of the population (15 percent).[2] At first glance this seems strange, because people age 19 to 29 should have the most opportunities to get health insurance through employment or by being eligible for an individual policy. Closer analysis reveals that, until the advent of HSAs today, going without health insurance may have been a deliberate choice for some of them.

The premium paid for traditional low-deductible health insurance is partly for protection ("insurance") against an unforeseen event, and mostly for prepaid medical expenses. But, most individuals age 19 to 29 consume almost no medical expenses—they need only high-deductible protection. Inexpensive, high-deductible, HSA-type policies allow these individuals to pay for only what they need—protection against a medical catastrophe. Once they learn about these policies, many of them will decide to buy health insurance, since they will no longer have to waste money on prepaid medical expense coverage that they don't need.

In the first 14 months that high-deductible HSA-qualified health insurance became legal, more than 1 million Americans opened an HSA—and 37 percent of these people were previously uninsured.[3]

The reason, as illustrated throughout Appendix A, is that HSA-qualified individual/family health insurance policies are available in 2006 at prices that are, on average, about half the price of traditional individual/family policies, and about one-fourth the price of employer-sponsored group health insurance.

Average Monthly Cost of Individual/Family Health Insurance Policies (2006)[a]

	Employer-Sponsored Plans (2006)	Traditional Policy (Lower Deductible)	Health Savings Account Policy (Higher Deductible)
Single	$ 375	$173	$ 92
Family	$1,166	$541	$266

[a]See Appendix A for details.

Preface

1. As explained throughout this book, all states (except New Jersey, New York, Massachusetts, Maine, and Vermont) now allow insurance carriers to sell individual/family policies at much lower rates to healthy people.

Chapter I

1. Himmelstein, David, Elizabeth Warren, Deborah Thorne, and Steffie Woolhandler, "MarketWatch: Illness and Injury as Contributors to Bankruptcy," *Health Affairs*, 2 February 2005, 5 May 2005.
2. Car-Accidents.com home page, 2005. Car Accidents.com, 5 May 2005, www.car-accidents.com.
3. American Heart Association home page, 2005, American Heart Association, 5 May 2005, www.americanheart.org.
4. American Diabetes Association home page, 2002. American Diabetes Association, 5 May 2005, www.diabetes.org.
5. Tiscali Money home page, 2005, Tiscali, 5 May 2005, www.tiscali.co.uk.
6. U.S. Department of Labor, Bureau of Labor Statistics, *Labor Force Statistics from the Current Population Survey—Unadj Median Weeks Unemployed*, 1995–2005, 5 May 2005, www.bls.gov/webapps/legacy/cpsatab9.htm.
7. Himmelstein, David, Elizabeth Warren, Deborah Thorne, and Steffie Woolhandler, "MarketWatch: Illness and Injury as Contributors to Bankruptcy," *Health Affairs*, 2 February 2005, 5 May 2005, http://content.healthaffairs.org/cgi/content/full/hlthaff.w5.63/DC1.
8. Except in some states where employers with less than 50 employees are pooled together or considered the same as individual/family policies.
9. U.S. Census Bureau, *Statistical Abstract of the United States: 2004–2005*, Section 3, 2004, 5 May 2005, www.census.gov/prod/2004pubs/04statab/health.pdf.
10. The legislation creating Health Savings Accounts was a 17-page amendment added to the Medicare Prescription Drug Improvement and Modernization Act of 2003.
11. Health Reimbursement Arrangements (HRAs) may reimburse employees only for medical expenses listed in Section 213(d) of the IRS Code. Health insurance premiums were added to 213(d) in 2004. However, until 2005, many carriers offering individual and family health insurance policies prohibited their policyholders from accepting reimbursement from employers.

Chapter 2

1. Survey of 82,000 individual/family health insurance policies sold by eHealthinsurance during a six-month period in 2004. *The Cost and Benefits of Individual Health Insurance Plans,* 12 October 2005, eHealthInsuranceServices, Inc., 5 May 2005, http://image.ehealthinsurance .com/ehealthinsurance/expertcenterNew/CostBenefitReportFinal101204 .pdf.

2. *Survey Shows Private Health Insurance Premiums Rose 11.2% in 2004,* 9 September 2004, Kaiser Family Foundation, 5 May 2005, www.kff.org/ insurance/chcm090904nr.cfm.

3. Zaneben.com is owned by my family and several associates. This is a company I founded after I lost my health insurance while my wife was pregnant (see preface for details). I am the chairman of this company.

4. This is assuming that my annual premium rises 6 percent per annum for 21 years and the initial base is lowered by $720 per year ($60 per month).

5. *Survey Shows Private Health Insurance Premiums Rose 11.2% in 2004,* 9 September 2004, Kaiser Family Foundation, 5 May 2005, www.kff.org/ insurance/chcm090904nr.cfm.

6. "The Factors Fueling Rising Healthcare Costs," American Association of Health Plans, April 2002, *PriceWaterhouseCoopers,* 5 May 2005, www.aahp .org/InternalLinks/PwCFinalReport.pdf. This age/cost relationship is directly reflected in the average monthly premium per single person of the 82,000 individual and family policies sold by eHealthInsurance in 2004.

7. Blue Shield of California home page, October 2003, *Blue Shield of California—Shield Spectrum PPO Savings Plan 2400,* 5 May 2005, https://mylifepath.com.

8. *The Cost and Benefits of Individual Health Insurance Plans,* 12 October 2005, eHealthInsuranceServices, Inc., 5 May 2005, http://image.ehealthinsurance .com/ehealthinsurance/expertcenterNew/CostBenefitReportFinal101204 .pdf.

Chapter 3

1. While this is generally true today, in the 1980s and 1990s legal loopholes in ERISA allowed corporate raiders to personally appropriate billions from worker pension accounts. For example, in 1985 respected businessman Mort Zuckerman and his friends purchased for $160 million cash equity the company that published *U.S. News & World Report* magazine. Over the previous decades, *U.S. News* and its employees had contributed $170 million more to the company's pension fund than the fixed obligation that then existed from the company to the future retirees. This was called an *overfunded pension account.* Under ERISA, the owners of the company, who were and still are the trustees of the company's pension account, were allowed to return this excess $170 million to the company and then give it to the new stockholders (themselves). The new owners did this within hours of buying the company, effectively walking away with a $10 million cash profit

and 100 percent ownership of one of the greatest companies in America—paid for entirely by the employees of *U.S. News & World Report* and their past labors.

2. ERISA's ability to supersede state insurance laws is confusing. ERISA first states that ERISA supersedes state and local laws when it comes to employer benefit plans. Then, ERISA states that nothing in ERISA exempts employers from complying with local insurance, banking, and security laws. However, ERISA then explicitly states (the "deemer clause") that employer-sponsored health benefits plans are not deemed to be insurance. I am indebted for this simplified explanation of how ERISA supersedes state insurance regulations to Professor Alison D. Garrett of Faulkner University's Thomas Goode Jones School of Law. From 1994 to 2004, Professor Garrett was with Wal-Mart Stores, Inc., serving in various executive capacities, including vice president and general counsel of the corporate division and vice president of benefits.

3. "Health Benefits Summary Plan Description," ChevronTexaco Human Resources home page, 1 January 2004, ChevronTexaco, 5 May 2005, http://hr2.chevrontexaco.com/spd/pdf/Health.pdf.

4. U.S. Department of Labor, Pension and Welfare Benefits Administration. *Health Benefits Under the Consolidated Omnibus Budget Reconciliation Act (COBRA)*, August 2002, 5 May 2005, www.dol.gov/ebsa/pdf/cobra99.pdf.

5. On May 26, 2004, the Department of Labor published final regulations for COBRA, which will become effective for all plan years beginning on or after November 26, 2004. Phillips, David H., and Dana R. Scott, "Think You Know COBRA? Think Again," *Gallagher, Callahan, & Gartrell,* July 2004, 5 May 2005, www.gcglaw.com/resources/benefits/cobra.html.

Chapter 4

1. In March 2005, I also experienced firsthand what happens when someone doesn't pay LabCorp. Although I had sent the company a check for the full amount of its last invoice, which it cashed, its computer systems failed to credit the amount to my account. For two weeks I received daily phone calls and letters from "LCA Collection Service" threatening legal action. Each time I phoned, I received voice messages that disconnected me after being put on hold. Finally, by e-mailing numerous LabCorp senior executives in its investor relations department, I was able to get someone at LabCorp to respond, apologize, fix its broken voice-mail system, and turn off its automated collection machine.

2. "HMO or PPO: Picking a managed-care plan," Consumers Union of U.S. Inc., 2001–2005, 6 May 2005, www.consumerreports.org/main/detailv2.jsp?CONTENT%3C%3Ecnt_id=329183&FOLDER%3C%3Efolder_id=162687.

3. Anthem BCBS of Ohio Home Page, December 2004, Anthem BCBS of Ohio—Short Term Rate, 6 May 2005, https://seca.anthem.com/ratequote/app; Applicant (M/35) from Columbus, OH 44107.

Chapter 5

1. *Employer Health Benefits: 2004 Summary of Findings,* 2004, Kaiser Family Foundation and Health Research Educational Trust, 6 May 2005, www.kff.org/insurance/7148/loader.cfm?url=/commonspot/security/ getfile. cfm&PageID=46287.

2. Ibid.

3. Taub, Stephen, "Microsoft Cuts Health Benefits," *CFO.COM,* 24 May 2005, 6 May 2005, www.cfo.com/article. cfm/3014003?f=related.

4. U.S. Department of Health and Human Services Centers for Disease Control and Prevention, *Health, United States, 2004,* 2004, 6 May 2005, www.cdc.gov/nchs/data/hus/hus04trend.pdf#027.

5. *Your Most Valuable Asset Is Income,* 2005, New York Life, 6 May 2005, www.newyorklife.com/cda/ 0,3254,8931,00.html.

6. U.S. Social Security Administration, *SSA Basic Facts,* May 2002, 6 May 2005, http://permanent.access. gpo.gov/lps7845/10080.html.

7. For more information about Group Policy Quotes (taken 26 April 2005 from e-mailed policy brochure), contact UnumProvident Corporation at www.unumprovident.com, phone (877) 322-7222.

8. For more information about Individual Policy Quotes (taken 26 April 2005 from call with Shauna), contact UnumProvident Corporation at www .unumprovident.com, phone (877) 322-7222.

9. Peterson, Chris L., and Bob Lyke, "Health Care Flexible Spending Accounts," *Congressional Research Service Report for Congress,* 1 November 2004, 6 May 2005, http://hutchison.senate.gov/RL32656.pdf.

10. Unspent FSA funds are supposed to be distributed pro rata the following year to plan participants as an FSA contribution bonus, less any employer expenses associated with the administration of the FSA plan. However, practically speaking, employers end up keeping these funds once they have allocated overhead to plan administration costs.

11. U.S. Internal Revenue Service, *Internal Revenue Bulletin: 2005-16 Rev. Rul. 2005-24,* 18 April 2005, 6 May 2005, www.irs.gov/irb/2005-16_IRB/ ar08.html.

Chapter 6

1. John Goodman, president of the National Center for Policy Analysis, has been called "the father of medical savings accounts" by Congressman Bill Archer. I have also been referred to as the "father of health savings accounts"—I received an honorary Ph.D. in April 2004 from Parker College for my work in promoting Health Savings Accounts in Congress and in *The Wellness Revolution* (John Wiley & Sons, 2002). Decker, Jonathan P., "A Better Way to Pay for Healthcare," *The Christian Science Monitor,* 10 May 2004, 6 May 2005, www.ncpa.org/abo/quarterly/20042nd/clip/ 20040510cs.htm.

2. A few states do not allow a deduction from state-taxable income for HSA

contributions although these states are soon expected to amend their tax codes to do so.

3. The HSA Insider home page, 2004–2005, The HSA Insider, 6 May 2005, www.hsainsider.com/fact_sheet.pdf.

4. 8.0 percent compounded daily (8.3 percent annual yield). 1728 Software Systems home page, 2000, 1728 Software Systems, 6 May 2005, www .1728.com/annuity.htm.

5. Technically, you are allowed to open your HSA with a nominal deposit up to 60 days before you have HSA-qualified health insurance, but you cannot contribute to your HSA until your HSA-qualified health insurance is in place.

Chapter 7

1. *Risk Pools—Affordable Health Insurance for Medically Uninsurable Individuals,* 7 October 2003, Health Insurance Resource Center, 6 May 2005, www.healthinsurance.org/riskpoolinfo.html.

2. "Maryland Health Insurance Plan," Maryland Health Insurance Plan home page, 1 December 2004, Maryland Health Insurance Plan, 7 May 2005, www.marylandhealthinsuranceplan.state.md.us/premium.pdf.

3. "What Were These States Thinking? The Pitfalls of Guaranteed Issue," Ed. Bunce, Victoria Craig, May 2002, *Council for Affordable Health Insurance's Issues and Answers,* 6 May 2005, www.cahi.org/cahi_contents/resources/pdf/guaranteedissue.pdf.

4. California Healthy Families home page, 2000, Healthy Families—Monthly Premiums, 6 May 2005, www.healthyfamilies.ca.gov/English/about_cost .html.

5. Healthy NY home page, 2004, Healthy NY—MVP Health Plan, 6 May 2005, www.ins.state.ny.us/website2/hny/rates/html/hnyalban.htm.

6. "Health Benefits Summary Plan Description," ChevronTexaco Human Resources home page, 1 January 2004, ChevronTexaco, 5 May 2005, http://hr2.chevrontexaco.com/spd/pdf/Health.pdf.

Chapter 8

1. Revell, Janice, "The Great State Health-Care Giveaway," *Fortune,* 19 April 2005, 6 May 2005, www.fortune.com/fortune/articles/0,15114,1050835,00.html.

2. Ibid.

3. *The Cost and Benefits of Individual Health Insurance Plans,* 12 October 2005, eHealthInsuranceServices, Inc., 5 May 2005, http://image.ehealthinsurance .com/ehealthinsurance/expertcenterNew/CostBenefitReportFinal101204 .pdf.

4. Medicare also covers certain disabled persons under age 65 and people who have end-stage renal disease (permanent kidney failure requiring dialysis or a transplant).

5. Medicare at a Glance, 29 April 2005, Kaiser Family Foundation, 6 May 2005, www.kff.org/medicare/loader.cfm?url=/commonspot/security/ getfile.cfm&PageID=52974.

6. Ibid.

7. Congress did this because allowing Medicare consumers to have no deductible on their medical expenses would defeat most of the public policy reasons for Health Savings Accounts.

8. These figures are automatically adjusted (discounted) for present value because the $78.20 monthly base premium is increased every year by the federal government.

9. The Congressional Budget Office estimates that 16 percent of Medicare enrollees will have chosen Medicare Advantage Plans by 2013, while Health and Human Services (HHS) estimates 30 percent. *Medicare at a Glance,* 29 April 2005, Kaiser Family Foundation, 6 May 2005, www.kff.org/ medicare/loader.cfm?url=/commonspot/security/getfile.cfm&PageID =52974.

10. There are some limited exceptions—if your Medigap policy was purchased before 1990, state law before 1990 might not have required Medigap policies to be "guaranteed renewable."

11. *The Medicare Prescription Drug Benefit–Fact Sheet,* 14 March 2005, Kaiser Family Foundation, 6 May 2005, www.kff.org/medicare/7044-02.cfm.

12. Average Daily Cost for Nursing Home Care by State, 2001, March 2002, GE Financial, Long Term Care Division, 6 May 2005, www.aarp.org/ bulletin/longterm/Articles/a2003-10-30-dailycost.html; $150 per day in 2001 increased 50 percent; medical costs rose 53 percent from 2001 to 2005.

13. Huddleston, Cameron, "Why You Need Long-Term Care Insurance," Kiplinger.com, 26 September 2002, 6 May 2005, www.kiplinger.com/ basics/archives/2002/09/story26.html.

14. "Do You Need Long-Term Care Insurance?" *Consumers Union of the U.S. Inc.,* November 2003, 6 May 2005, www.consumerreports.org/.

15. Long-Term Care Insurance and Tax Deductions—ID, New York Life, January 2005, 6 May 2005, www.newyorklife.com/cda/0,3254,12628,00 .html.

Chapter 10

1. "This analysis showed an increased risk of suicidal thoughts and behavior from 2% to 4% in people under 18," *About Zoloft: Common Questions.* 2005, Pfizer Inc., 9 May 2005, www.zoloft.com/zoloft/zoloft.portal? _nfpb=true&_pageLabel=common_questions.

2. Glenmullen, Joseph, "Prozac Backlash: Overcoming the Dangers of Prozac, Zoloft, Paxil, and Other Antidepressants with Safe, Effective Alternatives," *Dr. Joseph Mercola Online,* 2005, 9 May 2005, www.mercola.com/ 2000/apr/9/prozac_backlash.htm.

3. Krugman, Paul, "Passing the Buck," *The New York Times Online,* 22 April 2005, 9 May 2005, www.nytimes.com.

4. Americans spend more than $27 billion a year on medical malpractice, according to the Congressional Budget Office. As noted in Appendix D, the average individual health insurance premium for a healthy individual is $92 per month, or $1,104 per year ($27 billion per year divided by $1,104 per year equals 24.5 million), U.S. Congressional Budget Office, *Limiting Tort Liability for Medical Malpractice,* 8 January 2004, 9 May 2005, www .cbo.gov/showdoc.cfm?index=4968&sequence=0.

5. Pilzer, Paul Zane. *The Wellness Revolution.* New York: John Wiley & Sons, 2002, 2003.

6. Ibid.

7. "Health," *The Merriam-Webster Reference Library.* Dallas, TX: Zane Publishing and Merriam Webster, 1996.

8. Pilzer, Paul Zane. *The Wellness Revolution.* New York: John Wiley & Sons, 2002, 2003.

9. American Osteopathic Association, 1090 Vermont Ave. NW, Suite 510, Washington, DC 20005. Phone 800-962-9008, www.osteopathic.org.

10. The American Association of Naturopathic Physicians, 3201 New Mexico Ave. NW, #350, Washington, DC 20016. Phone 866-538-2267, http:// naturopathic.org.

Chapter 12

1. U.S. Department of Labor, *Field Assistance Bulletin 2004-1,* 7 April 2004, 17 May 2005, www.dol.gov/ebsa/regs/fab_2004-1.html.

Epilogue

1. Employer Health Benefits 2004 Annual Survey, 2004, The Kaiser Family Foundation and Health Research and Educational Trust, 30 May 1999, www.kff.org/insurance/7148/loader.cfm?url=/commonspot/security/ getfile.cfm&PageID=46206.

2. Johnson, Kelly, "Minute Clinic Offers Fast, Convenient Medical Treatment for Common Illnesses," *ABC Newspapers,* 12 May 2005, 30 May 2005, www.abcnewspapers.com/2005/May/12clinic.html.

3. CBS News home page, 24 April 2005, CBS News *60 Minutes,* 30 May 2005, www.cbsnews.com/stories/2005/04/21/60minutes/main689998_ page2.shtml.

4. Krugman, Paul, "Passing the Buck," *New York Times Online,* 22 April 2005, 30 April 2005, www.truthout.org/docs_2005/printer_042205H.shtml.

5. "A 2003 study in *The New England Journal of Medicine* estimated that administrative costs took 31 cents out of every dollar the United States spent on health care." Krugman, Paul, "The Medical Money Pit," *New York Times Online,* 15 April 2005, 30 April 2005, www.truthout.org/docs_ 2005/printer_041505H.shtml.

6. U.S. 109th Congress, 1st session, *The Health Care Choice Act,* HR 2355, by John Shadegg, 11 May 2005, 30 May 2005, www.govtrack.us/ congress/billtext.xpd?bill=h109-2355.

7. U.S. 109th Congress, 1st session, *The Health Care Freedom of Choice Act,* HR 66, by Christopher Cox, 4 January 2005, 30 May 2005, www .govtrack.us/congress/billtext.xpd?bill=h109-66.

8. Congressmen receive full federal health benefits from the day they are elected, but unlike other higher-grade federal employees who vest after 10 years, members of Congress get their benefits vested after only 5 years.

Appendix B

1. *"The Uninsured: A Primer—Key Facts about Americans without Health Insurance,"* 18 December 2003, Kaiser Family Foundation, 7 May 2005, www.kff.org/uninsured/4085.cfm, November 2004, www.kff.org.

2. Rhoades, Jeffrey A., "Estimates for the Civilian Noninstitutionalized Population Under Age 65," *Medical Expenditure Panel Survey,* 2002, 7 May 2005, www.meps.ahrq.gov/papers/st19/stat19.pdf.

3. "AHIP Announces One Million HSAs Sold," Galen Institute, 5 May 2005, 7 May 2005, www.galen.org/ccbdocs.asp?docID=795.

About the Author

Paul Zane Pilzer is a world-renowned economist, a multimillionaire software entrepreneur, an award-winning adjunct professor at NYU, and the author of two *New York Times* best-sellers and dozens of scholarly publications on economics. He was an appointed economic adviser in two White House administrations and has testified before Congress on health insurance issues. A former commentator on National Public Radio and CNN, Pilzer speaks each year to hundreds of thousands of people, and more than 10 million audiotapes of his speeches have been sold.

Pilzer received his MBA from Wharton. At age 24, he was appointed an adjunct professor at New York University where he taught for 20 years. While employed as Citibank's youngest officer at 22 and its youngest corporate vice president at 25, Pilzer started several entrepreneurial businesses—earning his first $1 million before age 26 and his first $10 million before age 30. Over the past 25 years, he has started and/or taken public five companies with hundreds of employees. He is the Chairman and co-founder of Extend Benefits LLC, one of the nation's leading suppliers of individual health benefits to corporate America.

Pilzer predicted the $200 billion savings and loan crisis of the 1980s years before official Washington was willing to listen. The book he wrote about the fiasco, *Other People's Money,* was critically acclaimed by the *New York Times* and *The Economist.*

After reading Pilzer's book, *Unlimited Wealth,* the late Sam Walton, founder of Wal-Mart, said that he was "amazed at Pilzer's business capacity" and his "ability to put it into layman's terms." Pilzer's *God Wants You to be Rich: The Theology of Economics,* which explained the Judeo-Christian foundation of our economic system, was a *New York Times* business best-seller. In *The Wellness Revolution* Pilzer identified the newly emerging wellness industry—for this book he received an *Honorary Doctorate in Public Service.*

Pilzer lives in Park City, Utah with his wife and four children where they are all avid snowboarders, mountain bikers, and chess players.